A New Kind of Public

Studies in Critical Social Sciences Book Series

Haymarket Books is proud to be working with Brill Academic Publish (www.brill.nl) to republish the *Studies in Critical Social Sciences* book series in perback editions. This peer-reviewed book series offers insights into our curr reality by exploring the content and consequences of power relationships un capitalism, and by considering the spaces of opposition and resistance to th changes that have been defining our new age. Our full catalog of *SCSS* volu can be viewed at www.haymarketbooks.org/category/scss-series.

A New Kind of Public

Community, Solidarity, and Political Economy
in New Deal Cinema, 1935–1948

Graham Cassano

Haymarket
Books
Chicago, IL

First published in 2014 by Brill Academic Publishers, The Netherlands.
© 2014 Koninklijke Brill NV, Leiden, The Netherlands

Published in paperback in 2015 by
Haymarket Books
P.O. Box 180165
Chicago, IL 60618
773-583-7884
www.haymarketbooks.org

ISBN: 978-1-60846-493-7

Trade distribution:
In the U.S. through Consortium Book Sales, www.cbsd.com
In the UK, Turnaround Publisher Services, www.turnaround-uk.com
In all other countries by Publishers Group Worldwide, www.pgw.com

Cover design by Ragina Johnson.

This book was published with the generous support of Lannan Foundation
and the Wallace Action Fund.

Printed in Canada by union labor.

10 9 8 7 6 5 4 3 2 1

Library of Congress Cataloging-in-Publication Data is available.

For Dad

Contents

Acknowledgements

First, and most important, I must acknowledge the intellectual companionship of my partner, Rosalind Hartigan. Thank you, Bia, for listening and for teaching me a few things about movies. In addition, I have received intellectual support, critique and advice from too many comrades, readers, and colleagues to name. A partial list must include my editor, David Fasenfest, a constant resource and a good friend. Thank you to David Roediger, Jennifer Klein, and Rick Wolff for their support and encouragement over the years. Conversations with my friends and colleagues Troy Rondinone, Jim Berger, Brian Schuth, George Sanders, and Mark P. Worrell, helped me develop the ideas in this monograph. Melina Lescoe provided editorial assistance. Amanda Nichols Hess of Oakland University's Kresge Library provided important research assistance. Brian Schuth and Denis Wall provided proofreading and editorial assistance. Joyce Goldenstern helped assemble the index. While I am grateful for all the assistance I have received, any mistakes or missteps within these pages are the author's responsibility. Finally, I need to thank Jay Meehan, Jo Reger, and all my Departmental colleagues and students at Oakland University for their kind support over the years.

Introduction
A Sociological Approach to New Deal Cinema

The Problem

For twenty five years I've had a movie on my mind....

Let me begin with my experience of the problem. A late 20th century movie house in Cambridge, sitting in the balcony. I'd seen Hollywood westerns. I knew what to expect. And those expectations left me entirely unprepared for the projections about to unwind.

FORT APACHE[1] (1948) is told from a variety of points of view. What struck me at the time, however, was the voice its director, John Ford, gave the Apache. They weren't represented as children. They weren't represented as savages. Instead, they were an aggrieved people battling the twin forces of colonization and corruption. And, as John Wayne's Captain York argues throughout most of the film, the Apache were in the right. But more startling than the sympathetic representation of the Apache, the film's final scene has Captain York consciously whitewashing the genocidal image of American imperialism the previous scenes had so convincingly evoked. After spending the first two acts of the film speaking to American power for the Apache, in the final shot Captain York leads his cavalry to hunt down Cochise. York turns his dead, imperious commander, Colonel Thursday (Henry Fonda), into a falsified legend, and, more important, a martyr for American nationalism. Anticipating the final lines of Ford's later film, THE MAN WHO SHOT LIBERTY VALENCE (1962), York would have the press conceal reality, and for the sake of the nation, "print the legend." FORT APACHE recognizes the power of propaganda, explains its uses and operation, and, yet, at the same time, seems to participate in the very process it critiques. In fact, I couldn't understand the film's conclusion. But my mystification provoked a series of questions that have since driven my research: Was FORT APACHE a critique of imperialism? An endorsement? What made York shift identities at the end, becoming the very thing he'd despised throughout the picture? What does it mean that the picture itself deconstructs York's

---

1   For clarity's sake, I use small capitals to designate film titles within the body of this work. In the table of contents, chapter titles, and subtitles, I use italics. When film titles appear in quotations from other works, I use italics, small capitals, or quotation marks, following the style employed by the cited text's author(s).

transformation? And how would its original audience understand that internal deconstruction?

The films of the 1930s and 1940s are all too familiar to twenty-first century audiences. The commercialization of certain styles (think of marketed imagery from CASABLANCA (1943) or film noir), the popularity of certain directors from the period (Hitchcock, Welles, Kazan), and the influence of these commodified tropes upon contemporary forms of entertainment, all lead to a situation in which the twenty first century viewer understands early twentieth century film through contemporary forms of thought and experience. While I do not mean to denigrate the commercial afterlife of early cinema, nor the identity tropes its marketing produces, such an anachronistic viewpoint conceals the more diffi-cult and contradictory moments in individual films. In order to break the spell of contemporary experience, this study acknowledges the fundamental estrangement between the society and practices of the twenty-first century, and the society and practices that gave birth to early sound cinema. But to complete the circuit from familiarity to estrangement to understanding, I argue that the cinematic product, like any cultural artifact, can be situated within the field of cultural, historical, and social forces that gave it original force. In other words, by understanding FORT APACHE as a discursive contes-tant fighting for position in the field of its times, its final scenes begin to make sense. And within this cultural study of popular art under capitalism, I have resisted directly functional and deterministic arguments in favor of an elabora-tion of discursive, cultural, political, and historical *relations* (Cassano 2005a).

Writing in the 1940s, Adorno and Horkheimer argue that cinematic repre-sentations are fundamentally important to the creation of a society of mass spectators, politically disabled, and satiated with amusement. While "industri-alized as well as popular culture may wax indignant at capitalism," (Adorno and Horkheimer 1987: 141) these stereotyped critiques never threaten the fun-damental stability of the culture industry.

> What is decisive today is...the necessity inherent in the system not to leave the customer alone, not for a moment to allow him [sic] any suspi-cion that resistance is possible. The principle dictates that he should be shown all his needs as capable of fulfillment, but that those needs should be so predetermined the he feels himself to be the eternal consumer, the object of the culture industry. Not only does it make him believe that the deception it practices is satisfaction, but it goes further and implies that, whatever the state of affairs, he must put up with what is offered.....
> Pleasure promotes the resignation which it ought to help forget.
>
> ADORNO and HORKHEIMER 1987: 141–142

To the extent that Adorno and Horkheimer provide a Marxist interpretation of the culture industry, and cinema more particularly, it is a thoroughly *functionalist* and *determinist* Marxism that is on display. I've quoted the above passage at length to illustrate two aspects of that functionalist determinism. First, while individual cinematic products may mock or critique the economic system, the cinematic apparatus as a whole sustains that system. That is to say, even if individual films overtly challenge some aspect of capitalist society, the audience's predetermined reactions disable any critical impact. Cinematic content and its formal expression reinforce capitalist behavior and values in a relatively unproblematic functional manner. Second, Adorno and Horkheimer posit a relatively unproblematic relation between the film's intent and its audience's reception. With the presumed intention of subduing and anesthetizing its audience, as well as inculcating capitalist aspirations and values, the film accomplishes this task with frictionless ease, turning the audience into a passive receiver of its politicized aesthetic content.

What I find most remarkable about the functionalist and determinist argument put forward by Adorno and Horkheimer, as well as their general dismissal of anticapitalist social action, is the fact that these judgments emerge from one of the most politically tumultuous moments in u.s. history (Cassano 2009c, 2006; Worrell 2009, 2006). Indeed, the authors first published *Dialectic of Enlightenment* in 1944, and the picture of the passive, resigned working class seems at odds with the post-World War Two upsurge in u.s. strike activity. From Adorno and Horkheimer's perspective, the general strikes of 1946 would have seemed quite impossible. Yet they took place (Lipsitz 1994). In fact, nothing was automatic in securing the silence of American dissidents, advocates, activists, and workers. It took concerted effort on the part of the state apparatus, and a new Red Scare, to (however briefly) create an enforced conformist passivity (Storrs 2013). And the intensity of this state reaction itself gives some sense of the potential power of working class discontent and the modes of political and cultural activity such discontent could potentially produce (Schrecker 1998; Ceplair and Englund 2003).

This study argues that a functionalist perspective is not particularly useful for the study of New Deal Cinema precisely because it ignores the contingencies of history. A close examination of the field of 1930s and 1940s cinema shows a contested set of representations competing for symbolic power over the audience. Most representations simply reinforced dominant values and behaviors and built their narratives on capitalist aspirations. But some contested capitalism itself and did so in a powerful and popular language. Moreover, films were able to do this precisely because of transformations in the cinematic audience. The consequences of the Depression, and the political responses to it, produced an audience ready to find symbolic resources for understanding and navigating their world. Many participated in the labor movement or the Popular Front. Many more were shaped by the cultures of these new social movements. And this new audience made new, potentially critical, pictures possible (Denning 1998).

Further, while Adorno and Horkheimer posit the functional identity between the picture's intended meaning and its force for the audience, they provide no evidence for that assumption. No such evidence is possible. Different audiences will react to the same cultural product in different ways. Those reactions, and the possible meanings they find in the cultural object, will depend upon their own position as readers, viewers, participants. In short, the audience's reaction is overdetermined by social forces (Althusser 1971; Resnick and Wolff 1987; Cassano 2005a). Moreover, the individual impact of any particular cultural representation will be reinforced by, contradicted by, and shaped by innumerable other cultural representations, from the same cultural sphere (art, cinema), or from different cultural spheres (politics, religion, gender relations). Adorno and Horkheimer's functionalist determinism has no place for the unstable interaction of various intersecting fields of symbolic struggle.

Thus, while I utilize the theoretical instruments provided by Marxism in the study of cinematic objects, it is a Marxism that rejects the functionalist determinism still widely utilized by sociologists of culture. Instead, this approach begins from the premise that every cultural artifact is overdetermined, the effect of multiple causes, and the cause of multiple effects (Resnick and Wolff 1987; Markels 2003). Because I question the methodological efficacy of assuming an identity between the meaning of the cinematic artifact (and the larger cinematic apparatus), on the one hand, and the audience, on the other, I necessarily abandon a long valued trope in cinema studies: What the audience *really* experienced. I do not claim unique or privileged access to how any particular audience experienced any particular film. Instead, in the pages that follow, I argue: (1) for the abandonment of the phenomenology of the audience; but (2) that every film, as a meaningful structure, carries its own imagined audience, as well as its cultural context, within itself. As a cultural artifact, it is meaningful in relation to a series of other cultural objects, ideas, and practices. And, in its attempt to make meaning to others, it carries those references within, so to speak. *The film projects its context.* And (3) in the case of New Deal Cinema, the context of economic and cultural crisis appeared in the cinema of the time. Further, (4) some of these cinematic representations were both popular and contained radical critiques of conventional cultural and economic practices. More than simply reflecting the political and cultural struggles of the 1930s and 1940s, cinema refracted those struggles in its own language, and offered that language to its audience as a prism through which to view their communities (Volosinov 1973).

Symbols, Experience, and Overdetermination

Near the end of his career, thinking about the power of culture to shape experience, C. Wright Mills offered this correction of Marx and Engels' line from *The German Ideology*, "Life is not determined by consciousness, but consciousness by life" (1988: 47).

> The consciousness of men [sic] does not determine their material existence; nor does their material existence determine their consciousness. Between consciousness and existence stand meanings and designs and communications which other men have passed on—first, in human speech itself, and later, by the management of symbols. These received and manipulated interpretations decisively influence such consciousness as men have of their existence. They provide the clues to what men see, to how they respond to it, to how they feel about it, and to how they respond to these feelings. Symbols focus experience; meanings organize knowledge, guiding the surface perceptions of an instant no less than the aspirations of a life time.
>
> MILLS 1959: 405–406

Human reality is symbolically mediated. Symbols are both selective and constructive. They select elements of outer and inner experience that therefore become meaningful and real. Through that process of selection and meaning generation, human consciousness constructs an organized (and relatively contingent) reality. But Mills is making this semiotic argument in service to his concern with the various concealed forms power takes in late 20th century western society.

Forces of domination and exclusion are produced unknowingly and automatically through the imposition of symbolic boundaries on lived experience.

> Debate is limited. Only certain views are allowed. But more than that, the terms of debate, the terms in which the world may be seen, the standards by which men judge of their accomplishments, of themselves, and of other men—these terms are officially or commercially determined, inculcated, enforced.
>
> MILLS 1959: 413

History is the history of symbolic struggles over the definitions of experience, possibility, and community. And hegemonic power operates by attempting to graft its standards of judgment onto the dominated as a kind of enforced "common sense." At the same time, this *conflict theorist* presents a rather *functionalist* vision of late 20th century society. In a language and attitude that echoes the nihilistic functionalism of Adorno and Horkheimer, Mills presents the struggle over the boundaries of reality as a *fait accompli*.

> The virtual dominance of commercial culture is the immediate ground of America's cultural scope, confusion, banality, excitement, sterility. In this overdeveloped society, the mass production, the mass sale, the mass consumption of goods has [become] the Fetish of both work and leisure. The pervasive mechanisms of the market have indeed penetrated every feature of life—including art, science and learning--and made them subject to pecuniary evaluation.
>
> MILLS 1959: 418

A dominant representational system, or "cultural apparatus," shaped by pecuniary considerations and commercial concerns, imposes its definitions of reality, value, and desire upon social subjects, now transformed into pacified consumers.

While he shares Mills' perspective on the power of symbolic life to shape experience, V.N. Volosinov contests this functionalist perspective on symbolic struggle. Every social symbol or sign is "an arena of class struggle."

> Class does not coincide with the sign community, i.e., with the community which is the totality of users of the same set of signs...Thus various different classes will use one and the same language. As a result, differently oriented accents intersect in every ideological sign.
>
> VOLOSINOV 1973: 23

In other words, different social groups use one and the same sign differently, deploy it with different "accents," and so potentially transform its meaning. But the "ruling class strives to impart a supraclass, eternal character to the ideological sign, to extinguish or drive inward the struggle between social value judgments, to make the sign uniaccentual" (ibid.: 23). So for Volosinov, too, the cultural apparatus attempts to standardize perception and judgment. But to this he adds the argument that the dominated have the capacity to react and challenge hegemonic boundaries of sense and practice.

While the dominant groups in a social order attempt to secure their domination by setting limits to symbolic meanings, this is just one phase in an ongoing struggle. Ruling groups attempt to impose limits to the sign, and subordinated groups resist. This resistance leads to the "inner dialectic quality" of the sign, the fact that as a living and moving aspect of social struggle, any symbol has the potential to shift and change in meaning.

> This inner dialectic quality of the sign comes out fully in the open only in times of social crises or revolutionary changes. In ordinary conditions of life, the contradictions embedded in every ideological sign cannot emerge fully because the ideological sign in an established dominant ideology...tries...to stabilize the preceding faction in the dialectical flux of the social generative process, so accentuating yesterday's truth as to make it appear today's.
>
> VOLOSINOV 1973: 23–24

Domination operates by concealing the flux inherent in language and imposing a false stability upon symbols. But history's events can have a destabilizing impact upon the boundaries of discourse, creating fissures for symbolic resistance. These moments, when latent symbolic struggles emerge more or less into the open, present paths of potential transformation. They are crises in the sense that old values are questioned, and new possibilities, however unstable, emerge to challenge the hegemony of previously constituted discursive prisons.

Like Mills, Volosinov argues that reality without symbols is indeterminate; that symbols set determinate limits to experience and define the boundaries of the real. But that process of determination and definition is a social struggle, and, because various and contradictory meanings intersect in the same symbol, symbols are inherently "multi-accentual." In other words, symbols are *overdetermined* by multiple, intersecting, and sometimes contradictory meanings, accents, and uses.

Interpellative Intention

For its contemporary audience, the function of early cinema was certainly to "entertain." But entertainment itself is a social process, and through its entertainments film communicates messages about community. Every film, like every other cultural commodity, attempts to limit and circumscribe a kind of reality. And in doing so, the film selects some aspects of that reality to count as fundamental, meaningful. Thus, in one way or another, every film communicates a series of social meanings, including attempts to articulate, and sometimes to challenge the normative boundaries of, class, race, gender, social status.

In the early 20th century, both the culture workers behind cinematic productions, and the cultural apparatus that produced and distributed those commodities, understood this potential function of the movie. From the perspective of the culture worker, Popular Front playwright and later member of the Hollywood Ten, Albert Maltz, wrote a scathing critique of the film BLACK FURY (1935) for the New York Times. Maltz argues: "An author is a propagandist by what he [sic] says or fails to say. He is a propagandist for one cause or another, directly or indirectly, by the very nature of the 'slice of life' he selects or fails to select" (Maltz 1935). Maltz's analysis of the power of cinema to potentially shape perspectives on life was shared by Joseph Breen, representative of the Hays Office. In response to some of the more risqué early sound pictures, as well as new anxieties and fears of working class revolt provoked by the an extended economic downturn, after 1934 Breen was empowered to enforce a draconian Production Code that had specific provisions regarding the representation of moral, social and political themes (Leff 1991; Jacobs 1997; Leff and Simmons 2001). And, precisely because he shared Maltz's theory of the potential power of cinema, Breen himself was deeply involved in censoring the representation of the conflict between labor and capital in BLACK FURY (Walsh 1986; Black 1994). Whatever their political differences, however, Albert Maltz and Joseph Breen both subscribed to a proto-Althusserian theory of cinematic potential: Film teaches lessons about the proper paths of desire, normative forms of community and solidarity, and the duties of mothers, husbands, workers, citizens, senators, lovers and kings. In short, film interpellates its audience.

Interpellation is a communicative process that involves a "call" and a "response." In Louis Althusser's original formulation, ideology "'acts' or 'functions' in such a way that it 'recruits' subjects among the individuals (it recruits them all), or 'transforms' the individual into subjects (it transforms them all) by that very precise operation which I have called *interpellation* or hailing, and which can be imagined along the lines of the most commonplace everyday police (or other) hailing: 'Hey, you there!'" (Althusser 1971: 174). By sanctioning certain beliefs, rites and practices, the ideological apparatus calls certain subjectivities into being (Wolff 2005). It addresses the subject as citizen, or woman, or white man, and by recognizing itself in that call, the self becomes subject to the boundaries marked by that identity.

> Assuming that the theoretical scene I have imagined takes place in the
> street, the hailed individual will turn round. By this mere one-hundred-
> and-eighty-degree physical conversion, he [sic] becomes a *subject*. Why?
> Because he has recognized that the hail was 'really' addressed to him, and
> that 'it was *really him* who was hailed' (and not someone else).
>
> ALTHUSSER 1971: 174

In this communicative process, the subject comes to recognize itself through
an interpellating gaze. And, focusing upon the mass media, Althusser adds,
"Experience shows that the practical telecommunication of hailings is such
that they hardly every miss their man [sic]" (ibid.: 174). Mass media as interpellation calls various kinds of subjectivity into being from the flow of social
becoming. Thus, even entertainment can be a kind of pedagogical process in
which the self learns the appropriate boundaries of socially sanctioned behavior, attitudes and experiences.

Although Althusser utilized the theory of "overdetermination" in his analysis of capitalism, his analysis of the process of interpellation can sometimes
suggest a functional determinism. While he initially represents interpellation
as a communicative *process*, his further interpretation of the term contains
less clarification than reification.

> Naturally for the convenience and clarity of my little theoretical theatre
> I have had to present things in the form of a sequence, with a before and
> an after, and thus in the form of a temporal succession.... But in reality
> things happen without any succession. The existence of ideology and the
> hailing or interpellation of individuals as subjects are one and the same
> thing.
>
> ibid.: 174–175

Perhaps in service to the structuralist insistence of the priority of the synchronic over the diachronic, Althusser de-temporalizes intepellation. But by
eliminating temporality, he simultaneously eliminates social process (which is
necessarily temporal or diachronic) and substitutes a reified synchronic social
structure that doesn't so much "call" subjectivity into being as impose subjectivity upon passive, unresponsive (almost comatose) selves.

Yet precisely because it is a kind of pedagogy, interpellation is a temporal,
diachronic process. In my use of interpellation, I deconstruct its rigid reification as a synchronic event, and restore the two *stages* of this social *process*,
the call and the response. Such an emphasis upon the process beneath interpellation restores the lived contingencies of historical social, economic, and

cultural struggles. Just because a cultural object offers a particular call does not ensure it will receive the response it intends.

From the perspective of this study, film is an *interpellative machine*. Movies attempt to sanction and call into being a series of social classifications and perceptions. But whatever messages films attempt to send, their reception is in part determined by the life and community processes that shape the audience. A rural audience in the Midwest won't necessarily read HIS GIRL FRIDAY (1940) in the same way as a working class audience in Detroit. Different elements may be emphasized, different schemes of life deployed, in a dialectical struggle over classification systems, symbols, and meanings. Film studies quite often come up against this "problem of the spectator." If the meanings specified in any particular study are valid, to whom are they valid? Who is watching *this* movie? Psychoanalytic and feminist film theorists were quite right to find in traditional film criticism an unspoken masculine viewpoint. But whether the gaze is an unspoken masculine point of view, or a critical and self-consciously feminist spectatorship, theorists often continue to posit an audience within their studies. As a reader, however, I am always left with the questions: Who is this posited spectator? An empirical person, shaped by her or his own particularities of class, gender, sexuality, and community? Is the spectator a Kantian transcendental ideal? A Weberian ideal type?

While I do not mean to discount the value of previous cinema studies, I leave this problematic aside by asking a different set of questions. Rather than asking what the cinematic commodity meant to a particular audience, and so implying some phenomenology of the audience beyond the scope of this study, I ask: What does this interpellating machine *attempt to do*? Rather than examining the particular impact of a particular film upon some particular audience, or upon an ideal typical audience, this study attempts to uncover the *interpellative intention* of the picture. This intention is not identical with the intention of any particular author, director, producer, or culture worker. Nor is it identical with the experience any particular audience has of any particular film at any particular moment. Rather, it is the chain of meanings, and the systems of classifications, the film puts to work in its interpellative call. And interpellative intention can be separated from the *interpellative force*, the response of particular subjects to the call. These two concepts, intention and force, reintroduce temporality, and thus, social process, into Althusserian interpellation.[2]

---

2 Further, *interpellative intention* is itself potentially overdetermined and contradictory. Precisely because the meaning of a picture does not necessarily coincide with the conscious intention of a particular writer, director, or producer, meanings can become unstable, classifications contradictory, norms uncertain. And here, the synthetic generalities of theory

While interpellative intention does not necessarily demonstrate the interpellative force of a cultural object, it does reveal the social imagination the object carries within. That is to say, in order to make sense to an audience, a cultural artifact imagines the reaction it will produce (Mead 1967). In imagining that reaction, it imagines the audience itself. In short, the object carries an imaginary audience within. And to explore the object's interpellative intention is to reimagine the audience to whom it hoped to communicate.

Context

Many studies of the semiotics of cinema look at film language as a finished product: as a dead set of techniques, a grammar. Even sensitive and serious scholars might use a film by John Ford from 1940 and a film by Martin Scorsese from 1973 in the same sentence in order to illustrate some technical point. But such a use of cinematic examples makes sense only from the perspective of explaining Scorsese (since he responds to Ford), and does little to explain Ford's work. This is what Volosinov rightly called the philologist's perspective. "The *isolated, finished, monologic utterance*, divorced from its verbal and actual context and standing open not to any possible sort of active response but to passive understanding on the part of a philologist—that is the ultimate 'donnee' and the starting point of linguistic thought" (Volosinov 1973: 73). While the philological (or formal, or grammatical or, even, synchronic) understanding of cinema has its uses, such an approach teaches nothing about the original *social sense* of the cinematic artifact.

Twentieth century cinema was a field of commodities. But the individual film was also a particular sort of commodity. As a participant simultaneously in the cultural and economic fields, that is as a commodity meant to generate profits, and, at the same time, as a system of images and sound meant to generate meaning, each movie was a machine for manufacturing sense. Indeed, its success in the economic field (the generation of profits) depended to some large extent upon its success in the field of culture, upon the picture's ability to become *meaningful* for an audience.

---

must be modified by the particularities of historical experience. During the 1930s, for instance, American Hollywood cinema inhabited a cultural region somewhere between the cultish and dogmatic portrayal of sanctioned American norms and a carnivalesque skepticism revealing deep seated questions about American capitalism, traditional gender roles, and racial classifications.

As a meaningful object in the cultural field, the film assumes for its very success (at the process of communication) the doxic attitudes implicated in the habitus of its audience. The system of these doxic attitudes, or the doxa, represents the taken for granted naturalization of social categories, concepts and practices (Bourdieu 1992: 164). This doxic experience sets sensible limits to common reality by representing socially constructed classifications as natural and necessary. But the doxa is not a reified, disembodied structure. Rather, it exists to the extent that it has become an "embodied social programme of perception" (Bourdieu 2001: 11). Concepts and classifications depend upon a bodily habitus. Indeed, "It is through the training of the body that the most fundamental dispositions are imposed" (Bourdieu 2001: 56). The socially constructed "order of things," what is "normal, natural, to the point of being inevitable," both structures and is structured by "the habitus of agents, functioning as systems of schemes of perception, thought and action" (Bourdieu 2001: 8).

Every film assumes (and, to some extent, projects) the doxic experience of its imagined audience. Consider, for example, a brief scene from Pierre Etaix's homage to early cinema, Yo Yo (1967). Late in the picture, after the central character, Yo Yo (Etaix), has become a famous television clown, he returns from the studio to his corporate offices. In a recurring gag, every time he opens his office door, there is a deafening mechanical clatter from an invisible typing pool. In order to catch Etaix's gag, the audience had to understand a coded message. For viewers in the late 1960s, that code was easy and obvious. Mechanical contrivances like type-writers were a part of their living habitat. And this evocation of the "typing pool" carried a number of other associated signifiers in its train. While the typists aren't shown, the sound of the typing evokes the metonymic image of women's hands hitting the keys. For the audience in both Europe and the United States, the "typing pool" was a sign of proletarianization of women, and the increasing participation of women in office service work throughout the early to mid-Twentieth century. In short, this brief gag contained within it the industrial revolution and the radical mechanical and *social* changes that marked the world inhabited by Etaix and his audience. And to understand the gag is to understand the social, economic and historically fashioned world its writer and its audience inhabited.

Just as the interpellative intention carries within it a mediated understanding of the audience, so too the cinematic object contains the system of references, practices, norms and desires meaningful to that audience. Through its dependence upon the doxic order, the film projects its context. To make sense the film must reproduce the spectator's habitus. It must accept the socialized boundaries of discourse and desire. However, film's function is not simply reproductive, but productive as well. Whether communicating a narrative or selling an actor's profitable persona, the successful cinematic object attempts to *add* to reality and, accordingly, remake some element of the spectator's habitus.

In attending to individual cinematic products, what this study necessarily also explores is the cultural context within which the film becomes meaningful. The approach is quasi-ethnographic, when the function of the ethnographer is understood in Clifford Geertz's sense: "The ethnographer does not, and...largely cannot, perceive what his [sic] informants perceive. What he perceives, and that uncertainly enough, what they perceive 'with'—or 'by means of', or 'through'...or whatever the word should be" (Geertz 1983: 58). Likewise, in order to understand the interpellating intention animating the film, this study explores what the film's imagined audience *perceives with*: their historically constituted structures of life; their habits and dispositions; in short, their cinematic habitus.

The Force of Imagined Things

Since film is a kind of sign or utterance, a participant in a web of communication, it carries within itself (1) the social context of the utterance, the web of meanings against which its contribution makes sense; and (2) an imagined audience to receive its meanings. Thus, in order to elucidate some of the more remote moments in any particular cinematic artifact, I necessarily interrogate the (internalized) context of the utterance itself, the cinematic habitus.

Remarkably, the scientific discovery of the term "habitus" begins with cinema. Marcel Mauss first formalized the term (though, perhaps, the pragmatists' use of "social habits" conveys a similar sense) as a way of describing the system of socialized bodily and cognitive dispositions that constitute the self's socialized environment. He recounts its origin:

> A kind of revelation came to me in hospital. I was ill in New York. I wondered where previously I had seen girls walking as my nurses walked. I had the time to think about it. I realized that it was at the cinema. Returning to France, I noticed how common this gait was, especially in Paris; the girls [sic] were French and they too were walking in this way. In fact, American walking fashions had begun to arrive over here, thanks to cinema. This was an idea I could generalize. ...Thus there exists an education in walking, too.
>
> MAUSS 1979: 100

Like Etaix's typing pool, Mauss's discovery of a bodily habitus, couched in revealing sexist language, contains within it a new web of social practices, capacities, and limitations, as well as Mauss's own anxieties about women's increasing importance in work and social life. But above all, what this narrative example points to is the completion of the circuit from *interpellative intention* to *interpellative force*. Cinema remade Mauss's world.

Writing in the 1930s, Mauss was not alone among his contemporaries in taking note of the impact of cinema upon the physical habits of the audience. Robert and Helen Merrell Lynd (1937) document the emerging importance of this new national media for the local inhabitants of Middletown (Muncie, Indiana).

> If the older generation takes its movies as an anodyne, and small children as an exciting weekly event, adolescent Middletown goes to school to, as well as enjoying, the movies. Joan Crawford has her amateur counterparts in the high-school girls who stroll with brittle confidence in and out of "Barney's" soft-drink parlor, "clicking" with the "drugstore cowboys" at the tables; while the tongue-tied young male learns the art of swift, confident comeback in the face of female confidence....
>
> LYND and LYND 1937: 262

The Lynds argue that film-going is a pedagogical process, calling new subjectivities into being. And they find evidence for its force in the influence of film upon the physical dispositions of the "girls who stroll with brittle confidence," as well as upon the everyday language and cultural reference points for the adolescent community.

Just a few years earlier, a number of Herbert Blumer's adolescent respondents reflected upon the influence of movies upon their bodies. "Right there I decided I would adopt a definite walk and be more careful about standing straight; either I would get my imitation from some screen star or from some story description" (Blumer 1933: 39–40). For both Blumer and the Lynds, this influence upon slang and posture was indicative of a deeper influence upon social attitudes and "schemes of life" (Blumer 1933). Based upon their empirical and theoretical work, Mauss, Blumer, and the Lynds would all agree with Bourdieu: "It is through the training of the body that the most fundamental dispositions are imposed," including perceptual and conceptual dispositions (2001: 56). And this training was taking place through cinema. For different reasons, the Lynds and Blumer regarded the power of cinema to undermine American norms as a particularly distressful phenomenon. But while many commentators in the 1930s feared the force of cinema and the mass media, others saw possibilities presented by this potentially critical new form of mass communication.

A New Kind of Public

While this study does not posit the particular impact of any particular film upon an audience, it does rely upon the established significance of movies within the American cultural conversation. This significance was heightened during the period when cinema was the only available mass medium for the dissemination of the sound moving picture, as during the age of New Deal Cinema.

By New Deal Cinema, I mean Hollywood productions released between 1934 and 1948. This period is conveniently bookmarked by two events: First, the new power given to the Hays Office under Joseph Breen (1934); second, the testimony of the Hollywood Ten before the House Un-American Activities Committee (1947). While both events were attempts to re-impose a normative order on Hollywood's imagination factory, the Hays Office was not entirely successful in its move to exclude radical dissent from cinema. On the other hand, the Red Scare of the late 1940s and 1950s was much more effective in silencing critics of American economic inequality (Leff 1991; Ceplair and Englund 2003).

The rise of sound cinema after 1927 coincides with a period economic, social and cultural transformation in the United States brought on by the Great Depression, the rise of Fascism, the Second World War, and a new Red Scare. The premise of this study is that traces of these critical transformations, and the cultural anxieties that accompanied them, can be found in cinematic artifacts. Not every film during the 1930s and 1940s dealt directly with social and economic crisis. But many did. More still treated economic and social issues in barely disguised allegorical forms. And in addressing the consequences of economic crisis, film often told stories about solidarity, about class identity, and about social conflict. These narratives became contestants in the cultural struggle over the identity of the "working class."

When, in 1935, Helen and Robert Lynd returned to Muncie to complete their second study of the community, *Middletown in Transition* (1937), they found a city struggling with the collective consequences of the Great Depression. Despite the manifest impact of the downturn in the business cycle, community leaders and the Republican dominated press consistently downplayed that impact in the years between 1929 and 1935. A brighter day was always just around the corner. And the causes of the Depression were portrayed, often, as primarily "psychological." As one newspaper editorial put it early on,

"If tomorrow morning everybody should wake up with a resolve to unwind the red yarn that is wound about his old leather purse, and then would carry his resolve into effect, by August first, at the latest, the whole country could join in singing, 'Happy Days Are Here Again'" (Lynd and Lynd 1937: 17). At the same time, despite an upsurge of labor activity, the union movement in Muncie was decimated by a combination of factors, including the municipality's "open shop" policy, a continuing "welfare capitalism" in some of the largest manufacturing firms, and, perhaps most importantly, the shocking inability of the traditionalist American Federation of Labor (AFL) to use the continuing economic crisis as an organizing wedge. For Middletown's "working class," the city's majority, this led to disillusionment with traditional labor organizations, and a general sense of fear and insecurity as the effects of the Depression made "getting a living" an increasingly precarious endeavor. Moreover, the ideological forces arrayed against workers, combined with a long tradition of American republican liberalism, led many and perhaps most workers to see their plight as an individualized phenomenon, the result of personal failure, and not the consequence of systematic processes at work. As the Lynds put it, "this fear, resentment, insecurity, and disillusionment has been to Middletown's workers largely an *individual* experience for each worker, and not a thing generalized by him [sic] into a '*class*' experience" (ibid.: 41).

While laborers were disillusioned and isolated in 1935, already, by 1936, some Middletown citizens from the working class Southside neighborhoods began to show signs of growing class awareness. "The fact that, as one worker describes it, 'We workers licked the big bosses here [in Middletown] by our majority for Roosevelt [in 1936]' may foreshadow some increase in South Side morale." (Lynd and Lynd 1937: 44) In this instance, Roosevelt's 1936 victory became the symbolic representation of a "working class" community, a totemic emblem of social solidarity. (On the significance of FDR's image for working class formation, see Roscigno and Danaher 2004: 32–45.) A working class community was being forged; and this construction depended, at least in some part, upon the representations offered by mass culture and mainstream cinema.

1935 and 1936 were pivotal years in American social history. In response to the economic crisis, new cultures of solidarity were emerging around the labor movement and the Popular Front, resulting in what Michael Denning (1998) has called a "laboring of American culture." To the extent that these new social movements were, indeed, popular, their constituencies intersected with movie house audiences. And this cultural contingency produced the remarkable result that a capitalistically funded and distributed medium, cinema, satisfied its audience with a number of pictures that were both successful and, nonetheless, critical of class distinctions, racial hierarchies, and traditional gender roles.

In 1936, on the eve of filming his radical indictment of whiteness, THE HURRICANE (1937), John Ford revealed his Popular Front sympathies when he told an interviewer for *New Theatre*: "there's a new kind of public that wants more honest pictures" (Eisenberg 2001: 258). The argument of this study is that Ford was not alone in responding to this new kind of public. Despite the overt efforts of the Hays office, the years between 1936 and 1947 produced a number of films that examined the social and economic inequalities in the United States from a critical perspective. On occasion, these cinematic critiques veered from progressive liberalism and Catholic corporatism into radical politics.

While I don't mean to suggest that critical perspectives dominated Hollywood productions, the fact that some of the most successful films of the 1930s and 1940s included radical critiques of social and economic inequality demonstrates the cultural power of this new kind of public searching old economic and social questions for new answers. And, in fact, one of the most pressing questions addressed by New Deal Cinema was: who belonged to this new kind of public? Or, put another way, what were the boundaries of community? Each of the films I interrogate in this study explores the boundaries of community and solidarity. And in exploring the boundaries of community and solidarity, the films make explicit and implicit statements about who belongs, who does not belong, and, at the same time, offer explanations for the social and economic inequalities within the community. In short, these films attempt to generalize social trauma into a shared, "*class*' experience."

Let me return for a moment to Albert Maltz's critique of BLACK FURY. He writes:

> Mr. Harry Irving, co-author of "Black Fury," in replying to my charge that "Black Fury" was anti-labor propaganda, said "We were not trying in any way to generalize conditions by our portrayal of a slice of a miner's life."... Mr. Irving, whether he likes it or not, is giving us a general picture of a miner's life. And it is my contention that from first to last the impression given of a miner's life...is incredibly false and distorted. It makes no difference what he intended to do...He has generalized in spite of himself.
>
> MALTZ 1935

For Maltz, cinema has a synthetic, generalizing affect. "The dramatist creates a world for his [sic] audience and when the play pretends to be realistic, as 'Black Fury' does, the audience inevitably identifies the world of the play with the

world of real life." The work of cinema is to create a world of imagined boundaries and classifications. Here Maltz Prefigures C. Wright Mills' argument. For
Mills mechanisms of mass communication make it "often impossible to distin-
guish image from source." He continues: "So decisive to experience itself are
the results of these communications that often men do not really believe what
'they see before their very eyes' until they have been 'informed' about it by
the national broadcast, the definitive book, the close-up photograph, the official announcement" (Mills 1959: 407). The cultural apparatus thus becomes a
mechanism for "establishment of the definitions of reality" (ibid.: 412) Like
Mills afterward, Maltz sees in cinema the dangerous possibility that the imagined world of the dramatist will become a template for understanding "the
world of real life."

With his contemporaries, Harold Blumer, the Lynds, and Marcel Mauss,
Albert Maltz argued cinema had the capacity to reach into and refashion reality. Precisely because of its "generalizing" affect, made manifest in the bodily
dispositions of its audience, Blumer, the Lynds, and Maltz feared cinema's
potential representational power. Marshalling that same force, however, John
Ford and other filmmakers during the New Deal, used movies, sometimes self-
consciously, to attempt to produce precisely the generalized 'class' experience
the Lynds found absent in Muncie. New Deal Cinema was an arena of struggle,
and one of the stakes of that struggle was a definition of the working class as
community.

Working Class Community

Historians often talk about "class" without offering a definition of the term.
Social theorists can be much more logically consistent in their interrogation of
the concept, but sometimes lose sight of the historical contingencies that
shape class experience. Since this narrative inhabits the mid-range between
historical studies and abstract theorization, I should clarify how I employ the
terms "class," "working class," and "proletarian."

Karl Marx is the touchstone for class theory. But throughout his career, Marx
deploys multiple definitions of social class. For instance, *Capital* (1967) focuses
primarily upon elaborating a conception of class as the process of the extraction of surplus value (Resnick and Wolff 1987). In *The German Ideology*, however, Marx, with Frederick Engels, offers a tripartite, sociological analysis of
class processes. First, class is always *relational*. That is, one class develops in
relation to another class with which it struggles. Second, Marx and Engels
argue that classes are always *communities*. For instance, in their definition of

"ancient" or "state" communism, they write: "The citizens hold power over their laboring slaves only in their community, and on this account alone, therefore they are bound to the form of communal ownership" (Marx and Engels 1988: 44). In other words, in a society based upon slavery, the ruling class becomes a community precisely in order to preserve their power over the slaves. At the same time, the slaves form a community in relation to their masters, based upon their common experience of brutal exploitation. And, third, all class relations are based upon *exploitation*. Marx and Engels define exploitation, in the broadest sense, quite simply: "enjoyment and labor, production and consumption," they write, are separated, with one class able to consume the social surplus, and the other bound to produce that surplus (Marx and Engels 1988: 52).

As powerful as Marx and Engels tripartite theory of class can be, their critic, Max Weber, argues that they conflate two analytically separable terms: "class" and "community." Weber does *not* reject Marx's theory of exploitation, only the former's tendency to conflate these two separable and often practically separate categories. In a passage that anticipates the postmodern Marxism of Resnick and Wolff (1987), Weber writes: "a class does not in itself constitute a community. To treat 'class' conceptually as having the same value as 'community' leads to distortion.... Yet, if classes as such are not communities, nevertheless class situations emerge only on the basis of communalization" (Weber 1946: 184).

For Weber, economic exploitation potentially produces systematically structured "life chances." These "life chances" can become a basis for (communal) political action, but for that to happen the class must *become a class community*.

> The degree in which 'communal action'...emerges from the 'mass actions' of the members of a class is linked to general cultural conditions, especially those of an intellectual sort. It is also linked to the...*transparency* of the connections between the causes and the consequences of the 'class situation'.
>
> WEBER 1946: 184

In other words, for a class community capable of political action to emerge, "the results of the class situation must be distinctly recognizable" (Weber 1946: 184). One basis for class formation is the transparency of the processes of exploitation and systematic inequality. Such a transparency depends upon "general cultural conditions," that is, upon representations, signs and symbols.

These two lessons I draw from Weber: First, there is no necessary connection between exploitation, inequality and community formation. Second, class community formation depends upon the transparency of the connection between the economic exploitation of a class of social actors, and the economic misery and social discontent of those actors; that is to say, upon cultural and symbolic processes. With communalization, there is a necessary moment of cultural representation. Individualized experience must be generalized into a class experience for a class community to emerge.

But there's a third aspect of Weber's argument that is implied by his theory. The process of "communalization" itself creates the "class situation." After all, communalization depends upon interpellation. That is, social actors are called upon to recognize themselves as subjects within the community. And this recognition is part of a symbolic process. Cultural symbols attempt to teach their audience how to think about class, race, gender, and community; who belongs, and who should be excluded. In the very process of speaking to an audience, these representations attempt to forge a community.

Some signs succeed in capturing their audience's vision; others fail. But one way or another, it is through cultural processes that social subjects learn to navigate their world, including the world of social inequalities. There have been moments in u.s. history when the discontent of American workers, translated into cultural processes, produced re-alignments of political and economic power. As Michael Rogin (2002) argues, the 1930s were such a moment, a moment when the American working class, as a cultural community, possessed more power than it ever had before. Like Rogin, I am interested in the representation of class during this period in large part because representations, especially popular representations, helped social actors think about their own class positions, helped them navigate the complex connections between the causes and the consequences of class situations, and, indeed, helped bring about the very class situations that were being symbolized.

The moments of radical analysis, as well as various other modes of social and economic critique, I find in Hollywood cinema have several aspects in common. They project the gap between two class communities, one with wealth and privilege, the other without. And they provide critical explanations of that divide, with the more radical representations underscoring the contradictions within the system of privilege and exclusion. All these films attempt to tell stories about the boundaries of community, who belongs together, who exploits, and who suffers.

Whether radical, or, more often, not, Hollywood productions of the 1930s and 1940s that addressed issues of dispossession, exploitation, inequality, and the Great Depression, attempted to shape working class desires and identity on a national scale. In a parallel process, Roscigno and Danaher (2004) have shown how hillbilly musicians like Ella May Wiggins, the Dixon Brothers and Dave McCarn, helped forge a regional class identity in the Carolinas that enabled the 1934 General Textile Strike. Mediated, in part, by the explosive growth in radio stations, hillbilly music gave strikers in isolated mill towns a sense of broader solidarity. In these songs they recognized their own struggles and realized that other workers faced the same "class situation." These hillbilly songs helped "generalize" individual experiences into a "class experience."

While many of these tunes simply generalized the alienated experience of the cotton mill worker (as in the Dixon Brothers' "Weave Room Blues" and "Weaver's Life"), others went further and attempted to explain the class situation they described (Lomax, Guthrie and Seeger 1999: 130–133). These songs attempted to add to the "transparency of the connections between the causes and the consequences of the 'class situation.'" And when it successfully connected its representation of cause to its representation of consequence, a song could "serve as a guiding force in addressing grievances" (Roscigno and Danher 2004: 74). For instance, Dave McCarn's "Serves 'em Fine" (1931) provides a quasi-Marxist narrative of dispossession and wage slavery (on McCarn's life and music, see Huber 2008: 162–215).

> Now, people, in the year nineteen and twenty
> The mills run good, everybody had plenty.
> Lots of people with a good free will
> Sold their homes and move to the mill.
> We'll have lots of money, they said,
> But everyone got hell instead.
> It was fun in the mountains rolling logs,
> But now when the whistle blows we run like dogs.
> It suits us people and serves us fine
> For thinking that the mill was a darn goldmine.

After establishing this narrative of a community dispossessed through an illusory "free-will," McCarn goes on to describe the periodic shut downs, the uncertainty of work, and the fact that the companies "don't pay nothing and they do us dirty." In short, he describes the radical economic contradictions at the base of communal struggles (Cohen, Seeger, and Wood 1976: 234–235).

But, like much radical analysis in New Deal cinema, McCarn provides a kind of Hollywood ending to the song that evades any direct examination of political transformation.

Now all you mountaineers that's listening to me
Take off your hats end holler "Whoopee."
For I'm going back home in the land of the sky
Where they all drink moonshine and never do die.
I'll take my dogs while the moon shines bright,
Hunt coon and possum the whole darn night.
If you can't get the money to move away,
It's too bad folks, you'll have to stay.

Rather than engaging in union or class struggle, McCarn returns to his lost utopia, leaving community behind. "If you can't get the money to move away/ it's too bad folks, you'll have to stay." He emphasizes this broken community in the last chorus, where "It suits *us* people, serves *us* fine" becomes "It suits *you* people, serves *you* fine..." Thus, while the song presented a radical vision of an exploited working class community, and thus potentially contributed to bringing that community into being, the only solution it provided to these contradictions was a tragic, individualized utopia. Like other cultural artifacts, McCarn's song is torn by contradiction and ambivalence. But, as in some Hollywood cinema, the quasi-utopian conclusion underscores the narrative of dispossession and community destruction that precedes it. "Serves 'em Fine's" ironic joy leaves its listener with the sour aftertaste of exploitation and pain.

The Hollywood Cultural Apparatus

Cinema attempts to mediate the representation of reality. Again, like other forms of cultural expression, cinema encounters an overdetermined reality, and selects from that reality certain elements and aspects. Through that process of selection, cinema comes to emphasize some aspects of reality as meaningful and significant, while others disappear from view. In that sense, every film produced during the Depression makes what Maltz calls a "generalizing" argument. Whether a Marx Brothers comedy or a "prestige" picture like THE GRAPES OF WRATH (1940), films mark the boundaries of an internalized reality, and through the process of communication attempt to secure the audience's recognition of the validity, necessity, and value of those boundaries.

I have argued that it is difficult, if not impossible, to precisely measure the cultural impact of any particular cinematic production. Every artifact, product, commodity, contributes to the circulation and construction of a culture. Measuring the particular force of any particular point in that circulating system is difficult. There is a reciprocal relationship between the individual cultural objects that constitute the cultural system or apparatus, on the one hand, and the apparatus, on the other, which itself has a share in constituting the meaning of each individual object. Cinematic productions depend upon what they imagine to be their audience's sense of the common world. At the same time, films attempt to intervene in the shaping of that common sense, reinforcing some norms, sometimes contesting others. For instance, while the dominant racist depiction of African Americans in New Deal Cinema emerged, in part, from the hegemonic culture of white supremacy in the early 20th century, that imagery further reinforced racism, teaching the lessons of white supremacy to new immigrants and their children. But if New Deal cinema usually reinforced hegemonic norms and supported the conventional apparatus of inequality within the United States, there were also moments when it challenged, subverted, and rejected the dominant conceptions of white supremacy and masculine domination, as well as the dominant explanations of class inequality.

Depression era anxieties and conflicts appear in some of the earliest sound productions, like GOLD DIGGERS OF 1933 (1933). But 1936 was a pivotal year in American cinema's confrontation with the Depression; and its significance was marked by the unequalled success of Charlie Chaplin's MODERN TIMES (1936). MODERN TIMES was the most financially successful film of the year, and one of the most successful of Chaplin's career (Balio 1995: 405). More important, the film's imagery and narrative projected a shocking critique of capitalist production and industrial alienation. The film begins in a factory, where the Tramp (Chaplin) faces constant speed-ups. In order to make him a more productive worker, the factory owner experiments with a feeding-machine. This apotheosis of Taylorism allows the worker to continue laboring, even as his energy is mechanically replenished through a kind of industrialized force feeding. When the Tramp escapes to the bathroom to catch his breath, the factory owner appears on a giant video monitor and tells him to get back to work. And, in one of the most visually stunning indictments of modern alienation, another worker is sucked into his machine, and fed through the huge gears as if a cog in the works.

In a number of ways, Chaplin's critique echoes Dave McCarn's "Serves 'em Fine." Like McCarn, Chaplin illustrates speed-ups, worker mistreatment, and the arbitrary power of management. Like McCarn, Chaplin resolves the film by allowing the Tramp and his companion, Gamine (Paulette Goddard), to escape capitalist alienation through flight down a country road. And like McCarn's conclusion, Chaplin's final scene is less a Hollywood resolution than an imaginary evasion that underscores the critique that preceded it. But there is also an important difference between Chaplin's and McCarn's narrative. While "Serves 'em Fine" illustrates the impact of capitalism upon a community, and its consequent destruction, MODERN TIMES concentrates upon the alienating impact of capitalist production on the lone worker. Community hovers around the edges of Chaplin's picture, but it isn't his central concern.

Chaplin's depiction of the irreconcilable conflicts between the individual and a mechanized capitalism has a kind of radical sociological foundation, but in this study I have focused upon films that more explicitly explore the boundaries of community. For instance, THE GRAPES OF WRATH argues that the capitalist system of production and distribution is itself at the root of communal disruption and the destruction of tradition. And while the film's final scene provides some modicum of Hollywood comfort to the audience, the problems faced by the Joads are never solved. Indeed, the only solution the film imagines comes in the form of Casy's dream of collective action and Tom's promise to follow in the preacher's path.

A number of factors produced New Deal cinema as a field of cultural struggle allowing for a somewhat surprising diversity of perspectives, including moments of radical critique. First, as John Ford's remarks make clear, New Deal filmmakers and producers were thinking about their audience. Recognizing the anxieties, desires and hopes of an audience was central to a film's success. So, to some extent, cinema, driven by the competitive pursuit of profit, had to recognize the world its audience recognized. And that was a world of social struggle, inequality, and financial insecurity. Hollywood could dream these realities away, as in THE WIZARD OF OZ (1939), but the power of that dream came in part from the drab realism of Dorothy's farm. At the same time, new social movements were stirring, and as the United States entered what Michael Denning (1998) calls "the age of the CIO," a new kind of audience, schooled in the fires of struggle, demanded new forms of cinema.

This need to meet the audience's demands (even as film attempted to shape their desires) produced a semi-autonomous workforce of cultural artisans. Producers, directors, and writers worked within the limitations imposed by the Production Code, and by their financial masters, but within those limitations retained some degree of autonomy, sometimes more, sometimes less, depending upon the particular power of the producer, writer, and director. That power, in turn, depended upon the culture worker's prior successes. Hence, if only to enhance personal symbolic power, the Hollywood culture worker had an interest in appealing to the audience, even when that appeal sometimes bit the hand of capital. Further, precisely because they were culture *workers*, Hollywood directors and writers were engaged in many of the same social and economic struggles engaging their working class audience. In particular, the 1930s brought labor struggles to the fore, as screenwriters and directors transformed their guilds to unions. And, just as in much of the rest of the United States, interaction with labor brought ideas, images, and analyses from the Popular Front into some mainstream Hollywood pictures (Ross 1941; Nichols 1947; Ryskind 1994; Nielsen 1995; McBride 2001).

I do not mean to suggest that most, or even many, New Deal films offered radical critiques of the economy and society. Instead, I simply mean to show that there was a cultural space for such a critique, even within an industry committed, by definition, to the reproduction of capitalism. The films I examine that have moments of radical analysis were all financially successful. A number were among *Variety*'s Top 10 in the year they were released. While financial success is an uncertain measure of the interpellative force of any particular film, it does suggest there was an audience ready for (perhaps hungry for) radical challenges to hegemonic forms of domination. At the same time, any film that goes largely unseen necessarily loses interpellative force.

While Hollywood cinema sometimes produced radical critique, that radicalism was soaked in contradictions. In particular, radical economic critique was often built upon a traditionalism that emphasized privileges bound to white supremacy and masculinity. But these contradictions were not unique to New Deal cinema. In fact, much left discourse, and even the language of the Popular Front itself, had a masculine inflection and was often built upon an unspoken and unconscious white supremacy. While the limitations of Hollywood's radicalism were not exactly coincident with the contradictions that shaped the Popular Front, the relation between these two discourses draws the attention of much of this study. The language of the radical left in the 1930s emerged within a dominant culture of white masculine privilege, and, like cinema, refracted that discourse; sometimes contesting it, but often reinforcing it.

Like the cultural productions of the Popular Front, like radio broadcasts, like local newspapers, cinematic symbols attempt to focus experience, to teach the audience how to read the world. Cinema attempts to mediate reality. An analysis of New Deal cinema provides a method less for understanding the *experience* of its audience then for unpacking the *categories that sought to focus that experience*. To the extent that cinema attempts to represent "the working class," or to speak to "working class experience," those representations are, of course, shaped by the cinematic apparatus itself. But every cultural attempt to give voice to working class experience is necessarily mediated. Whether an article in a Popular Front journal, a hillbilly music performance, or a film, every representation of working class experience is both a claim and an appeal. It claims "*this* is working class experience,"; and in that claim is an appeal that attempts to get "the working class" to recognize the symbolic boundaries it projects. A lifetime in the archives won't illuminate what the working class "really" experienced. Instead, researchers find *versions* of that experience, contested representations, contradictory realities, events transformed by interests or memory. Rather than looking for what the working class or working class experience "really" was, this study seeks a way into the struggle over the representational systems that, during an era of economic and social crisis, tried to define its boundaries and to organize its lived meanings.

Plan of the Work

This study proceeds in a roughly chronological sequence, beginning with BLACK FURY (1935) and ending with FORT APACHE (1948). At the same time, some reference will necessarily be made to films produced before 1935 and some produced after 1948. As a methodological rule, I give special attention to fissures, contradictions, and gaps in the cinematic narrative, since such lacunae often reveal the social obsessions that animate the film's imagined audience. Perhaps not surprisingly, these obsessions center about questions of race and gender. During a time when the racial order was shifting, and a new popular sense of immigrant whiteness was beginning to emerge, New Deal cinema refracted that emergence (Roediger and Barrett 2002; Roediger 2005). And as the Great Depression's economic turmoil transformed gender relations and opened new possibilities for women in the formal labor market, New Deal cinema refracted that transformation as well (Cohen 1990; Lynd and Lynd 1937).

Chapter 1 examines two films about organized labor, BLACK FURY and RIFFRAFF (1936). During the course of the 20th century, only a handful of sound films directly examined labor struggles. Thus, while neither BLACK FURY nor RIFFRAFF provide a radical indictment of capitalism, it's significant that these relatively sympathetic portrayals were produced in the wake of the passage of the Wagner Act in 1935. Like the newspaper stories of the time, but with a different inflection, both films attempt to frame the viewer's understanding of labor, capital, even "exploitation" itself (Rondinone 2010). More important from the perspective of this study, both films make explicit arguments about race, community, and the status of immigrants in the U.S. While BLACK FURY offers a relatively progressive representation of these new immigrants, and argues for their full inclusion within a new, broadly defined "white" community, RIFFRAFF's narrative turns on an unspoken nativism that represents immigrants as gangsters, Lotharios, and thugs. At the same time, while RIFFRAFF explicitly rejects Marxism, including the Marxian theory of economic exploitation, as so much hot air, it projects an alternatively gendered perspective on labor struggles. RIFFRAFF argues that masculine domination, secured through bonds of love, conceals women's economic exploitation in the household. Both BLACK FURY and RIFFRAFF reject any radical analysis of class relations in favor of an idealized corporatism in which the various classes cooperate to produce a functional totality. But RIFFRAFF recognizes that such an idealized economic vision is founded upon the continued hidden exploitation of women within the community.

In Chapter 2, I look at MY MAN GODFREY (1936). This popular film also provides a corporatist solution to the economic problems of the Great Depression, but adds something distinctive: an argument for the social necessity of the speculative investor or venture capitalist. Godfrey, as one of the Depression's "forgotten men," becomes a mediator between classes. But in order to achieve this mediating position, he must be gendered as a woman. By depicting Godfrey's gendered transformation, the film challenges the strict, hegemonic division between male and female. Godfrey's success comes from his ability to participate in both gender schemes. And this gendered mediation also allows Godfrey to mediate class relations. While MY MAN GODFREY criticizes the excesses of capitalism, and satirizes the life styles of the ruling class, it ultimately rejects radical analysis of those conditions in favor of a corporatism that affirms the social necessity of "Captains of Finance" (Veblen 1994). At the same time, that affirmation takes the form of a carnivalesque and critical inversion of gendered norms.

Chapter 3 interrogates the Astaire-Rogers' musical, SWING TIME (1936). One of the most popular films of its year, SWING TIME begins with a radical indictment of the American leisure class, using a visual rhetoric that seems to intentionally evoke the work of Thorstein Veblen (1994). While the first half of the film continues this critique, often invoking the symbols of the new union movements and the Popular Front, in the second half of the film that critique is repressed by an ambivalent display of white supremacy. On the one hand, the film argues that working class culture is built upon the labor of black cultural workers (swing music), and, at the same time, the film is unable to tolerate that debt. Thus, it concludes by endorsing an unstable white supremacy that both acknowledges and conceals the dependence of the white working class community upon black creativity.

With Chapter 4, I turn to John Ford and Dudley Nichols' radical indictment of colonialism and "whiteness," THE HURRICANE (1937). I argue that this film demonstrates Ford's emerging Popular Front sympathies, as well as his mobilization of his own sense of Irish ethnicity in the formation of his understanding of colonialism and race making. THE HURRICANE is one of the only films of the early 20th century to make explicit reference to "whiteness," and, I argue, the film does so in a context that anticipates the work of Frantz Fanon (1967). Despite this radical critique of colonialism and the construction of imperial whiteness, Ford and Nichols remain committed to an anti-black white supremacy within the boundaries of the U.S. This remarkable contradiction and blindness provides some insight into the limits of racial critique in the early 20th century, as well as the limits of Ford's own radical traditionalism.

While the first four chapters provide close readings of individual films, Chapters 5 and 6 take a slightly different approach by looking at bodies of work. In the case of Chapter 5, I study Ginger Rogers' work for RKO studios between 1939 and 1941. What I discover is that many of these films were directed or written by artists later blacklisted during the Red Scare. And, indeed, Popular Front rhetoric and ideas repeatedly surface in Rogers' work during this period. On the one hand, Ginger Rogers marks the high point of a kind of proletarian Hollywood cinema, with films like KITTY FOYLE (1938) and TOM, DICK AND HARRY (1941) written by Popular Front radicals. But to the extent that radical depictions of class inequality or class conflict penetrated these pictures, those politics remain premised upon a kind of radical paternalism that seems especially worried by women's increasing participation in the formal labor market (Stansell 1987). In addition, while writers like Dalton Trumbo and Paul Jarrico sometimes attempted radical representations of opposed class communities, none of these Popular Front culture workers in Hollywood directly confronted capitalism's economic imperatives and forms of exploitation.

Though often regarded as a Cold War liberal, John Ford provides perhaps the only example of a mainstream, popular Hollywood picture that directly confronts capitalism as a systematic process, THE GRAPES OF WRATH. In Chapter 5, I examine John Ford's transformation over time, from a sympathetic fellow traveler with the Popular Front, to a Cold War nationalist who represses class conflict in favor of a militaristic collective fiction of solidarity. In this sense, FORT APACHE represents the last of Ford's Popular Front films. When York turns away from his commitment to justice, and toward an uncritical nationalism, Ford turns away from his concerns with class and inequality. Yet this is a turning that acknowledges the very repression it attempts to accomplish. In this sense, Ford's work during the 1940s reveals the contradictions, ambivalence, and shifting alliances that shape his politics, his world, and, perhaps, his audience.

Several significant findings emerge from this research. First, based upon the evidence of films like SWING TIME, MODERN TIMES, KITTY FOYLE, and THE GRAPES OF WRATH, New Deal Hollywood cinema allowed a remarkable diversity of political responses to the Great Depression, including moments of radical critique and radical economic analysis. Thus, despite the overt efforts of the Hays Office, American cinema sometimes questioned the very economic system that generated its profits at the box office. But, second, when radical economic themes did penetrate the Hollywood cultural apparatus, those radical representations were often founded upon a moral traditionalism that celebrated white supremacy and masculine domination. Again, these contradictions were not unique to Hollywood movies. But their presence did shape the political projections of solidarity advocated by the films, usually excluding women and non-white subjects. Yet not all New Deal films subscribed to an uncritical white nationalism, nor projected an uncritical celebration of masculinity. BLACK FURY and THE HURRICANE both challenge white supremacy, with the latter film openly critiquing the very concept of "whiteness." Despite corporatist politics of class cooperation, and a shared anti-Marxism, RIFFRAFF and MY MAN GODFREY both respond to transformations in the economic and social order by challenging reified forms of masculine authority.

Thus, like other forms of popular culture, Hollywood representations were always overdetermined by competing interests, meanings, and political themes (Meyerowitz 1994). This overdetermination would be largely invisible to a functionalist Marxian analysis. Tensions and contradictions in the cultural apparatus suggest that, in order to maintain commercial power, Hollywood attempted to meet a new kind of audience. Evidence for the openness provoked by the search for this audience appears in Gingers Rogers' films of the late 1930s and early 1940s, many of which had some connection to Popular Front artisans, and contained explicit reference to Popular Front ideas and class inequality. Thus, to the extent that this audience demanded new kinds of pictures, those demands sometimes intersected with popular demands for a new kind of economy and society based upon new forms of social and economic justice. This new kind of public was made possible, in part, by the cultures of solidarity that emerged in response to the economic and social dislocations of the Great Depression. When those cultures of solidarity decayed, cinema itself refracted the loss of promise that ended the age of the CIO. John Ford's films between 1940 and 1948 track that transformation, and chart the melancholy appeal of Cold War forms of solidarity once the best hopes of labor had been dashed. With his self-conscious turn away from Popular Front themes and ideas, Ford trades the collective dream of social justice for a garrison state that shelters ethnic Americans within barricades built by a newly fabricated white identity.

CHAPTER 1

Black Fury (1935) and RiffRaff (1936)[1]

By 1937, after the successful settlement of the General Motors sit down strike, industrial unionism, as a social movement, reshaped the lives of working Americans.

> Across industrial America the GM settlement transformed the expecta-tions of workers and managers alike.... [Most workers] were fearful bystanders whose union consciousness would crystallize only after the CIO had stripped management of its capacity to penalize their union loyalty. Thus, in almost every industrial district, workers poured into the new unions...They shouted "CIO, CIO, CIO!"
>
> LICHTENSTEIN 2002: 51

For union consciousness to crystallize, a principle of hope and solidarity was necessary. The dream of the CIO served precisely that function. For this new industrial union movement to take hold, workers needed to know about the CIO victories. But information, of course, is never unfiltered. It is always mediated, always framed. For workers throughout the United States, the mass media helped shape information about organized labor, and helped frame its struggles (Martin 2004, Puette 1992, Rondinone 2010, Luhmann 2000). In the mid-1930s, these mass sources of information were three-fold: the printed word, radio, and cinema.

Two years before the CIO-GM settlement, the Lynds find that for Muncie, Indiana (aka "Middletown") "information in this culture tends to reach the public largely 'with the compliments of' business." (Lynd and Lynd 1937: 378) The local business friendly newspapers batter organized labor and attempt to frame the discourse around labor. "Labor 'atrocities' tend fairly consistently to be featured on page one, and its equities and victories to be played down and relegated to an inside page" (ibid.: 382–383). The press tends to frame all strikes as injurious to the public interests, and all strikers as radicals (see also Rondinone 2010: 90–105). "When a front-page picture is shown of police or troops 'mussing up' strikers, the caption is likely to feature the word 'Radicals,'

---

1   This chapter is a considerably expanded version of material originally published in "'Hunkies,' 'Gasbags' and 'Reds': The Construction and Deconstruction of Labor's Hegemonic Masculinities in Black Fury (1935) and Riff Raff (1936)" Left History 13: 2, November 2008: 65–94. A revised version of this essay was also reprinted in Cassano 2010.

so that the picture portrays the forces of law and order putting down an un-American, anarchistic brute threat from the underworld—and this makes sense to Middletown, even to most workers" (Lynd and Lynd 1937: 383). At least in 1935, like most cities in industrial America, Muncie had an anti-labor press that attempted to frame labor struggles as fundamentally un-American.

At the same time, the Lynds find a struggle between the local world portrayed by the local press, and the wider national culture. "The presence of more syndicated material in Middletown's press is working further—hand in hand with movies, radio, nation-wide fashion services, automobile mobility, important standards in education, Federal sponsored relief policies, and many other aspects of its culture—to make Middletown identify itself with the wider America that surrounds it" (Lynd and Lynd 1937: 378). As the Lynds indicate in their title, Muncie was in a state of transition, from one kind of culture to another: from a localized, isolated culture, to a more cosmopolitan culture based in shared forms of work and shared forms of entertainment. Hence, the representation of labor by local newspapers competed with these other forms of representation in a struggle to frame the discourse around organized labor. This chapter explores some of the ways in which New Deal cinema attempted to depict organized labor and the way those frameworks of interpretation intersected with and sometimes contradicted the attitudes evinced by the leisure class that in America, as in Middletown, delivered information to the public "with the compliments of business."

In the history of twentieth century (post silent) cinema, only a handful of films were made about organized labor, and fewer still about strikes (Walsh 1986; Rogin 2002; Puette 1992:12–31)).[2] Hence the significance of the fact that two films about organized labor and strikes emerged within less than a year of each other between 1935 and early 1936. BLACK FURY (1935) was produced in the wake of the passage of the Wagner Act, and seems to consciously point toward the formation of the CIO. RIFFRAFF (1936) is a lighter take on the same material, perhaps produced as a satire of the previous film. Through these pictures, Hollywood producers and artisans were attempting to interpellate their audience and set boundaries for acceptable discourse. Both films make arguments about racial identity, and about who belongs in the working class. Both films offer sympathetic portrayals of organized labor, and set limits to political debate. And those boundaries foreclose radical analysis of the economic conditions portrayed. Nonetheless, RIFFRAFF, the more overtly conservative of the two pictures, manages to challenge, subvert, and deconstruct dominant gender

---

2 Ross (1999) finds considerably more cinematic interest in labor during the silent era.

norms, even as it imagines a white-only working class, and advocates class compromise, craft unionism, and "'moral" capitalism.

BLACK FURY takes the side of New Deal liberalism toward unskilled union-ized workers, but confines women to the household, and, at best, to an auxil-iary status in labor struggles. This sympathetic vision of industrial unionism sets imaginary limits to labor solidarity by excluding women from full partici-pation in the movement. On the other hand, RIFFRAFF offers an economic justification for traditional, AFL craft unionism, attacks militancy and commu-nism, but does so with a visual rhetoric that employs a much more compli-cated notion of women's gendered roles in the household and the workforce. Because, in part, RIFFRAFF is the product of two powerful women screenwrit-ers, Frances Marion and Anita Loos, it examines labor struggles from the per-spective of the excluded woman and manages to pierce the veil of ideology that surrounds this male dominated discourse. The result is a picture that deconstructs the labor movement's hegemonic masculinity, reveals "radical paternalism" to be a screen for masculine domination, and, consequently, rejects radicalism itself upon those grounds.

Radical Paternalism and Labor's Solidarity

Following the lead of Eric Hobsbawm's groundbreaking study, "Man and Woman: Images on the Left," (Hobsbawm 1998) labor historians and cultural theorists have explored the themes of "masculinity" and "femininity" in radi-cal political discourse and in labor's visual iconography. For instance, Elizabeth Faue's Community of Suffering and Struggle devotes a pivotal chap-ter to "Gender, Language, and the Meaning of Solidarity, 1929–1945," in which she argues women were represented as part of the laboring community, but almost never as laborers. Examining political cartoons from labor newspa-pers, Faue finds women portrayed as proletarian republican mothers, adjuncts and necessary auxiliaries in the masculine confrontation between labor (or the "community") and capital. Men appear as radical paternalists defending their community of "dependent" wives and children. Gerstle's study of the Woonsocket, Rhode Island labor press during this same period parallels Faue's, and supplements her findings, adding the celebration of the patriarchal nuclear family to labor's iconographic arsenal (Faue 1991; Gerstle 2002: 193; Melosh 1991). The literature and theory of the Popular Front period draws the attention of Paula Rabinowitz in her monograph, Labor and Desire (1991). She pays particular attention to the Popular Front's "pronatalist rhetoric"—that is, the celebration of the proletarian mother—as well as the depiction of capital as effete, feminine, and homosexual. In short, much left and labor discourse was founded upon a kind of "radical traditionalism" (Thompson 1993) that critiqued capital in the name of traditional forms of racialized and gendered privilege. Perhaps in order to highlight the invidious character of radical traditionalism, Stansell renames the gendered version of this discourse "radical paternalism" (Stansell 1987).[3] While the collapse of social democratic hopes during the post-World War Two period had a complex and decidedly overdetermined set of interacting causes, these scholars suggest that among the various determinates was what might be called a *failure of imagination*. The inability of workers and activists to escape hegemonic gendered and raced norms, and thus to see women and racial "others" as full members of the working class "community," circumscribed the boundaries of solidarity and thereby restricted possibilities for political agency and collective resistance.

Radical paternalism thus simultaneously resists and helps to secure the reproduction of capitalist processes of exploitation. As a trope, this version of working class "masculinity" associates duty to the community (the laboring man as the protector of the weak, helpless and dependent) with both wage labor (through his hard work, he shelters and provides for his family) and with an invidious prestige that makes the man a lord within his household. Meanwhile, this version of the trope of "femininity" subordinates women, but validates that subordination by figuring domestic partners as essential supports in the manly struggle against capital's assaults. Women are discouraged from participating in wage work and capitalist processes of exploitation even as they are encouraged to labor within the household. And while men are compensated for their efforts through wages, women labor within the household

---

3 It is vital not to lose sight of the complex, often contradictory functions inherent in the discourse of radical paternalism. Radical paternalism, and radical traditionalism more generally, help shape narratives of class conflict that figured the forces of capital as enemies of the laboring "community." When capitalist processes of surplus extraction impinge upon "traditional" communal values and practices, this appears as a violation of the community's moral compact. It gives energy to organizing efforts, and strengthens the solidarity of laborers resisting processes of exploitation through sit-downs, strikes, slow downs and sabotage. The activated worker isn't just fighting for himself; he's fighting for all the values he and his fellows hold dear. At the same time, included in those community "values" are processes of domination that invest an invidious prestige in certain community members (e.g. "white" males), while subordinating some (women) and entirely excluding others (e.g. African Americans) from membership in the group. This is the double edge inherent within working class radical traditionalism—as both a form of solidarity and a system of domination (see Chapter 6 of this volume).

out of "duty" to their family and, perhaps, out of "love" (Fraad, Resnick and Wolff 1994; Cassano 2010).[4]

The day BLACK FURY opened at the Strand in New York City, Albert Maltz's radical attack upon the coal industry, *Black Pit*, was continuing its run at the Theatre Union.[5] "Although 'Black Fury' is immersed in the same materials as the militant Theatre Union melodrama 'Black Pit,'" wrote the New York Times' critic, Andre Sennwald, "you would be phenomenally naïve if you expected that it adopts the same bias as that angry product of the left-wing theatre of action" (*New York Times,* April 7, 1935). Both Sennwald and Maltz (1935) recognized the rupture between the radical representation of class struggle in the Theatre Union, and the "conservative propaganda" found in the Strand. But while BLACK FURY did not offer a radical representation of class struggle, there was nonetheless a profound continuity between the systems of signs populating that film and the messages that sometimes constituted labor's self-representation (on the history of censorship and revision that shaped BLACK FURY's screenplay, see Walsh 1986; Black 1994: 252–260). Whatever the overt political differences between BLACK FURY and the products of the labor press and Popular Front artists, on a symbolic level they often shared a common set of constructions that often represented labor as inherently "masculine," while women were represented as necessary adjuncts and subordinates in labor's manly struggle with capital. Yet even as it reinforces traditional concepts of gender, the film subverts and challenges elements of the normative racial order.

Black Fury and the Construction of Whiteness

BLACK FURY is overtly a film about class and class struggle. But as a film about class, it is simultaneously and necessarily a film about gender, about the proper

---

4   The postmodern Marxian economists, Stephen Resnick and Richard Wolff, reject the notion that any single class process encompasses all the complexities of contemporary social formations. Thus, they offer a model in which various, competing, and sometimes contradictory class processes simultaneously exist together. They find that in some forms of household association, feudal processes of exploitation help perpetuate the subordination of women. In the imagined (and interpellating) "traditional" family in which women labor out of love or duty, the household lord (e.g. the man) appropriates the surplus of his loving vassal. "The feudal form is appropriate because it requires no intermediary role for markets, prices, profits, or wages in the relation between the producer and the appropriator of surplus labor." (Fraad, Resnick and Wolff 1994: 7). The household as imagined by radical paternalist discourse is almost an ideal type of this feudal form of exploitation.

5   Maltz later gained some notoriety as one of the "Hollywood Ten" targeted by the House Un-American Activities Committee (Ceplair and Englund 2003; Schrecker 1998: 321).

place of women in relation to working men. At the same time, as a film about class and gender, BLACK FURY is also (and perhaps necessarily) a film about "race" and racial constructions. The film appeared eleven years after the restriction acts put an end to the great, post-1890 immigration wave that brought masses of Southern and Eastern Europeans to the United States. In the late 19th and early 20th century, these "new" immigrants were often represented in popular and scholarly discourse as racially separate from the native-born Anglo stock that made up much of the American laboring population. But with the influx of new immigrants, racial categories slowly began to change. A new language of "ethnicity" emerged to describe these foreigners who were not quite "white," yet not entirely "black." In the binary racial divide that had captivated the American political imagination since the eighteenth century, Italians, Jews, Greeks, and Slavs became what historian David Roediger (2005) calls "in-between peoples," neither wholly white nor entirely "other." For these "in-between peoples," race-making was a "messy process." Racial categorizations didn't change overnight, but evolved slowly, in response to changing social, political, and economic conditions. By 1935, some representations of "ethnicity" suggested a conditional "whiteness" for the new immigrants (that is, if they were properly "Americanized"), while other representations continued to associate new immigrants with racial alterity. BLACK FURY takes a "progressive" position regarding these new immigrants.[6] Although neither the word "race," nor "ethnicity" appear in the film, the narrative posits an invisible boundary that separates "white" Americans from the immigrants who populate the coal fields, while, at the same time, criticizing that very boundary (on the Americanization of the "new immigrants," see especially Barrett 1992; Mink 1995; on the "inbetween" racial status of the "new immigrants" and "whiteness" see Roediger and Barrett 2002; Roediger 2005; Brodkin 1998).

BLACK FURY begins with a shift whistle sounding and an industrial montage: first, from a distance, farmland in the foreground, the viewer sees the smoke stack; then, dissolve, now the camera's closer, watching a coal car roll up the tracks toward the lens; then, dissolve, coal pouring out of a shoot, the camera pans to the wasted landscape surrounding the company town; then, dissolve, miners, faceless in the shadows, leaving home for the mines; then, dissolve, a scene of domestic support, as a mother and daughter prepare a meal for their men. Mike comes into the kitchen, yawning.

---

6   The term "hunky" was applied to many different ethnicities. But since the root of this particular slur comes from the term "Hungarian," it's worth noting that *Black Fury*'s director was the Hungarian born Mahala Kurtez, who, once in Hollywood, changed his name to Michael Curtiz (Beauchamp 1997: 306).

"Where's Joe?"

"He's not up yet," Mike's wife responds, "I woke him the same time as you....
Ah, that fella. Every morning the same thing,—Joe" she knocks, "he never want
to get up."

Joe Radek loves to sleep. His precious slumber might simply be the result of
his hard day's labor, but there's something else at work. As the film will shortly
reveal, Joe sleepwalks through life, hardly aware of the labor struggles around
him. He is a dull-witted "hunky" miner whose greatest hope in life is to marry
his sweetheart, Anna Novak, and settle down on a pig farm. Like Radek, the
workers in the mines are overwhelmingly "in-between peoples": Italians, Slavs,
Southern Europeans. African American extras are present at the union meetings and in the mines, but they have no speaking parts. Thus, the central concern of the narrative is with these "new immigrant" ethnics and their
second-generation children. Anna Novak, with her short hair and perfect
English, represents this Americanized second-generation.

Later, in the bowels of the mine, when a manager insists upon a speed-up,
Joe's happy to comply. But Croner, a disgruntled miner with an Eastern city
accent, begins to sound off.

> Here's me shoveling gum, you yourself pulling down slate. They call that
> 'dead work' so we don't get paid for it. Look at Pratt and Butch over there
> laying track. They've been breaking their backs all morning carrying rails
> and banging spikes...more dead work. And we can't even begin to earn a
> nickel for ourselves until all that dead work's done.

As the audience will soon learn, Croner is an agent provocateur, trying to incite
a strike so his Pinkerton agency can profit off the turmoil. Nonetheless, the
audience, like some of the miners themselves, is swayed by Croner's argument
and sees the obvious injustice of miners' working for nothing. These lines and
others scattered throughout the film clearly attempt to solicit the audience's
sympathy for the miner's condition. In these terms, the film offers a clear
defense of what might be called a *responsible* unionism. The conservative
union leadership serves an important function, protecting the interests of
workers under the slogan "Half a loaf is better than none."

After the scene is set, a love affair between Joe Radek and Anna Novak drives
the subsequent narrative forward; and, in particular, a racial dialectic of desire
sets the plot in motion. Joe wants Anna; but Anna doesn't love Joe. Instead, she
has a secret affair with a white, native-born company cop. As the incarnation of
the Americanized "second generation" immigrant, Anna lusts after whiteness
and cannot understand why, when she looks white, she isn't. The scene opens

with a close-up of a poster: "Auspices—Federative Mine Workers—Tommy Poole secretary—DANCE—Slovak Hall—September 22nd." Inside, Joe laughs and drinks and waltzes with Anna to an old-world tune played by a band in lederhosen and feathered hats. As he hops from foot to foot, Joe says: "Old country dance more better than American jazzbo hot stuff mama, no?" Anna replies with a silent and sad smile. Three company cops come in the door.

> The first says, "come on Slim, I'll buy you a drink of that hunky bug juice." "Nothing doing," says Slim, "one of us has got to stay sober in case these hunyaks wind up in a brawl."

As this exchange makes clear, whether the miners were conceived as a separate "race" or "ethnicity" matters less than the fact that they are on the other side of the boundary demarcating "whiteness." A cultural divide cuts across the community, with the cops, as "white" men, on one side, and the "hunkies" and "hunyaks" on the other.

Once Joe departs, Anna learns that Slim is leaving Coal Town for a new job.

> Oh Slim you can't leave me here alone. You promised me, if you ever had a chance to get out of Coal Town you'd take me with you.... You said yourself, if I stay here I'll just be another worn out miner's wife. Pinchin' and starvin'. Tryin' to raise a bunch of squealing kids. I don't want to spend the rest of my life like that.

A series of binary oppositions structure and reveal the overdetermined meaning of racial categorizations. On one side of the divide, poverty, dirt, foreigners with old world customs; on the other side, abundance, cleanliness, American modernity. Slim is the symbolic incarnation of "whiteness." He represents Anna's escape from poverty, from degradation, from Coal Town. In this context, "whiteness" is more than simply a racial marker; it is, simultaneously, a "class" and a "gender" marker. Anna doesn't want to be "just...another worn out miner's wife." She lusts after the escape from "pinchin' and starvin'" promised by a white woman's identity and the freedom from the confined domesticity of a "hunky" woman "tryin' to raise a bunch of squealing kids." For Anna, Joe represents the "old world," racial alterity, poverty, and patriarchy; while Slim symbolizes "Americanism," freedom, abundance, and assimilation.

Anna Novak runs away to Pittsburgh, trailing Slim. When Joe discovers her betrayal, he breaks down and soaks his trouble in alcohol. That night, with Mike at his side, Johnny Farrell, Vice President of the FMW, speaks to the assembled miners. Within the union hall, the "new" immigrant miners are portrayed together with African American miners. Although the African American extras have no lines, the director and cinematographer take particular care to emphasize the presence of black miners at the union meeting. This rare cinematic representation of inter-racial labor solidarity provides further evidence that BLACK FURY participated in a broader symbolic discourse of solidarity that challenged dominant racial representations. During the 1930s, African Americans and "white" or "ethnic" actors rarely shared the screen. When African Americans did appear in Hollywood productions, they were nearly always portrayed as comic characters, maids, butlers, and servants of various types. In BLACK FURY, African Americans are active agents; and, although silent, their presence in the coalfields beside "hunky" miners violates the silver screen's "Jim Crow" conventions. Farrell's talk echoes Mike's earlier defense of a responsible unionism. "What answer are you gonna make to the men when their wives and children are starving?" Again, concealed in these words, an appeal to the workers' masculine identity.

In answer to Farrell's challenge, Croner says, "We'll tell 'em that if they wanna win, they gotta starve." Joe stumbles into the meeting, drunk and angry. He hears fragments of Croner's speech and says "Joe Radek not afraid to fight!" Mike tries to stop him. But Croner points to Radek, "There's your answer, Farrell. We're through with your whole rotten outfit." Then, saying "take this back to headquarters," Croner throws his union button at Farrell. Following his lead, half the miners in the room pelt Farrell and the other union officials with their buttons. The next morning, Joe awakens, hung over in Croner's room.

Croner says, "You gotta step out and be somebody. A big shot. Then she'll be sorry she walked out on ya. Joe you're a smart guy. You can be a big shot...." Croner plays on Joe's desire for Anna in his attempt to marshal the miner for his plan. In these lines, there's an implicit recognition that Anna desired Slim for the status elevation that he would provide. Later, after Joe's been elected President of the new, insurgent union he says to Croner: "President more better than coal policeman, no?" For Anna's sake, for her desire, Joe wants to be a "big shot."

Black Fury's Paternalism

When the strike begins and scabs appear, Radek finds himself ostracized by his fellow workers. Meanwhile, the cinematic iconography of the strike evokes the "masculine" representations of labor strife, as angry miners charge the coal cops and throw stones and insults toward the scabs. The camera offers a close up of a miner's wife, baby in her arms, careworn expression on her face, as she says to another woman, "I remember the last strike." With those words the audience realizes that Radek has betrayed his community, and, more than that, he betrayed his own masculinity, and his responsibility, *as a man*, to protect dependent women and children.

The final blow comes with Mike's blood sacrifice. While attempting to protect the honor of a young woman, Mike is beaten to death by a group of marauding coal company cops. Coming to his friend's aid, Joe ends up injured and in the hospital. While Joe recovers, Anna returns to Coal Town. She visits Joe in the hospital, but Joe won't respond to her pleas for forgiveness until he learns that the miners had decided to end the strike. Joe can't stand the thought of Mike's sacrifice being in vain. He gathers a load of dynamite and Anna helps him plant the charges. A stand-off follows, with Joe deep in the mines, and, as the audience knows from the montage of newspaper headlines that cross the screen, in the process Joe wins back the affection and admiration of his community. As Joe begins to blow some of the charges, the mine manager begs Anna to talk Joe out of the mine, but she responds: "This is Joe's fight and he's got to fight it his own way." By calling this "Joe's fight" Anna effaces her own labor, and ultimately, her own identity. Her labor was an essential support for Radek's siege. But Anna subsumes her identity within Joe's. There is a profound continuity between BLACK FURY's representation of the woman's role within labor struggles and the broader discourse of organized labor. It was as if Anna, during her sojourn away from Joe, had stumbled upon these words from the labor press:

> You too must realize that, in this struggle for a decent living, for the right to educate your children and give them a fair chance to continue to live peacefully after you have passed on, you must take your place beside your husband. *His struggle is your struggle. His wages are your livelihood.* Stand shoulder to shoulder with him and fight.
>
> Quoted in FAUE 1994: 89, emphasis added

We don't know what happened to Anna while away from Coal Town. But whatever happened, she returned having learned the proper place of a workingman's woman. Because his wages are her livelihood, his struggle is her fight too; but as an auxiliary worker in the important manly struggle for social justice.

BLACK FURY is hardly a radical representation. In a scathing response to screenwriter Harry Irving's contribution to the film, Albert Maltz calls the picture "prejudiced against labor."

An author is a propagandist by what he [sic] says or fails to say....
Mr. Irving despite his artistic intentions has constructed a picture with
the following propaganda: Militant workers are stoolpigeons; there is no
real basis for strikes; miners are stupid sheep who spend their time drinking or being led by the nose; and mine operators are fair-play boy scouts
who counsel their hired thugs not to use violence.

MALTZ 1935

Maltz's judgment of the picture is accurate enough. No doubt, BLACK FURY's
"realism" patently falsifies the reality of working peoples' experience in other
ways as well. During the 1930s, with male employment episodic at best among
many in the laboring classes, women moved into the formal economy in record
numbers, often becoming the household's primary breadwinner (Porter
Benson 2007; Lynd and Lynd 1937; Cohen 1990). But in BLACK FURY not a single woman works outside the household. Rather, evoking a golden age that
probably never existed, men, and men only, work in the "formal economy,"
while women take their "rightful" place as domestic laborers, caring for children and cleaning up after the men. Yet, for all its imposed limitations, the film
does take the side of New Deal liberalism by representing unionization as a
positive ideal, even as it attempts to resist the dominant racial categories that
excluded new immigrants from mainstream American society. Remarkably,
RIFFRAFF, a comic and sometimes anti-immigrant response to the Warner
Brothers' social problem film, nonetheless comes much closer to representing
the "reality" of women's experience during this period.

RiffRaff

When RIFFRAFF was released in January of 1936, it created none of the cultural ferment that greeted the release of BLACK FURY.[7] Yet RIFFRAFF closely
parallels BLACK FURY's narrative, at least for the first few reels; but with some
important differences. For instance, in order to situate the stories in decidedly
working class contexts, both films begin with a shift whistle and a montage
reflecting the early morning activities of the communities. But before the shift
whistle blows, BLACK FURY sets the tone for its narrative with the soundtrack
of a driving march, drums and horns creating an ominous aura. Before Riffraff's
shift whistle sounds, the audience experiences a very different montage.
After the Metro lion roars and the credits appear, pastoral and comic music

---

7 RIFFRAFF opened to generally positive reviews and grossed over a million dollars, a tidy sum
when movie ticket prices ranged from a nickel to a quarter. (Beauchamp 1997:327).

introduces a caption, *"Early morning on the waterfront,"* followed by idyllic scenes of the "white" working class fishing community as it rises from an evening's slumber. A man stretches outside his fishing shack. A woman lowers a beer bucket from a second store window to the cigarette stand on the first. Then a close-up of a smoke stack shrouded in smog and the sounding of the shift whistle. Shanty tunes play as the montage continues, illustrating the work of faceless men around the docks, hauling nets and setting tackle. Dissolve to a "lush" stumbling home to his shack on the dock. Cut to inside the shack, a blond woman standing before a washbasin, while the drunk stumbles in the door, stage left. The first lines of the film come from the woman as she rings out a piece of cloth:

"Stinko again."
"Is that a way to talk to your father?"
"Where was you all night?"
"I was lookin' for a job."
"What was you tryin' to do? Sneak up on it in the dark? Gee, if you was ever to get one, I'd drop dead." The scene cuts to a bedroom, where two children are stretching. They shake Hattie (Jean Harlow) out of her sleep.

These opening moments of the film are so close to the introductory scenes of BLACK FURY that RIFFRAFF appears almost to be a remake of the previous film. But as the narrative unfolds, the audience realizes that the Jean Harlow/Spencer Tracy vehicle is not so much a remake as a *response*, dialogically engaged in a political and social argument with the prior film. The terms of that engagement are announced in the opening moments. Not only does the music suggest that RIFFRAFF is somehow less serious, less ominous than BLACK FURY, but the visual montage of "white" workers beginning their day on the docks tell the audience that this is a film about *"our"* community. If BLACK FURY is about *"them,"* new immigrants, foreigners, racialized "others," RIFFRAFF is about an imagined "us" (in the *herrenvolk* sense) skilled, white craft workers. But something else, more significant still, emerges from these opening scenes. While BLACK FURY's montage ends with a shot of Joe Radek's slumbering close-up, thus communicating to the audience that *this is his story*, Riffraff's opening passage ends with Hattie's peacefully sleeping face. *This is her story*, a version of BLACK FURY told from the point of view of the women in the working class community.

Women's Exploitation in the Household

Hattie lives with her sister Lil, their younger brother, their father, Pop, Lil's husband and daughter. As we learn from the sequence above, the women in the household do the majority of the work. Pop is unemployed. Lil sees to the domestic chores in the household. Hattie works in a cannery. We never see Lil's husband at work, though we know he's a musician and probably out of work or underemployed. Thus, at least in this household, women are workers, while men are represented as dependent wastrels. The first words in the picture, that comic exchange between Lil and Pop, offer a symbolic representation of a central social trauma caused by the Great Depression. Lizabeth Cohen argues that "Unemployment among husbands forced many wives and children into the work force during the 1930s as the sole support of their families.... When the male breadwinner suffered prolonged unemployment, traditional authority relationships within the family, between husbands and wives and between parents and children, began to break down" (Cohen 1991: 247). Rather than taking this breakdown of patriarchal authority as a cause for mourning, however, RIFFRAFF's comic presentation suggests that the loss of male authority is an occasion for celebration.

From the first shot of Lil washing, RIFFRAFF situates women *as workers*. True, BLACK FURY opens with a similar representation. But while the women in BLACK FURY labor—"naturally"—for workingmen, RIFFRAFF's women labor for lazy scoundrels. Although Lil tells Pop to get his own morning coffee, she ends up pouring for him. And, moments later, in a parallel scene, Pop asks Hattie for "two bits." Although she replies, "ah go ask the government," she instantly reaches into her purse and gives him the quarter. In both cases, women's surplus is appropriated by a man whose marginal authority carries only a vestige of prestige. He doesn't—and can't—order them to give him the fruits of their labor. They give out of love. They produce a surplus. He lives without working. Thus, the film begins with a theory of exploitation constructed from a woman's gendered perspective (Fraad, Resnick and Wolff 1994; Cassano 2010; Resnick and Wolff 1987; Marx and Engels 1988). The fact that the film offers parallel portrayals of women working—Lil laboring at home and Hattie in the cannery—suggests that both women are being exploited, though the form of exploitation varies.

This focus on women's labor in the household as well as in the formal economy highlights a central absence in BLACK FURY. By portraying women's work as a natural duty, BLACK FURY essentially effaces the processes of exploitation that happen within the household. On the other hand, RIFFRAFF"s narrative offers an implicit critique of the exploitation implicit in the "traditional," male dominated household. At the same time, the film argues that household exploitation remains concealed precisely because it remains outside the bounds of conventional labor discourse. Much labor and left discourse remained blind to non-capitalist surplus production within the household; and this blindness on the part of the traditional left had representational consequences. Perhaps the fact that the women behind RIFFRAFF—screenwriters Anita Loos and Frances Marion—didn't recognize themselves in radical discourse influenced their dismissive attitude toward militant labor and political radicalism.

Both women had been writing screenplays since the days of silent cinema, and by the 1930s Frances Marion was among the highest paid writers in Hollywood. In addition, both women were active in the re-formation of the craft union, the Screen Writer's Guild, with Marion elected vice-president in 1933 (Beauchamp 1997: 307). Anita Loos' experiences with organized labor began during the "red summer" of 1919, when the Actors Equity Association was transformed from a toothless guild into an authentic union. Loos' husband at the time, John Emerson, helped lead the actors' strike; and the labor strife had a significant impact upon the young writer.[8] While she clearly admired the fact that "the actors' strike of 1919 was one of the first ever to be organized by white-collar workers," her account of the period takes an ironic, distinctly jaundiced form. Although the strike begins as a "struggle for better working conditions,"

> ...it soon evolved that the strike would give them [striking actors] a more imposing stage than they ever occupied before. And when strike activities began to give actors more publicity than they could earn onstage, the call to strike was sounded.... Never had actors, *en masse*, attained so many headlines or had more fun, for the strike turned every producer into a villain, and every striking supernumerary became a star.
> LOOS 1966: 253

The strike was a stage; the strikers acting their parts for publicity and personal prestige. In the end, it was clear to Loos that the struggle wasn't for justice—just for power. "Actors were now entering into the twentieth century's melodramatic switch of power; no longer underdogs, they now had their turn to trample on the boss, and this is only fair, considering the many centuries that the converse had been true." And to this rather Machiavellian view, she adds a touch of anti-communism (seemingly via NINOTCHKA (1939)): "I had seen an early demonstration of the triumph of the underdog in Berlin, where Soviet commissars, 'in town on business,' were spending government funds on German baby dolls with all the abandon of capitalistic sugar daddies"

---

8   The Actors' Equity strike is the subject of the final chapter of Loos' first autobiography, *A Girl Like I* (1966: 252–275).

(Loos 1966: 263). Loos' ambivalent attitude toward the strike and the strikers plays out in Dutch Muller's desire to use the coast's labor troubles as a wedge to win personal status. And the film's anti-militant attitude may have something to do with Loos' experience of a strike that "split up families and old friendships" and divided a community of "artists" who fancied themselves beyond politics (Loos 1966: 254). Consequently, in RIFFRAFF Marion and Loos offer an ambivalent but sympathetic portrayal of craft unionism, from a woman's perspective. This perspective deploys an ironic androcentric iconography that deconstructs the labored paternalism it puts on display.

Women's Exploitation in the Cannery

On her way to the cannery, Hattie finds the men crowded on the dock, listening to a radical organizer's harangue. The scene cuts to an office interior. Nick, the dark-skinned southern European cannery owner, hangs his hat on a hook. One of his thugs, "Flytrap," agitated and pacing, tells the boss that the workers are ready to strike. But Nick, apparently more interested in the fox stole he just purchased for his girl, doesn't seem to care.

> ...Look Flytraps, look. The men signa a five year agreement with me to work on certain percentage without pulling walkout, didn't they?...Is plenty tough for Nick, poor fellow. So what he gonna do? Nick is gonna for to bring in cheap labor and catch the fishes at half the price.

This sequence stands as a stark contrast with the presentation of the capitalists in BLACK FURY. Here Nick's image is much closer to the labored representation of capital as effete, with his primping and vanity. To this, RIFFRAFF adds a distinctive racial cast. Nick is a racial other, and his accent and malapropisms, an echo of Chico Marx's riff on Italian ethnicity, suggest an almost minstrel-like character (Roediger 1999). Moreover, the film plays upon the cinematic and cultural image of the ethnic gangster, and Flytrap's offer to "smoke" the union organizer solidifies the impression that Nick is somehow "connected." So while RIFFRAFF approaches the historical "reality" of New Deal labor struggles—Nick wants to provoke the men into violating their contract so he can bring in cheap labor—this racialized representation of capital circumvents class critique.

The scene cuts to "Ptomaine Tony's," an eatery where Dutch sits at the counter flirting with the waitresses. The union leader, Brains, comes in, followed by

Dutch's side-kick, Lew.[9] Like Flytrap, Brains is worried that the men are about to strike; and he's particularly disturbed that his fellow workers are listening to the radical organizer. "He's a 'red' if I ever saw one."

"Why that gas bag," growls Dutch, "I'll break him in half. I'll show them dumb-dumbs."

Dutch pushes his way through the men and confronts Red Belcher. "Ah shut up and get offa that barrel. Where do you think you are, Roosha?" From the distance, Hattie watches with a group of women. As Dutch begins, one says "oh my, what a man." Hattie mockingly rolls her eyes and the scene cuts back to Dutch.

> When we was kids we used to fight like wildcats. But if an outside gang come in we stuck together and threw 'em out. [Laughter.] Brain says that Nick wants us to strike.... He thinks we're suckers. But we ain't. We ain't gonna fight. And I'll sock the first guy in the puss who says we are.

At that point, a riot erupts, with Dutch leaping into the fray. As a cop grabs Dutch and begins to drag him away, Hattie, in a balcony above, yells "watch out below, it's a bomb" and throws a tuna can. The cop releases Dutch, grabs the can and begins to throw it to the bay before realizing the trick. As the men return to their boats, the "strike" over, at least for now, Hattie says "come on, Lil, I'm gonna show that big lug who saved his skin." After the riot dissolves, a newsreel crew stops Dutch.

> Mr Muller, will you say something to the Metrotome news while we take your picture?

The similarities between the opening minutes of this picture and the beginning of BLACK FURY are unmistakable. Like Joe Radek, Dutch Muller is a dense workingman, relatively indifferent to the union. And, like Joe, Dutch has a close friend and advisor, a "responsible" unionist, Brains. Furthermore, an agitator, Red Belcher ("that gas bag") goads the men to break a five-year contract, and strike. Dutch, like Joe, takes the side of his friend, and through a display of masculine prowess, persuades the men to stay on the job. But important differences appear in the framing of this conflict.

Hattie's narrative perspective orients the entire scene, and her consistent parody of Dutch's "masculinity" and self-importance undermines the patriarchal iconography. Hattie sees through Dutch's narcissism, and the audience sees Dutch through Hattie's eyes. Like Anna Novak's, Hattie's efforts—in this

---

9 "Lew" is played by Vince Barnett, an actor who had previously appeared in BLACK FURY.

case, her improvised "bomb"—are central to Dutch's success—his escape from the police; but in this instance, Hattie resists Dutch's attempt to erase her part in the process. Standing before the newsreel camera, talking about what *he* decided, what *he* did, Dutch is dumped into the bay by a fish Hattie throws. With that, the audience learns how to read Dutch's masculinity and Hattie's agency. She's no demur product of old world custom willing to defer to male authority. Thus, from its first moments, RIFFRAFF inverts the typical iconography of a laboring community consisting of manly workers and their dependent women and children. With the single exception of Brains, men in the picture are consistently represented as either dependent good-for-nothings or vain gasbags, while women support families and sustain the community, even as they are systematically blocked from formal participation in the union and the life and death communal decisions made by men.

RIFFRAFF disrupts normative systems of gendered representations; but it doesn't abandon patriarchal tropes. Rather, it re-orients the spectator's perspective by imagining gendered constraints through Hattie's eyes. And the film goes further still by envisioning women as workers, even industrial workers. After Hattie dumps Dutch in the bay, an industrial montage: first, a shot of rolling gears and belts; then cans rolling down a chute; a man tending a machine as it chops tuna; a woman's hand pressing tuna into cans; cans passing on an assembly line before another woman controlling quality; a group of women standing in front of tables, cleaning fish from a fresh catch; a line of uniformed women standing over a mechanized belt, and Hattie, rushing in from the docks, taking an empty place on the line. Unlike BLACK FURY, where women work, but exclusively within the confines of the household, RIFFRAFF extends this gendered division of labor. The docks and the union hall represent the men's world. The industrial cannery represents feminine space. The montage that precedes the dialogue offers a single male representation, and the man seems to be servicing a machine. In other words, men do the "skilled" craft labor, while women do the low status, and low paid "unskilled" line work. Furthermore, an exchange between Hattie and the foreman ("you're gonna get the gate [get fired]," says the foreman) suggests that these women workers don't share the union standards that protect the male dockworkers.

Hattie is led from the line to Nick's office. She slams the door as she enters. Rather than firing her, Nick gives Hattie a new fox stole. This sequence introduces the racial dialectic of desire that drives the rest of RIFFRAFF's narrative forward.[10] Once again, as in BLACK FURY, there are indications that Nick lusts

---

10   The racial dialectic of desire that I'm documenting was only one cinematic pattern among
      many. During the 1930s, the so-called "new immigrants" were represented on both sides of

after Hattie because of her metonymic connection to "whiteness." After all, Nick has money and power. But he lacks something. As he says to Hattie, "you got what it takes for Nick." The audience doesn't know exactly what "it" is. We do know that Nick socializes with the otherwise exclusively white workers who make up his tuna fleet. We also know that Nick is decidedly vain, vain enough to hang a picture of himself prominently in his office. Finally, despite Nick's attempts to socialize with white workers and to put on a "white" mask—e.g. his attempts at rhetorical eloquence that come out as foreign malapropisms—he remains on the other side of a barrier. True, this "racialized" barrier has class overtones (after all, Nick is the capitalist); but it's hard not to see Nick's desire for Hattie as a desire for assimilation, acceptance, and "whiteness." And, at the end of the picture, when Nick has given up his desire for Hattie, we find him quite satisfied in the arms of another blond "factory girl," adding further evidence for this reading. But whatever Nick's racial ambitions, there is another aspect of his desire for Hattie that is unambiguously indicated. "You know, I like the way you dumped that Muller guy in the water. That was pretty good." Nick desires Hattie because she put Dutch in his place. That is to say, Hattie becomes a prize in the symbolic and material struggle between Nick Lewis and Dutch Muller. In fact, the struggle between capital and labor that will consume much of the rest of the film is driven forward by Nick's desire for Hattie, and Dutch's desire to claim what Nick wants.

Anti-Marx

The next scene finds Dutch on a tuna boat, away from Hattie's and Brain's moderating influences. Here, Dutch listens to Red's political invectives. And the filmmakers take this opportunity to attack and pillory Marxian value theory. Red tells Dutch that he "could do a lot" for the working men on the coast, and

---

the racial boundary separating "white" from "non-white" Americans. King Vidor's 1935 picture, THE WEDDING NIGHT, tells the tale of a romance between an unambiguously "white" writer (Gary Cooper as a Connecticut Yankee) and a blond haired Polish immigrant woman (played by Anna Stein). Despite the young woman's "white" appearance, the romance is, in part, derailed by the racial differences between the two lovers. At the same time, other films, like ROMANCE IN MANHATTAN (1935), starring Ginger Rogers, allow for intermarriage between "white" women and immigrants. And immigrant director Frank Borzage's THE BIG CITY (1937) has Spencer Tracy romance and marry a dark-skinned immigrant woman, with the active support of the community of "white" workers within which he lives. Finally, this racial dialectic of desire also plays out in films that address the "yellow peril." See especially Rogin (1992) and Marchetti (1994).

in a remarkable cinematic moment, quotes, nearly word for word, Marx's *Wage-labor and Capital*. In that text, Marx theorizes the relation between wages and production: "Wages, therefore, are not a share of the worker in the commodities produced by himself. Wages are that part of already existing commodities with which the capitalist buys a certain amount of productive labour-power" (Marx 1902: 24). Belcher, aboard the tuna boat, tells Dutch:

> "Wages are not the working man's share of a commodity he has produced. Wages are the share of a commodity previously produced of which the employer buys a certain amount of productive labor power. That's right, isn't it?"
> "Huh?...Oh sure, sure."
> "Alright. The wage-worker sells labor power to capital. Why does he sell it?"
> "Huh?...Why, because he's a sucker, that's why."
> "Now, look, is work an active expression of a man's life?"
> "Yeah," says Lew.
> "No," says Red.
> "No, you dope," says Dutch.

By the time this exchange occurs, the audience already knows that Red's loyalties lie with big ideas, not with the workers. Red uses Dutch's ignorance and arrogance, his desire to be a "big man," as a seductive wedge. But in that scene of seduction, the audience recognizes political deception; and the claims made by Red represent an obvious *inversion* of the truth. Thus, since Red is a liar and Dutch a fool, the film argues wages *are* the workingman's *fair share* of what he produces. At least for the skilled craft workers on the boat, labor *is* the active expression of a man's life. Here, again, let me suggest the possibility that this critical attitude toward Marxian discourse, and the Marxian theory of exploitation (represented by the screenwriters as so much hot air), may have much to do with the blindness that traditional Marxists often showed toward women and household exploitation. After all, from the first shot of RIFFRAFF forward, it is *women* who do the lion's share of the labor, both industrial and household production, while authority remains vested in the men who exploit and appropriate that labor (Fraad, Resnick and Wolff 1994; Cassano 2010). Because the formal language of Marxian exploitation seemed to bypass the experience of domestically laboring women, Frances Marion and Anita Loos portray it as hollow rhetoric, one more empty exhalation from a male gasbag. While I don't mean to suggest that a more inclusive Marxism would have opened a larger space for "radical" representations within American cinema, I would like to suggest the possibility that Marion's and Loos' attitude might be symptomatic of a broader cultural perception among American women that Marxism did not speak to their reality.

Race, Wealth, and Desire

Red's appeals to Dutch take root once Dutch recognizes Nick's desire for Hattie. And here, as in BLACK FURY, a racial dialectic plays out in the context of a communal celebration. The scene on the tuna boat ends with Red's words: "We need you Muller, you're a born leader." And before the last syllable fades, the tune "You are my lucky star" frames the sign: *July 4th. Entertainment! Dancing! Fireworks! Come one! Come All! Celebrate the 4th on board the Fairy Queen.* Hattie enters with Nick on her arm and his brown fox stole around her neck. When she sees Dutch at a table with one of the waitresses from Ptomaine Tommy's, Hattie takes the adjacent table, dragging Nick along. She means to inspire Dutch's jealousy. On the bandstand, a man attempts to silence the crowd. Then a newsreel rolls. The narrator, "...*Muller, a strong silent man, reluctantly offers his own modest comments on how he stops strikes.*" A shot of Dutch standing atop his boat. Meanwhile, in the dancehall, Flytrap says to Nick, "Hey boss, boss, you want me to knock his block off?"

"Ah leave him alone. He's full of escaping gas."

Cut back to Dutch on film, "*Well what I done was no more than anybody woulda done who used their brains in the same situation...I wanna say that I don't—*" then Hattie's flying mackerel slaps Dutch in the side of the head, he tumbles into the bay, and the dancehall audience explodes into laughter and applause. Dutch pretends not to care and leads his date out of the room, but Nick blocks his path. The struggle between Nick and Dutch over Hattie turns into a dice game. The men clear a table and begin to cast lots. At first, Nick wins cast after cast. When Dutch is busted, Hattie says "ah let him roll one more."

"You better go downstairs," says Nick.
"Hey, who are you ordering around?" asks Hattie. "I'm staying right here."

She moves close to Dutch and spits on his dice for luck. Dutch begins to win, taking most of his opponent's cash. Afterward, he and Hattie dance close on the floor while an angry Nick watches. He tries to break the two apart.

"Hey listen, big shot," Dutch says to Nick, "a little more respect outta you or I'll tie up your whole dirty waterfront."
At this point Brains intervenes, "You're heading for trouble, Dutch."

Dutch ignores Brains and downs Nick with a right hook. As the lights go out, the dance breaks into a riot. Grabbing Hattie by the arm, Dutch takes flight. Blue notes distant in the night, Dutch and Hattie escape the workers' brawl for the solitude of a docked tuna boat. Dutch takes Hattie's fox stole and tosses it to the sea. Her anger melts when Dutch takes her in his arms and they kiss. Still in his arms, her voice almost a whisper:

"You don't wanna marry me just 'cause Nick does, do ya?...You didn't dream about getting married 'till I told you about Nick, did you?"
"Ah, don't be screwy. I wanna marry you 'cause you spit lucky."

The audience knows better than to believe Dutch. Despite Hattie's clear affection, Dutch avoided her, or offered only flirtatious promises, until Nick provoked Dutch's desire. In other words, Dutch wanted Hattie precisely because Nick wanted her. And this passionate circuit is further complicated by Nick's own ambiguous social status. On the one hand, he represents a capitalist, and so commands Dutch's obedience, if not his respect. On the other hand, Nick is a racialized other, a dark-skinned southern European who desires Hattie precisely for her "whiteness." Nick wants Hattie because normative American culture valorizes and validates her "whiteness"; in turn, Dutch wants Hattie because Nick wants Hattie. And Nick has one more thing Dutch wants: Nick is a "big shot." What began as a scene of cinematic humiliation before the other members of the community, ends in Dutch's public victory over Nick when he seizes Hattie, and, in the subsequent sequence, marries her. And, when Hattie stands at the altar, she's wearing a *pure white* fox stole, this one a present from Dutch.

Like Anna Novak in the previous film, Hattie is offered a path out of poverty and away from her working class community. Although Hattie considers the possibility of an affiliation with Nick, the audience realizes that her central interest in her boss comes from his ability to inspire Dutch's desire. At the same time, like Joe Radek, Dutch is driven by the desire to be more than a simple worker, to be a big shot, a born leader, to have what Nick has. But Radek's desire for prestige was derived, ultimately, from his desire for Anna. Prestige became a symbolic compensation for his lost love. In RIFFRAFF, however, that same circuit is inverted. Dutch's desire for Hattie derives from his desire to be a big man, his desire for authority and prestige; and Hattie, as the object of Nick's passion, becomes a symbolic compensation for Dutch's lack of authority over himself and his labor. Finally, unlike Anna Novak, Hattie refuses to be a passive object passed from man to man. Rather, she continually resists the authority and impositions of both Dutch and Nick (she says to both men, "Hey, who are you ordering around?") and attempts to establish her own agency. But Hattie's power is continually circumscribed by gendered norms, and her agency, her resistance, necessarily takes subtle and often concealed forms.

Responsible Unionism

After the wedding, Dutch takes Hattie home to their love nest, a consumer's paradise full of electrical appliances and new furniture. Although Hattie is impressed, she's shocked by the fact that Dutch bought everything on the installment plan. And her shock turns to horror when Dutch tells her that he and the men have decided to strike. "Oh, come on squirt," he pulls her onto his lap. "Don't worry about the strike. Let me worry about it. It's my business," he says, nuzzling her neck, "you just look after your wifely duties."

Another montage follows, beginning with a newspaper headline: *"Muller calls strike."* Then, docked tuna boats; men fishing off the side of the docks for their family dinner; headline, *"Strike reaches tenth week"*; women and children moving through a bread line; headline, *"Scab fleet brings in tuna"*; close-ups of angry faces, women and men, yelling "scabs!"; finally dissolving to Nick's office, with Brains and Dutch negotiating.

> "Listen Nick," says Brains, "those scabs ain't fishermen. 50% of the load of tuna is spoiled already because they don't know how to pack them in ice after they catch them.... You need the men. They're real fishermen. You've never lost a pound of fish out of their catches yet."

Cut to the words, FISHERMEN'S UNION, LOCAL No. 14, the sound of angry male voices and, inside the hall, Dutch standing behind a table, Red at his side. The camera cuts away to the building's exterior. Outside the window, women with worried faces watch the men's deliberations. Hattie stands at the head of the gathered crowd. Back inside, Dutch is pounding his gavel, trying to restore order. "None of you got a right to think," yells Dutch, "I'm thinkin' for you." Cut to Hattie's worried face.

> Another voice, "I vote for a new leader. I nominate Brains McCall."

Again, the parallels with BLACK FURY are striking. Like Joe Radek, Muller, pushed by his desire to be a big shot, forces a strike and loses. At the same time, a significant difference comes to light. In BLACK FURY, the sympathetic attitude toward "responsible unionism" depends upon an argument for social justice. After all, the miners and their families are mired in poverty, and, added to that, the audience learns about the "dead work" the miners do without any recompense. RIFFRAFF, however, stages a very different justification for "responsible unionism." On the one hand, from the available evidence, it seems that fishermen and their families lead relatively comfortable lives. At one point, we see the interior of Brain's home, and it's the ideal of lower middleclass domesticity. There is poverty on the docks, but it seems especially prevalent among the cannery workers. They have no union. On the other hand, when the argument for unionism is made, it's made on the basis of the skills of the tuna men. The scabs are ruining the catch. They lack the skills of "real fishermen." The union makes sense because it promotes *industrial efficiency and secures capitalist profit.*

As in BLACK FURY, Dutch's desire to be a big man severs his relationship with the community. At the same time, the differences with the prior film are also instructive. Despite the fact that the union decisions impact the entire community, including the women, the strike is men's business. Dutch makes this quite explicit. ("Don't worry about the strike. Let me worry about it. It's my business.") Men are the community's agents; while women become passive observers, standing outside the window, watching the gasbags fight among themselves. Again, this perspectival re-orientation serves a critical purpose. For all his strutting and display, Dutch's masculinity is revealed as hollow. As Brains puts it, "I don't care whether you're running the union or not. Our families are starving." Dutch's masculinity isn't a shelter for the weak and the "dependent"; his paternalism isn't a defense of community. Rather, machismo serves as a vehicle for personal ambition; and he's perfectly willing to throw the men of the union, as well as the community's women and children, overboard, in his narcissistic pursuit of personal power. By underscoring the self-serving character of Dutch's masculinity, RIFFRAFF offers a veiled critique of the tired labored paternalism that effaced women's labor, made them subservient under the guise of "protection," and left the life and death decisions that affected the entire community exclusively in the hands of men.

After Dutch breaks with Brains and the union, the parallels between RIFFRAFF and BLACK FURY largely come to an end. Dutch returns from the union meeting to find the furniture man repossessing everything he'd bought on installment. Meanwhile, when Brains and Hattie attempt to bring Dutch back into the fold, they don't use a language of abstract or communal solidarity. That is, they don't appeal to Dutch's loyalty to his comrades and his community. Rather, the appeal is closer to a form of blackmail. "Well you get in wrong with the union and you'll see what you'll be doing with that shovel." The union is a "vested interest" controlling the most lucrative and high status jobs on the waterfront (Veblen 1964). It's not on the basis of class solidarity that Hattie and Brains make their argument; rather they appeal to Dutch's pecuniary self-interest. Moreover, when Dutch refuses he says, again, "That's my business." But Hattie knows better, and from her perspective, "It's my business, too." Again, Dutch's longing for status, prestige and power becomes a betrayal of his love for and solidarity with Hattie.

At the same time, both Dutch and Hattie remain prisoners of hegemonic and normative values and desires that intervene directly in their relationship. On the one hand, nothing stands in the way of their happiness; nothing, that is, but Dutch's pride. And in this context, "pride" is a synonym for "masculinity." Hattie can go back to work and support the household. But Dutch can't stand the thought of his humiliation. He can't stand the thought of failing in the eyes of the other men. He can't stand the thought of their laughter. In short, he's imprisoned by their gaze, by their expectations, by his own conception of hegemonic masculinity (Connell 1987).[11] But Hattie is as much a prisoner as Dutch. "Dutch, look at me. I love you, honey. I'd do anything in the world for you." He may be a gasbag, a blow hard, a swelled head "big I am," but Hattie can't escape her longing for the man.

Dutch won't allow Hattie to return to the cannery precisely because he's invested in the traditional trope of the male dominated household. He sees Hattie's participation in processes of capitalist exploitation as an implicit threat to his domestic authority; and the public display of his domestic authority is fundamental to his conception of masculinity. At the same time, Hattie is prepared to accept a "second shift," both as a household worker and as a wage laborer, precisely because she loves Dutch (Hochschild 2003). Her own attachment to a traditional trope and a traditional circuit of desire prepares her simultaneously for feudal exploitation (in the household) and capitalist exploitation (in the cannery). Unlike BLACK FURY, RIFFRAFF refuses to endorse Hattie's attachment to Dutch and the forms of exploitation that come from her love. Rather, the film's critical and ironic representations deconstruct the circuits of socially constructed desire that imprison its characters.

---

11   In my use of "hegemonic masculinity," I follow R.W. Connell's definition: "In the concept of hegemonic masculinity, 'hegemony' means (as in Gramsci's analyses of class relations in Italy from which the term is borrowed) a social ascendancy achieved in a play of social forces that extends beyond contests of brute power into the organization of life and cultural processes" (1987: 184).

This theme of imprisonment by desire helps explain the extremely odd suspended resolution that ends the film. After Dutch and Hattie part, Dutch falls on hard times. When Hattie learns that he's sick in a hobo jungle nearby, she steals money from Nick Lewis to give to Dutch. Although she's unable to find him, the cops find Hattie, and as she's being taken away, the arresting officer tells her "you'll get twenty years for this." The audience then learns that Hattie is pregnant, and she has Dutch's baby behind bars. Meanwhile, Dutch comes back to the waterfront and begs to be readmitted to the union, but to no avail. He learns of Hattie's imprisonment—though not of the child—and formulates an escape plan. When he visits Hattie in prison and tells her his idea, she's insulted and leaves the room angry. But working in the institution's kitchen, she has a conversation with two other inmates.

> "Ah, what's the use of kidding myself. I'll never get over it. What a sap I was for sending him away.... Oh, why do I keep on thinking about him? What do you do to forget a guy like that?" asks Hattie, rhetorically.
> "I cut his throat," responds her co-worker, "that didn't do no good." Fade to black.

These lines explain RIFFRAFF's otherwise incomprehensible transformation into a women's prison movie. Now the audience realizes that the prison house is a material embodiment of women's desire. Like Hattie, the other women are trapped by their longing for men who are no good gasbags. The hegemonic masculinity that imprisons men through its constraints and demands, simultaneously imprisons the women who love them.

When he returns to make amends with Brains, Dutch is a broken man. His suit is torn, his face dirty, his pride gone. Although Brains can't get Dutch back in the union, he does manage to find him a non-union security job, guarding the docks. And this sets up the final parallel with BLACK FURY. Recall, in the previous film, Joe Radek ends the strike by dynamiting some of the mineshafts and threatening to blow the entire works. Joe's manly and violent resistance makes him once again a hero in the community. RIFFRAFF inverts BLACK FURY's climatic moments. While Dutch is watching the docks, Red returns with two men from the hobo jungle. The three communists have come with a load of dynamite. They're going to blow the docks to pieces. Red says, "so if they aint going to let us work, we aint going to let them work." Dutch plays along, pretending to agree to the sabotage. But at the decisive moment, Dutch turns against his former comrades, beats them, and seizes the dynamite. By foiling Red's plot, Dutch saves the waterfront, and becomes a hero of the men, even winning the admiration of Nick Lewis.

Meanwhile, Hattie does indeed escape from prison and Lil hides her from the cops. While Hattie's hiding, the workers hold a party in Dutch's honor and give him back his union card. When he learns of Hattie's escape, he rushes to her side. She's ready to flee with him to Mexico. But Dutch will have none of it.

> There's something I gotta tell you. I just want you to know that I aint the big shot I thought I was. See, Belcher kept telling me I was Trotsky or somebody, but I ain't, see? I couldn't be...I know what I am now. I'm just the best tuna fisherman on this coast. And I can still knock the nut offa anybody who thinks he's big enough to say that I ain't. And that's all.

Recall, once more, BLACK FURY. When the picture ends, both Anna Novak and Joe Radek learned important lessons. Joe learned the value of solidarity, and the limits of his capacity as a leader. He learned how to moderate his desires. Anna learned the proper place of a working class wife, as adjunct and support for the workingman's struggle. RIFFRAFF, too, offers a tale of transformation. Dutch Muller learns that he's no Trotsky, no big shot. He's a skilled craftsman, and that alone should provide sufficient support for his masculinity. Dutch also learns the value of community. But the tone of that lesson is different. While Radek learns lessons of solidarity, Dutch learns that the union holds the power, and without its privileges, he's nothing. But where's Hattie's lesson? What did she learn? How was she transformed? In fact, Hattie didn't learn anything, *because she didn't need a lesson.* From beginning to end, Hattie was the voice of the community, of responsibility, of reason. Throughout the film, Hattie saw through the screens of masculinity. She mocked and parodied Dutch's blustering attempts to be a big man. But although Hattie saw through the cracks of Dutch's self-presentation, she remained trapped in a world controlled by men, and, more importantly, by a hegemonic masculinity. Thus, we have the remarkably odd end of the picture. The cops wait outside her door to bring her back to prison where she'll presumably finish her twenty-year sentence. Although Hattie pierces the veil of masculine ideology, there's no escape from its constraints.

Cinematic Contradictions

While BLACK FURY marks out the boundary separating white workers from "hunkies," it simultaneously criticizes that boundary. The constant repetition of racial slurs by cinematic villains, combined with the visible "whiteness" of Anna Novak, signifies the irrationality and injustice of this racial division.

And the representation of African Americans, as workers, silently resists Hollywood's "Jim Crow" standards. In fact, the film's racial politics anticipate the imagery of Philip Evergood's *Wheels of Victory* picture; and David Roediger's analysis of Evergood's work applies equally as well to the imagery in the Warner Brother's picture.

> Four centrally located and well-illuminated white workers huddle, exchanging words and the time of day. Looking wistfully at them from a catwalk is a patrolling black guard. The painting strikingly captures what civil rights leaders at the time called the need for a double V—victory over the Nazis abroad and victory over racial exclusion at home. But what the painting assumes is perhaps as important as what it argues. The four foregrounded figures, checking watches, stand for the included white worker. But just a quarter century before, during the World War I era, the dress and the sometimes orientalized and sometimes 'hunky' features of the four would have signaled their 'inconclusive' whiteness.... Clearly important processes of inclusion were occurring, shaped by the continuing exclusion of people of color.
>
> ROEDIGER 2005:134

Thus the film both figures and resists the racial boundary that separates "hunkies" from "whites." RIFFRAFF, however, offers an uncritically racialized worldview and presents a working community made up of native born and unambiguously "white" low wage industrial workers and privileged "skilled" craftsmen. And the portrayal of the union workers as both "white" and "skilled" had a clear political meaning at a moment in American history when the Congress of Industrial Organizations was attempting to build an *industrial* union movement with a largely "ethnic" and "immigrant" constituency (Zieger 1997; Denning 1998; Lichtenstein 2002).

At the same time, both films build upon a gendered rhetoric that places communal power primarily in the hands of men. But while BLACK FURY unambiguously endorses the labored paternalism that portrayed men as the protectors of the "dependent" and "helpless," RIFFRAFF, telling the same story through a woman's eyes, deconstructs hegemonic masculinity and reveals labor's paternalism as a screen for masculine domination. In particular, while BLACK FURY leaves women completely out of the industrial workforce, and represents household production as the natural "duty" of a "loving" wife, RIFFRAFF focuses squarely upon the question of women's exploitation, both within the industrial plant and within the household. Men live off women's surplus production, and women submit out of love and desire. During the opening moments of the film, Pop asked Lil for a cup of coffee, Hattie for two bits. Both women initially refused, and then silently surrendered. Both were imprisoned by their love. Traditional Marxian discourse remained as silent as these women on the question of the feudal household. Exploitation began at the factory gates. Perhaps it's not surprising that women who *did* recognize this form of exploitation, yet had no formal language through which to express that recognition, might perceive talk about (male) worker's exploitation as so much hot air.

Once again, I think that RIFFRAFF's implicit critique of gendered norms, traditional forms of desire, and household exploitation, have much to do with its origin. Let me return to screenwriter Anita Loos' autobiographical reflections upon gendered labor. Like Hattie, Loos faithfully fulfilled her "wifely duties." For instance, her "care work" (Fraad, Resnick and Wolff 1994; Cassano 2010) allowed John Emerson to pursue his organizing activities during the 1919 labor unrest. "Sometimes when he returned from late committee meetings John would be either too exhausted or too keyed up to sleep, so I spent hours ministering to him, treating his ailments, both real and imagined, listening to his outlines for the next day's campaign, or reading aloud the countless fan letters he had been too busy even to open" (Loos 1966: 260). Without her material and emotional labor, Emerson's strike might have failed. But Loos was hardly a "traditional" woman who surrendered her efforts with quiet fortitude. She was already an actress and writer, capable of supporting herself from her earnings. The fact that she worked in the formal economy as well as taking a "second shift" within the household helped fuel the anger she felt when others saw her as Emerson's "inconsequential little doll." After all, "John's 'inconsequential little doll' was his nurse, secretary, masseuse, collaborator, and friend beyond all other friends, *and had earned the better part of the family fortune*" (Loos 1966: 261, emphasis added). Not only did she participate in multiple class processes, as an earner she proved superior to her household "master." This overdetermined perspective put her in a privileged position to critique the traditional household and the forms of desire that sustained it. Yet as the passage above suggests, even as Loos bridled under feudal exploitation, she herself remained a prisoner of the traditional gender expectations associated with love. And while I don't mean to psychoanalyze Loos, it is possible that the anti-radical, anti-communist, and generally anti-left tone of her films represents a reaction formation on the screenwriter's part. Her uneasy relationship with organized labor, symbolically bound up with her uneasy and unequal relationship with her husband, perhaps provoked the portrayal of labor leaders and radicals as self-serving narcissists. Like Dutch Muller, John Emerson "frankly cared more for himself than for anyone else, and his main thought at all times was to see that he was comfortable and happy" (Loos 1966: 261).

During the 1930s, some participants in the labor movement continued the tradition of radical paternalism that had long animated much of its male constituency. In its public presentations, it often imagined women as "dependent" adjuncts in the manly struggle against capital, rather than as fully autonomous agents. That failure of imagination limited the labor movement's potential by setting artificial boundaries to organized labor's solidarity. True, women participated in the movement. But that participation was all but effaced from labor's public self-presentation; and women in the movement were often excluded from the highest leadership positions. At the same time, Marxian discourse seemed to have little to say to the experience of women, especially those outside industrial production. At best, it ignored the exploitation of women within the household; at worst, it endorsed the labored paternalism that justified such exploitation as the natural outgrowth of a woman's love for her family. Because of this exclusion, subordination, and blindness, radical politics and the labor movement appeared to many women as "men's business" and the screenwriters behind RIFFRAFF responded accordingly, offering a film that pilloried labor and the left for this continual refusal to burst the boundaries of hegemonic masculinity.

In the 1930s and 1940s, Hollywood itself was the site of multiple union struggles, and the owners of the studios, as well as their financiers in New York, were resolutely anti-labor (Horne 2001; Nielsen and Mailes 1995; Ceplair and Englund 2003). Thus, it is a testament to the meaning of labor struggles for working Americans (cinema's audience) that these themes not only penetrated mainstream studio productions, but that labor itself was cast in a positive light, as long as it remained "responsible," anti-militant, and anti-radical. Thus, Hollywood studios attempted to frame the discourse surrounding labor and interpellate a certain set of desires. At the same time, the complexities of collaborative production (between producers, directors, writers, actors) and the need to appeal to the audience, allowed for fissures in the ideological framework produced by the pictures. In the case of BLACK FURY, Hungarian born director Michael Curtiz manages to make a film that questions "whiteness," immigrant racial status, and even the exclusion of African Americans from representations of the working class. RIFFRAFF challenges the subordinated status of women in working class communities, and deconstructs labor's implicit radical paternalism and hegemonic masculinity. In short, while both films affirm capitalism, at least in its "moral" form, the affirmation accompanies a subversive set of questions that unsettle other ideological constructs.

But it wasn't only films with overtly political themes, like labor struggles, that took up the problems and contradictions brought on by the Great Depression. These themes also appeared in light comedy and musicals. In the next two chapters, I examine two such pieces of 'pure entertainment,' MY MAN GODFREY (1936) and SWING TIME (1936). SWING TIME dispenses with the idea of a moral capitalism, and portrays the leisure class in the Veblenian language of conspicuous consumption and invidious comparison. Against a morally corrupt leisure class, SWING TIME posits an oppositional community brought together through mass culture. But, in a remarkable moment of cinematic anxiety, SWING TIME both acknowledges the debt of this new mass culture to African American creativity, and represses that very acknowledgement using the language of blackface minstrel theatre. Thus, even as the film calls for a culture of solidarity opposed to the leisure class, it forecloses the channels of that solidarity by excluding the very agents who make it possible, black Americans. But before turning to some of these radical representations, I examine one more corporatist cinematic argument.

Like BLACK FURY, MY MAN GODFREY (1936) advocates a moral capitalism, and, like RIFFRAFF, does so in a language that challenges traditional conceptions of masculinity. In response to transformations in the social division of labor and the proletarianization of women, this comedy posits a new mode of masculinity, laboring at household tasks in an uneasy truce with powerful women. Thus, like these other films, GODFREY both refracts the anxieties of its imagined audience, and attempts to intervene in shaping that audience's point of view on capitalism, gender, and the role of the privileged classes during the Great Depression.

CHAPTER 2

My Man Godfrey (1936)

In his late autobiography, former socialist turned early neo-conservative, Morrie Ryskind rejects any attempt to interpret his work as screenwriter.

> A few years ago, I happened to receive an inquiry from an overly earnest (is there any other kind) young film scholar asking me to assist him with some insight into the allegorical implications of *My Man Godfrey*. As best that I could understand his request, the young man was constructing his thesis around the fact that the title character of Godfrey Parke...was supposed to be a representation of God. The key to understanding this assertion could be found in Godfrey's name.... *GOD-Free*...wasn't it artistic of me to have devised such a meaningful idea. Well, as this all came as news to me, the most that I could do for the young man was write back to him and inquire if he were certain that we were discussing the same movie. The desire to read some sort of symbolic message into the films of the thirties, when our only intent was to entertain, strikes me as a very strange endeavor.
>
> RYSKIND 1994: 124

While Ryskind's only intention may have been "to entertain," in constructing one of the more popular films of 1936, he offered representations of some of the most pressing problems of the Depression, including unemployment, a perceived "crisis" in masculinity, and the responsibility of the wealthy to the working class. In short, MY MAN GODFREY is centrally concerned with some of the central concerns of the working class. And, once again, it frames the social problems created and intensified by the Depression with a plea for a "moral" capitalism run by "responsible" entrepreneurs. Thus the film is a kind of mirror reflection of BLACK FURY, or, even more, RIFFRAFF, and, as those films demand responsible unionism, MY MAN GODFREY demands "responsible" capitalism.

Cinema is an institutionalized mechanism for interpellating social subjects. "And the stake of the social-ideological fantasy is to construct a vision of...a society which is not split by an antagonistic division, a society in which the relation between its parts is organic, complimentary. The clearest case is, of course, the corporatist vision of a Society as an organic Whole, a social Body in which the different classes are like extremities, members each contributing to the Whole according to its function—we may say that 'Society as a corporate

Body' is the fundamental ideological fantasy" (Zizek 1989: 126). When New Deal cinema discovered fissures in the corporate Body, it often attempted to resolve those real contractions using imaginary tools and corporatist fantasies. Thus, in BLACK FURY, the judge finds there never really was an issue in the strike, and, under the guiding hand of the Federal Government, worker and capitalist now work together for the benefit of all. After seeing the picture, Joseph Breen expressed his approval:

> The whole moral of the drama points to the folly of strife, to the desirability of peace, to the interdependence of capital and labor, and to the need of law and order. Intelligent capitalistic management and union labor are fairly presented; communistic agitation is not countenanced; and the government itself has a welcome hand in settling the trouble.
>
> Quoted in BLACK 1994: 260

These widespread and actively policed representational politics became the subject of parody in Preston Sturges' SULLIVAN'S TRAVELS (1942). That picture opens with a film within the film, a scene playing from the imaginary movie *O Brother Where Art Thou*. As the film within the film comes to an end, the director, John Sullivan (Joel McCrea), interprets his work for the production executives in the room and seems to be quoting Breen himself.

> You see, you see the symbolism of it! Capital and labor destroy each other. It teaches a lesson, a moral lesson. It has social significance!...This picture's an answer to the communists!

Sullivan is tired of directing light comedy like *Ants in the Pants*. He wants to create "serious" cinema about social problems. In addition to Breen, Sturges' primary target seems to be Capra (and perhaps John Ford), but the attitude he parodies penetrates the very fabric of 1930s cinema (Moran and Rogin 2000). While Sullivan wants to make a serious film built upon gritty realism ("but with a little sex," the producer says), in this chapter, I find the same corporatist politics at work in a light comedy.

MY MAN GODFREY was directed by Gregory La Cava, with Morrie Ryskind as lead writer. Although not one of *Variety's* Top-Grossing films of the year, its popularity was strong enough for the paper to report, "Because of the smash success of 'My Man Godfrey'...Gregory La Cava is being quoted at new top figures by Myron Selznick" (*Variety*, October 23, 1936). As I will argue in the next chapter, 1936 is a signal year for working class politics in America and for political economic themes in Hollywood cinema. By 1936, Hollywood producers, directors, and writers, perhaps in a bid to capture the attention of the "new kind of public" (Eisenberg 2001: 258) described by John Ford, were crafting a cinema that addressed class relations, capitalism, and the various consequences of the Depression. While I do not mean to suggest that every film made that year attempted to analyze, portray, or explain the causes and consequences of economic disaster, films like MODERN TIMES, MR DEEDS GOES to TOWN, SWING TIME, RIFFRAFF, and MY MAN GODFREY all did just that and all proved successful at the box office.

In the case of GODFREY, a close reading of the film does, indeed, reveal a corporatist vision of a functional social body and an argument for a "moral" capitalism. But within that vision, two aspects stand out as original. First, like RIFFRAFF, MY MAN GODFREY addresses the social crisis in gender relations brought on by the Depression. But while RIFFRAFF deconstructs and parodies traditional gender conceptions, MY MAN GODFREY proposes the gratifying fantasy of a man who rediscovers a (revised) manhood after journeying through the world of women's work. The second original contribution the film makes to the corporatist fantasy is the idea that Captains of Finance (investors, speculators and bankers) have an important function within the social whole. Thus, the film not only endorses a responsible capitalism, but finds an important function for the investor, the speculator, and the banker in the integrated, well-functioning society.

More generally, as a film about debt and responsibility (especially the wealthy class's debt to the Forgotten Men of the 1930s), MY MAN GODFREY also explores the mechanisms through which debt, competition, and exchange bind a community together. Thus, in service to an overall corporatism that celebrates the nearly mystical skills of the investing class, MY MAN GODFREY criticizes the irresponsibility of the idle rich, argues for a "moral capitalism," and resolves a real social contradiction (wage earning women contesting male authority within the household) with a Hegelian dialectic of service that transforms the main character's sense of manhood through the gendered experience of domestic labor.

Cinematic Corporatism

While there are clear differences between Italian corporatism, Canadian corporatism, American corporatism, as well as further differences within any given national-cultural context (Father Coughlin's corporatism was not FDR's), nonetheless, as far as the term has any meaning at all, it is useful to explore some of the common elements that unite these dissimilar moments. For the purposes of this study, I find that corporatism, as the pursuit of a "moral capitalism" (a phrase that is itself open to variable interpretations), combines an anti-Marxist theory of economic value with a functionalist theory of the social order.

In order to illustrate this corporatist theoretical structure, I'll begin in the European context and then look at the translation of these ideas in New Deal America. As I've already suggested, corporatism is premised on a particular theory of economic value. The French sociologist, Emile Durkheim, rejects the labor theory of value as articulated by both so-called "socialists" and the classical political economists. For Durkheim, the value of a product results from and belongs to neither the capitalist nor the worker. In fact, both positions represent "functions" within an organic social totality. And "value" both belongs to and is made by that functional totality. He writes:

> It is said that we should be free to dispose of the talents and energies involved in this labour. But are we able to dispose of our abilities with such freedom? Nothing can be more debatable. We do not belong to ourselves entirely: we owe something of ourselves to others, to the various groups we form part of. We give them and are bound to give them the best of ourselves; why should we not be equally bound (and with even better reason) to give them the material products of our labour.
>
> DURKHEIM 1992: 122

Durkheim interprets the labor theory of value through the terms provided by the natural rights tradition. Following Locke and Smith—but notably, not Marx—he considers the labor theory of value inseparable from an older, and, he thinks, outmoded conception of the human individual as a kind of Robison Crusoe, self-sufficient yet marooned amidst a sea of others. This rational actor produces value through hard-won labor and steady initiative, without the aid of other producers. For Durkheim, such a conception is nonsense. Society represents a storehouse of wealth and social value that has been socially created through time and space. The socially constructed human individual contributes to society's reproduction and partakes of its benefits. But any individual's contribution is mediated by the production and re-production of all the other actors who form the social totality. The image of the value-producing laborer as an isolated, self-sufficient individual is worse than a fiction.

Since every actor has a functional place in the social totality, class inequity, in itself, is not particularly problematic. For Durkheim, the central fissures in modern capitalism result from its emphasis upon this fiction of an isolated, rational actor. Thus, capitalism represents a condition of "moral anarchy," and classical political economy is based upon a "self-delusion" because "economic functions were studied as if they were an end in themselves, without considering what further reaction they might have on the whole social order" (Durkheim 1992: 15). The classical political economists trumpeted productive efficiency, but without concern for the costs to the social totality's integration. "But production is not all, and if industry can only bring its output to this pitch by keeping up a chronic state of warfare and endless dissatisfaction amongst the producers, there is nothing to balance the evil that it does" (1992: 16). And here's the key to Durkheim's critique of capitalism. He doesn't reject private property or market exchange, but he does demand that the "evil" done to social solidarity by these systemic processes find some "balance." After all, if "industry can be productive only by...unleashing warfare, it is not worth the cost." As an answer to this state of chronic dissatisfaction and unending economic warfare, Durkheim offers a limited, mediating solution. "There should not be alternating periods of over and under production. No regulated planning means no regularity" (ibid.). This functionalist image of a planned economy does not give the worker control over her labor. After all, she doesn't belong to herself. But it does attempt to remedy the "injustice" of an unequal distribution of social wealth. Durkheim is not merely making an abstract theoretical argument. Rather, his revision of classical liberal value theory has an essentially political purpose. Through these lines, Durkheim introduces his conception of a "third way" between capitalism and socialism: a corporatist politics that endorses a class-based social structure, but, at the same time, demands social justice for workers. Like SULLIVAN'S TRAVELS fictional director, Durkheim contrasts a society in which capital and labor destroy one another with a kind of "moral capitalism" in which class has a necessary function.

Writing in 1924, Durkheim's most gifted interpreter, Marcel Mauss, extends his uncle's argument by foregrounding the function of the state in a corporatist redistribution of social wealth.

All our social insurance legislation, a piece of state socialism that has already been realized, is inspired by the following principle: the worker has given his life and his labour, on the one hand to the collectivity, and on the other hand, to his employer. Although the worker has to contribute to his insurance, those who have benefited from his services have not discharged their debt to him through the payment of wages. The state, itself representing the community, owes him, as do his employers, together with some assistance from himself, a certain security in life, against unemployment, sickness, old age, and death.

MAUSS 1990: 67

Mauss anticipates both the structure and the ideological justification for the modern welfare state. While he conceives the social whole as a totality in which individuals are bound together through a web of mutual obligations, he believes—with Durkheim—that unregulated capitalism, and the "egoism" it produces, has distorted social morality, producing an anomic, sick, and decadent social structure. For Mauss, the key to restoring health to this structure lies in the development of a moral capitalism, a capitalism that justly compensates workers for their contribution to the whole. And, notably, Mauss underscores the function of the state apparatus in producing this re-distributive scheme. Once again, this corporatism represents a third way, somewhere between unregulated capitalism and the utopian imaginings of the socialists. Mauss says as much when he writes, "Over-generosity, or communism, would be as harmful to [the worker] and to society as the egoism of our contemporaries and the individualism of our laws" (1990: 69). The corporatism outlined by Durkheim and Mauss was premised upon a conception of the social totality fundamentally opposed to the ideas articulated by liberal economists. Rather than a collection of atomized individuals bound together through the innate propensity to "truck, barter, and exchange," Durkheim and Mauss conceive society as a totality that structures human dispositions, even the disposition to exchange. At the same time, however, they feared and resisted the mass workers movements of their time and opposed the theoretical and ideological positions of anarchism, radical social democracy, and Marxian socialism.

Not long after Mauss published his *Essai Sur Le Don*, this same corporatist politics received a striking visual elaboration in Fritz Lang's proto-fascist masterpiece, METROPOLIS (1927). Here I don't mean to suggest that Fritz Lang had a direct impact on American cinematic corporatism. Rather, I think this particular German film helps us gain a deeper understanding of the European corporatist imagining of the social totality. Lang and his wife and screenwriter, Thea von Harbou, illustrate the mechanized and alienated misery of the subaltern working-class, alongside the unconscious luxury of the rulers living above. When the son of a wealthy industrialist ventures into the caverns, he learns the misery of the working class. At the same time, deep in the bowels of the workers' city, he finds a hidden temple, where a young woman, bathed in light and standing before a sea of crosses, preaches a message of corporatist social justice. She retells the story of the Tower of Babel as an allegory of capitalist development and worker exploitation. Those who conceived the tower could not build it. "But the hands that built the Tower of Babel knew nothing of the dream of the brain that had conceived it." After the laborers destroy their own handiwork, the titles tell us, "people spoke the same language, but could not understand one another." The young woman ends her tale by saying

"Heads and Hands need a mediator. The mediator between Heads and Hands must be the Heart." The rest of the film illustrates the allegory of Babel. A common language exists, but not mutual understanding. The young man finds his heart by experiencing the workers' degradations. Although he does not abandon his class, he returns to it with a new understanding, a new ability to forge a common language. He will find a *third path*, somewhere between liberal capitalism and classless socialism. The Catholic imagery in this allegory is as undeniable as it is important. Just as Christ, by becoming human, mediates between the sacred and the profane, so the industrialist's son, by becoming a worker, mediates between the Metropolis and the caverns. Interestingly, however, this mediation only comes about after the workers rise up against their oppressors. But in destroying the machines, the laborers destroy their own city. And, in their haste, the mob forgets that they have left their children behind. Only one worker remains rational enough to stop their revelry and ask them: "Who told you to attack the machines, you idiots? Without them, you'll all die." The workers may be oppressed and exploited, but they need their machines to live, and they need the Heads that created those machines. While the leisure class above is indebted to the workers for its luxury, the workers, in turn, are indebted to the thinking class for their very lives. A net of mutual obligation binds them, but neither side recognizes the necessity of the other. They share a common language, but do not understand one another. Class conflict becomes a problem in communication.

Forgotten Men

In its formal structure, MY MAN GODFREY reiterates the political narrative contained within METROPOLIS, but in a distinctly Hegelian mode. The titular character (William Powell), various known as "The Forgotten Man," "Duke," "Godfrey Parke," "Godfrey Smith," and "Nobody," begins the picture living in a Hooverville, unemployed, and bitter. Later the audience discovers his previous identity, Godfrey Parke, a Boston Brahmin fallen upon hard times because of a broken love affair or failed marriage. Godfrey becomes butler to a family of wealthy "nitwits" and "scavengers" who have no capacity to see beyond their own privilege. While he is unable to educate the family, through his own subjection to their desires, he recognizes the value of his labor. This self-recognition allows him to utilize his social network and through the aide of a wealthy (though dull witted) friend, Tommy Gray, he transforms the city dump into a fashionable nightclub, "The Dump," employing his old comrades from Hooverville. The film's ending makes it clear that "The Dump" continues to depend upon the charity of Godfrey's friend and benefactor, with Godfrey as the club's owner and manager. As in METROPOLIS, the conflict raging between two communities demands mediation. Godfrey represents the mediator; his capacity to mediate comes from the fact that he began with wealth and power, traveled through poverty and invisibility, and so understands both worlds. Unlike METROPOLIS, however, Godfrey's function as mediator depends upon a new self-recognition, and it is precisely a renewed self-respect that enables him to transform the dump into "The Dump."

Early in the film, Godfrey is an "object," controlled and manipulated, but precisely through this objectification, he becomes a subject. And MY MAN GODFREY genders this Hegelian transition. In order to recover himself, Godfrey must first submit to feminine power, and in this submission, he is gendered as a woman. Thus, while MY MAN GODFREY obviously addresses the economic and political problems of the Depression, it also addresses a "crisis of masculinity" as men lose economic power through unemployment and job insecurity, and women achieve increasing economic independence as they become wage earners outside the household. When the film offers its fantastic resolution of the social problems of unemployment and homelessness, it also provides a fantasy that resolves conflicts over gender ideologies and new modes of expressing masculinity and femininity. In a sense, more than his role as mediator between the wealthy and the unemployed, Godfrey's most significant function is as mediator between new conceptions of masculinity and femininity.

In the picture, the wealthy, as a class, are represented as "hysterical," in the psychiatric sense, or, as one character says of the Scavenger Hunt that opens the picture, "the place slightly resembles an insane asylum." Alexander Bullock (Eugene Pallette), the Father (hereafter simply "Father") of the central female characters, responds, "Well all you need to open an asylum is an empty room and the right kind of people." In other words, the wealthy as a class are the "right kind of people" for an asylum, a mob, mad, hysterical. This trope, the asylum, recurs throughout the film as a description of the wealthy household of the Bullock family. And, in the household, the hysterical character of the leisure class invokes the traditional associations of hysteria, figuring the disorder as fundamentally feminine. The household is, in Father's words, "out of control," with power consistently represented as the prerogative of the household's women. Father is emasculated; and even Godfrey must submit to the women's discipline. In a sense, this submission does not end, and the final scene of the film suggests Godfrey's own masculinity has been reinvented by his experience of women's work.

The film's success was surely a product of a witty screenplay, the celebrity of the central actors, William Powell and Carole Lombard, and the evident craft of La Cava and the other artisans behind the camera. But like other films of the period, MY MAN GODFREY also represented the symbolic resolution of social trauma. And at least some of the draw of the picture may have come from its ability to interpret its audience's anxieties about changing roles of women and men during the early 20th century.

As I argued in the previous chapter, following Lizabeth Cohen, a challenge to unquestioned masculine privilege was one effect of the economic dislocations that characterized the 1930s. "The Great Depression was disrupting authority relations in the family, much as it had in the ethnic community and the factory" (Cohen 1990: 249). Men were thrown out of the labor force, and women "found it easier to find and hold work in the depression than their husbands," in part because their labor was cheaper, in part because they often "worked in service occupations as clerks, maids, and waitresses, which survived the hard times better than manufacturing jobs" (Cohen 1990: 246–247). For many working class women, this economic crisis offered the opportunity to achieve new freedoms through access to wage-earning, as well as new authority within the family. Thus, "traditional authority relationships within the family...began to break down" (Cohen 1990: 247). Men responded to these transformation in a number of ways, sometimes with conservative rage, resignation, or resentment. "A Chicago social worker...claimed more women were assuming dominating roles in the family, while their husbands grew resentful over their loss of status" (Cohen 1990: 248). But in its representation of gender politics, MY MAN GODFREY resists such simple resentment. The film's ending does not restore traditional gender relations. Instead, the film takes the economic disruption of traditional gender roles as an opportunity to explore new modes of masculinity and femininity.

Ostensibly, the film gravitates around a central trope of cinematic depictions of the Depression, the so-called "Forgotten Man." (This same "Forgotten Man" trope becomes a central figure in films like GOLDDIGGERS OF 1933 and SULLIVAN'S TRAVELS.) And while the film does attempt to address the social problems of unemployment and homelessness, for most of the audience, the "Forgotten Man" was simply a metaphor, beyond their range of experience. Unlike THE GRAPES OF WRATH and SULLIVAN'S TRAVELS, MY MAN GODFREY hardly attempts to portray the lived experience of poverty and unemployment. However, as Cohen's Chicago social worker suggests, in other ways many working class viewers had a more visceral experience of Forgotten Men. Again, from an early scene in the picture, at the Scavenger Hunt, Bullock (Father) wants to go home, but his wife and her "protégé," Carlo, refuse to leave. They still have items to retrieve for the hunt, a Forgotten Man and a bowl of Japanese goldfish. "I don't know anything about goldfish," Father says, "but if you want a Forgotten Man, you'll find me home in bed." As the film makes clear, Bullock is a forgotten man, powerless and sexless. Since his wife always seems to be accompanied by Carlo, Bullock's bed has been forgotten, along with his manhood. The other Forgotten Men, living in Hooverville, have preserved their masculinity, but at the price of respect from the broader community. Unlike Bullock, on the one hand, and the Forgotten Men, on the other, Godfrey journeys from misogynistic independence to powerlessness to a revised masculinity that maintains an uneasy truce with powerful women.

Two Communities

Like METROPOLIS, MY MAN GODFREY posits two communities, opposed to one another. Standing in the Hooverville beside the East River, Godfrey says to Tommy Gray (Alan Mowbray), "there are two kinds of people, those who fight the idea of being pushed into the river, and...the other kind." What he does not say, but what the film argues, is that the "other kind" are those who do the pushing.

The film begins with a Scavenger Hunt. The scavengers here are the idle rich, "the right kind of people" for an asylum. Godfrey, the Forgotten Man, lives as Duke (the name implying both the anonymity of a pseudonym and an emblem of noble rank) among his fellow vagrants. Into his world charge the young scavengers, Cornelia (Gail Patrick) and Irene Bullock (Carole Lombard). As part of the hunt, they need to retrieve a Forgotten Man. Cornelia approaches Duke/Godfrey first, offering $5 if he'll be her prize. After pushing Cornelia into an ash pile, Godfrey returns to the Waldorf Ritz Hotel with Irene, as *her* Forgotten Man. Irene wins the hunt, and Godfrey delivers her victory speech: "My purpose in coming here tonight was two-fold. Firstly I wanted to aide this young lady. Secondly, I was curious to see how a bunch of empty headed nitwits conducted themselves. My curiosity is satisfied. I assure you it will be a pleasure for me to return to a society of *really* important people."

In just over ten minutes, the wealthy are portrayed as "scavengers," the right kind of people for an asylum, and nitwits who turn human beings into objects of a hunt. At the same time, the men of Hooverville represent a "society of *really* important people." Later in the film, when Godfrey and Tommy return to the "Village of Forgotten Men," this representational opposition is amplified. Attempting to educate Tommy, Godfrey explains of the residents, "These men have no choice." But Tommy simply can't comprehend. "Do you mean to say that people actually live in his place?" he asks. To which Godfrey wryly responds, "Well, they go through the motions." We meet Godfrey's former neighbors, all men at work on household tasks, washing, watering flowers, carrying wood. In addition, this is a community built upon solidarity, as neighbors help one another move and rebuild. But this is exclusively a masculine community. Tommy still cannot understand Godfrey's interest in this community. "After all, things have always been this way for some people. These men are not your responsibility." But the film suggests the opposite. Through Godfrey, the wealthy will pay their debt to the Forgotten Men. Finally, exasperated, Godfrey says, "Tommy, there's a very peculiar mental process called thinking. You wouldn't know much about that. But when I was living here I did a lot of it. One thing I discovered was that the only difference between a derelict and a man is a job." Here is a representation not just of two communities, but two classes, opposed and antagonistic. And in this figure, the film inverts the usual representation of wealth and poverty. It is the callous wealthy who are empty headed scavengers; while the men who literally scavenge to survive in Hooverville are hard-working victims of economic circumstances beyond their control. But what the film finds most scandalous, perhaps, is the inability of the wealthy to recognize their responsibility for these Forgotten Men.

Responsibility and Recognition

The themes of debt, responsibility, and recognition run throughout the picture. In the "Village of Forgotten Men," Duke/Godfrey asks Irene to explain her Scavenger Hunt. "Well, a scavenger hunt is exactly like a treasure hunt, except in a treasure hunt you try to find something you want, and in a scavenger hunt you try to find something nobody wants."

"Like a Forgotten Man?"

But then, after looking at Godfrey's reaction, Irene adds: "You know I've decided I don't want to play anymore games with human beings as objects. You know its kinda sordid when you think it over." As the picture begins, Duke is forgotten by the wealthy, and Irene objectifies him in a human hunt. But in her recognition that "its kinda sordid when you think it over," she also recognizes, for an instant, Godfrey's humanity. Recognizing his humanity, she begins to recognize her own (and her class's) responsibility to the Forgotten Men.

At the same time, Irene is grateful to Godfrey for his help in defeating her chief rival, her older sister Cornelia, becoming, in his words, "a kind of Cornelia beater" for the rest of the picture. So Irene hires Godfrey as the family butler. Through this act, Irene not only offers Godfrey access to income, she transforms him from "something nobody wants" into an object of desire. *She* wants him. For this, Godfrey in turn feels deeply indebted, and throughout the picture calls himself "very grateful" for her sponsorship. Irene, in turn, regards Godfrey as her project, her "protégé." And, in direct contradiction to what Tony Gray will say at Village of Forgotten Men, Irene tells Godfrey:

"Do you know what you are?"
"I'm not quite sure."
"You're my responsibility."

Among the Bullocks, Irene is the only character to recognize this responsibility. And perhaps because Irene preserves her sense of indebtedness, her responsibility for a Forgotten Man, she is the only family member who preserves her social prestige at the end of the picture.

In order to elucidate the dialectics of debt and recognition that structure these symbolically invested exchanges, I return to the work of Marcel Mauss, now supplemented with ideas from Alexander Kojeve's lectures on Hegel. Mauss, because he helps explain the significance of debt and responsibility in the picture; Kojeve, because his interpretation of the Hegelian dialectic makes sense of Godfrey's own transformation from Forgotten Man to Captain of Finance. After this brief excursus on the "ancient morality of the gift" (Mauss 1990: 18) and the social dialectic of desire this morality implies, I will use these theories to provide context and meaning for the system of debt, desire and exchange that serves as the film's narrative architecture.

For Marcel Mauss, exchange, and the consequent mutual indebtedness, is the act that establishes social solidarity. In answer to the Hobbesian dilemma that haunts sociology, he writes: "To trade, the first condition was to be able to lay aside the spear" (Mauss 1990: 82). At the same time, as a method for establishing "mutual ties and alliance that...are comparatively indissoluble" (Mauss 1990: 33), exchange has an ambivalent aspect. The same force that binds social subjects to a community creates amongst them a mutual struggle for recognition and prestige. Every gift is a kind of challenge. "To refrain from giving, just as to refrain from accepting, is to lose rank" (Mauss 1990: 41). If a community member receives a gift and cannot repay that gift in full, he or she becomes indebted to the Giver. Because of the gift's social force, generosity generates prestige and "ranks of all kind are gained in a war of property" (Mauss 1990: 37). This struggle over prestige, and the authority prestige itself generates, is perhaps best illustrated through Mauss' discussion of a community chief's obligation.

He can only preserve his authority over his tribe and village...if he can prove he is haunted and favored both by the spirits and by good fortune, that he is possessed, and also possesses it. And he can only prove this good fortune by spending it and sharing it out, humiliating others by placing them 'in the shadow of his name'.... For in the American Northwest, to lose one's prestige is indeed to lose one's soul.

MAUSS 1990: 39

The chief is obliged by rank "to redistribute everything" (39), but in the process achieves the goal of the recognition of his prestige and consequent authority. "The potlatch, the distribution of goods, is the basic act of 'recognition,' military, juridical, economic, and religious. One 'recognizes' the chief or his son and becomes 'grateful' to him" (Mauss 1990: 40). Social prestige exists as the recognition of authority, and that recognition comes from debt. When I accept the other's generosity, I have fallen "in the shadow of his name" and owe myself to the other.

Mauss supplements this general theory of social solidarity with his later discussion of the socialization of individual subjects and the production of a social "habitus." And Mauss' discussion of "body techniques" and "habitus" makes it clear that his theory of prestige and recognition is also a theory of socialized desire. It is through a mechanism that Mauss calls "prestigious imitation" that the self comes to exist, and, in the process, comes to desire the other's desire.

Habitus represents the social subject's scheme of bodily dispositions and cognitive orientations. These "body techniques" are not individual idiosyncrasies, but "vary especially between societies, educations, proprieties and fashions, prestiges" (Mauss 1979: 101). In order to explain the acquisition of the ensemble of habits and dispositions that constitutes a socialized "self," Mauss uses the term "prestigious imitation."

The child, the adult, imitates actions which have succeeded and which he has seen successfully performed by people in whom he has confidence and who have authority over him.... It is precisely this notion of the prestige of the person who performs the ordered, authorized, tested action... that contains all the social element.

MAUSS 1979: 101-102

Mauss uses his notion of "prestigious imitation" to resist simplistic theories of identification. Whether in the case of a single child learning from a care-giver, or in the case of the spread of fashions and ideas, the self takes on attributes of the other. And actions, fashions, ideas become important, disseminated, popularized precisely because of the *prestige* of the actor, of the fashionable, of the bearers of ideas. The social subject identifies (in the psychoanalytic sense (Freud 1989b)) with the other, because of the other's power, prestige, authority; because the self *recognizes* the other. Recognition invests the other with the self's desire.

In order to explain the dialectic of desire implied by Mauss's theory, I turn to Hegel's interpreter, Alexander Kojeve. When, in the 1930s, Kojeve situated Hegel's work for a French audience often unfamiliar with *The Phenomenology*, he was, perhaps, conceiving Hegel as if in dialogue with the leading social thinker of the time, Marcel Mauss. Kojeve's engagement (and debate) with the *College of Sociologie* and its radical re-interpreters of Durkheim and Mauss, Georges Bataille, Roger Caillois, and Michel Leiris, would seem to add likelihood to such a possibility (Hollier 1988). But whether Kojeve had Mauss in mind or not, his discussion of the dialectics of desire, and his interpretation of Hegel's master/slave dialectic, resituates and clarifies Mauss's theory of the relationship between power, recognition, and desire. What Kojeve adds to Mauss' account of "prestigious imitation" is the very word that Mauss mysteriously passes over in silence: *desire*. Kojeve, like Freud (1989b), understands that any account of "prestigious imitation" or "identification" implies a social theory of desire. Through "prestigious imitation" the self performs the authorized action because s/he recognizes authority; and, further, through the act, asks for recognition in return. Indeed, by performing the authorized action, by imitating authority, the self enacts a two-fold desire. On the one hand, the imitation itself acknowledges a desire for the other's approval, for authority's endorsement. On the other hand, by imitating the other, the self remakes itself as the other's double, now desiring what the other originally desired. In both cases, the self becomes itself by acquiring the authorized attributes, dispositions, and attitudes of a social subject. In both cases, the self recognizes the other's prestige and, consequently, desires the other's desire.

The desire for the other's desire revealed by "prestigious imitation" is a recognition that desires recognition. By acquiring the other's values, the self looks for respect and recognition. "Therefore, to desire the Desire of another is in the final analysis to desire that the value that I am or that I 'represent' be the value desired by the other: I want him [sic] to 'recognize' my value as his value. I want him to 'recognize' me as an autonomous value" (Kojeve 1969: 7). The self wants to be recognized as an autonomous subject by an other invested with prestige. But the self begins as an object, imitating those with authority. In order to move from the status of object to subject, the self must engage the other in an allegorical "fight to the death for pure prestige" (Kojeve 1969: 7).

In this struggle between Master and Slave, Kojeve, following Hegel, argues that both seek the same prize, recognition. But with this contest, the Master's situation is "tragic," precisely because the Master has reduced the Slave to an object who works for the Master's desire. As an object, the slave is unworthy of respect. "Hence, [the Master] is recognized by someone whom he [sic] does not recognize.... [He] can be satisfied only by recognition from one whom he recognizes as worthy of recognizing him" (Kojeve 1969: 19). While "a Master will never be satisfied," "the satisfied man will necessarily be a Slave; or more exactly, the man who has ....passed through Slavery" (20).

The Slave's advantage lies in submission and service. The Slave recognizes the authority of the Master, and in submitting to the Master, the Slave surrenders "everything fixed-or-stable" within it. Through this "absolute liquefaction of every stable-support," the Slave prepares itself to become something (someone) new (Kojeve 1969: 21). Further, "in service" to the Master, "slavish Consciousness...overcomes its attachment to natural existence" (22). The Slave represses its own desire and cares, instead, for the Master's Desire, so transforming itself and its world. But through work, the Slave comes to recognize its own power and autonomy. "In the raw, natural, given World, the Slave is a slave of the Master. In the technical world transformed by his work, he rules—or, at least, will one day rule—as absolute Master" (Kojeve 1969: 23). By re-working the natural world, by using tools to remake the given, even doing so in the service of a Master, the Slave creates an artificial mirror. And in the reflection produced through the mirror of service and labor, the Slave recognizes itself and its autonomy.

To a point, Mauss and Kojeve offer parallel arguments. Kojeve's Master is Mauss's Giver; Kojeve's Slave, Mauss's recipient; every subject who performs "prestigious imitation," copying the dispositions of those with power, receives a gift (a habitus) and remains indebted. Yet, this debt is also a challenge. As Mauss implies with his analysis of authority in *The Gift*, "prestigious imitation" is an active process in which social subjects struggle for rank and recognition. This struggle takes a dialectical form as the fight between Master and Slave. And while the outcome of that struggle varies, those who save "face," who acquire a persona, who possess "soul," are transformed from objects into subjects. Kojeve, of course, adds a final element, foreign to Mauss's depiction: labor. The Slave ultimately overcomes not only the other, but the very need for the other's Desire. Through labor, the Slave discovers its own reality and so recognizes the Master's approval (recognition) as meaningless (empty). And it is precisely Kojeve's addition (by way of Hegel) to Mauss' analysis of debt that makes visible the meaning of labor and submission in MY MAN GODFREY.

Mastery and Servitude

When Irene makes Godfrey her "protégé," she begins a process through which both she, as Master, and Godfrey, as Slave, will become free. But in her initial mastery of Godfrey, Irene remains a slave to her identification with her mother.

> "You're more than just a butler, you're the first protégé I've ever had," she tells Godfrey.
> "Protégé?"
> "Yes, like Carlo."
> "Who's Carlo?"
> "He's *Mother's* protégé."

By making Godfrey "more than just a butler," into a protégé, Irene marks a point of identification with her mother. And this mark of identification is a mark of servitude, of prestigious imitation. At the same time, in assuming her mother's role, Godfrey has become her "responsibility," her *work*. As Godfrey is transformed through the course of the picture, Irene comes to see herself in that transformation. After all (in Godfrey's words): "A protégé has certain responsibilities also. For instance, if someone should ring for me now and I didn't answer, that would reflect upon you, because you're my sponsor." Godfrey's success or failure is Irene's responsibility, her reflection.

Godfrey, on the other hand, begins not as a Slave, but a Forgotten Man. He has not yet experienced the "absolute liquefaction of every stable-support" that will eventually restore his self-respect. By definition, a Forgotten Man ("something nobody wants") goes unrecognized. But as Godfrey says at the Scavenger Hunt, being a Forgotten Man "has certain advantages." In particular, he preserves a certain masculine independence, and a scrap of honor, living as Duke among the Forgotten Men.

Irene represents the society he thinks he's left behind. But when she recognizes the shame in treating him like an object ("kinda sordid when you think of it"), she recognizes him as worthy of recognition. Her gaze, tinged with recognition, produces gratitude. Duke's gratitude leads him to want to please Irene. As he says later in the film, "I've been trying to do things that I thought would make you proud of me." In short, to please Irene, he remakes himself. Duke becomes Godfrey Smith to make Irene proud. He desires her desire. And in desiring her desire, he purges his former self (Godfrey Parke), until all that's left are ashes. In the Village of Forgotten Men, Godfrey says:

"Tommy, observe yon structure on your left" (pointing to a shack) "that was the birthplace of the celebrated butler, Godfrey Smith."
"Where are the ashes of Godfrey Parke?"
"Scattered to the wind."

When the film opens, Duke pushes Cornelia into Godfrey Parke's ashes. But when Godfrey submits to Irene, "the absolute liquefaction of every stable-support" scatters those ashes to the wind.

Godfrey's submission to Irene's desire becomes a submission to her family. After all, a good protégé has certain responsibilities. And, although he functions as Irene's "Cornelia beater," he must submit to Cornelia as well. The film emphasizes this theme of submission in an early scene between Godfrey and Cornelia that borders on fetish pornography. Still angry at her humiliation in the ash pile, Cornelia sits upon the sofa and asks "have you a hankerchief? There's a spot on my shoe, will you see what you can do about it?" As soundtrack seduction music plays, a close up of Cornelia's leg, Godfrey kneels before the seated woman and polishes her sandal. She says, "I could have you fired, you know, but I like to see things wriggle." Godfrey submits. But it is precisely in his servitude that Godfrey begins to recognize his own capabilities.

In a later scene, Father asks Godfrey, "why do you stay here? I have to. You don't."

"It's much more comfortable than living in a packing box on the city dump, sir. Besides, I'm rather proud of my job here."
"You're proud of being a butler?"
"I'm proud of being a good butler, sir. And, I may add sir, a butler has to be good to hold his job here."
After a pause, Father again: "Say, who *are* you?"
"I'm just a nobody, sir."

As the film opened, Duke was something nobody wanted. Now, by becoming "a nobody," by surrendering everything "fixed-or-stable" within him and submitting himself to the other's desire, and, then, taking pride in working for that desire, Godfrey Smith becomes an object of the Master's desire. Father's mystified question ("Say, who are you?") signifies his admiration, his recognition that Godfrey Smith is someone worth recognizing.

But MY MAN GODFREY is not simply a psycho-sociological allegory of a subject returning to itself through work. This allegory has a gendered character. In order to become Godfrey Smith, Duke needs to surrender a certain limiting conception of independent masculinity. By working for women, and by doing work traditionally gendered as "women's work," Godfrey escapes Slavery.

"The only butler we ever had who understood women"

The film announces its subject matter, gender identity, in its very title. And it amplifies this message with its early concern for the Forgotten *Man*. But MY MAN GODFREY is less about particular men, than it is about manhood itself, about the social structure of masculinity. In order to chart the film's critique of traditional forms of masculinity, we need to look at *cops* and *hats*.

The first lines of the film invoke the police as symbols of authority over men. In the Village of Forgotten Men, Mike stands beside Duke—both men in fedoras—as they warm their hands over the fire. Duke asks: "Any luck today?" Mike says: "If them cops would stick to their own racket and leave honest guys alone we'd get somewhere in this country without a lot of this relief and all that stuff."

The next representation of the police takes place in the third act of the film, when Godfrey returns drunk from his lunch with Tommy Gray. Cornelia uses his drunkenness to attempt an act of revenge that is also a gift. She conceals a string of pearls in his bed and claims they were stolen. When the police arrive, they wear their fedoras as they interrogate the family concerning the "crime." Mother (Alice Brady) says to one of the cops:

> "If you're going to be rude to my daughter, you might at least take your hat off." The detective responds: "When we're on criminal cases, lady, we keep both hands free."

Here, the film slyly provides the key to its own cryptogram: *A man with his hat on has both hands free.* As if to amplify the gest, a few minutes after the scene with the police fades, a newspaper column appears, with the author's by-line figured prominently: *Hatton Man.*

With this key in hand, so to speak, earlier scenes make new sense. In the early scenes at Hooverville, Duke wears his fedora. But when he arrives for his first day at the Bullocks, the maid, Molly, tells him to "leave your hat by the door." He is then immediately subjected to a series of emasculating encounters with the women of the house. His hat is his masculinity. And a man without a hat is man whose hands are bound, *a man in service.* Godfrey is bound in service to women.

Moreover, in the representations of his service, Godfrey is shown doing work traditionally gendered as feminine. He provides meals. He cleans dishes. He makes beds. When Father Bullock asks him if he is proud of being a butler,

Godfrey is serving breakfast. Near the end of the film, in a pivotal scene, Godfrey is dressed in Molly's apron as he does the dishes. Irene tells him:

> "You look so cute in that apron."
> And it is as he washes dishes that he tells her, "I've been trying to do things that I thought would make you proud of me."

On the one hand, these "things" refer to the newly refurbished "Dump," a nightclub he's built with Tommy Gray; but, in addition, as the scene itself demonstrates, he attempts to satisfy Irene's desire ("You look so cute") and make her proud, by *wearing the apron* and *doing the dishes* ("a protégé has certain responsibilities").

While a film like RIFFRAFF deconstructs the discourse surrounding household labor, MY MAN GODFREY violates the norm itself by projecting the possibility that men might become useful again through labor traditionally ascribed to women. A man wears his hat to keep his hands free and so preserves his authority and independence. Not Godfrey. He is indebted to women, submits to their desires, and does women's work. Through this gendered submission, Godfrey sees both genders in a new way. As Mother says at the end of the picture (in tears):

> "You know I hate to see Godfrey go. He's the only butler we ever had who understood women."

And when Godfrey transcends service, his new masculinity no longer requires that he keep both hands free. A man who gives his hand in marriage can't keep both hands free. In the final minutes of the picture, Irene rushes into Godfrey's office, her driver following with food and wood. Although he's refused her marriage proposal on multiple occasions, Godfrey now stands dumbfounded as Irene calls in the Mayor to sanctify their union. The film ends just before the vows begin. Although Godfrey has rediscovered his manhood, he continues to recognize Irene's authority. She plays the masculine role. She proposes, she provides for the household, and Godfrey submits to her desire. Just as the dump became "The Dump," Godfrey returns to a reinvented manhood. His independence is now circumscribed, and he depends upon Irene, as she does upon him, for mutual recognition.

Obviously, Godfrey is a butler, and that transforms the meaning of his household work. But most of the film's audience had no experience of butlers, none of maids. And the scene of Godfrey wearing a woman's apron and doing women's work represents an imaginary resolution of a very real social crisis. With this projection of interdependent genders, and a man who comes to understand women by doing "their" work, the film both criticizes dominant gendered norms, and provides an imaginary resolution to persistent tensions in the households of its audience.

Captain of Finance

Of course, like RIFFRAFF, GODFREY's critique of dominant gender norms, and its fantasy of interdependent genders, is in the service of a kind of corporatist argument for a moral capitalism. After all, Godfrey's rehabilitation of "The Dump" is funded, in part, by the wealthy classes, in the figures of Irene and Tommy Gray. When, at the end of the film, Godfrey demands more funds from Tommy Gray, the latter protests:

> "I've still got an interest in this company, when do you start paying dividends?"
> "Well, we're giving food and shelter to 50 people in the winter and giving them employment in the summer," replies Godfrey, "What more do you want in the way of dividends?"

As mediator, Godfrey brings rich and poor together, and reminds the wealthy of their responsibilities to the Forgotten Men. But the film adds something to the representation of the corporatist aesthetic as it plays out in METROPOLIS. The earlier film saw a role for the creator-capitalist, as well as for the worker, in the corporatist solution to class conflict. But Godfrey acts as more than simply a mediator bringing together the industrial class (Tommy owns baked bean canneries) and the Forgotten Men. Indeed, it is through the work of his own ingenuity that Godfrey is able to generate the initial capital that goes into "The Dump." He does this not through production, but through stock speculation.

Unlike Tommy Gray, Godfrey is not a "Captain of Industry." Rather, he functions as what Thorstein Veblen would call a "Captain of Finance" (Veblen 1990). As a radical, Veblen's notion of contemporary social formations and conflicts was very different from the vision of idealized harmony projected by corporatism (Cassano 2009a, 2009b). According to Veblen, contemporary social life is driven by the contradiction between the interests of a productive industrial system meant to serve human need, on the one hand, and the interests of speculators, investors, and businessmen, on the other

(Cassano 2005b). He writes that "in point of material welfare, no nation and no community has anything to gain at the cost of any other nation or community." This because:

> In point of material welfare, all the civilized peoples have been drawn together by the state of industrial arts into a single going concern.... Any degree of obstruction, diversion, or withholding of any of the available industrial forces, with a view to the special gain of any nation or any investor, unavoidably brings on a dislocation of the system...and therefore a net loss to all its parts.
>
> VEBLEN 1990: 73

According to Veblen, when a system capable of serving human needs (industrial technology) is turned to the service of special "vested interests" (capitalists, investors), the result is a net loss for the productive system itself (Cassano 2008, 2005b). Capitalism is, by definition, unproductive. And "the captains of finance are working, at cross purposes and in collusion, to divert whatever they can to the special gain of one vested interest and another, at any cost to the rest..." (Veblen 1990: 73). Captains of Finance are worse than non-productive, they are systemic parasites, dislocating production and diverting social wealth into individual accounts.

Given the revival of radical Veblenian thought in the 1930s (see Chapter 3 below), perhaps it's hardly surprising that MY MAN GODFREY attempts to restore capitalism's legitimacy by representing the centrality of the investment speculator to the community's welfare. By positing a fundamental social function for Godfrey, the film argues that Captains of Finance are as important to the corporatist compact as Captains of Industry and workers.

Maussian themes return in the penultimate scene of the picture, when Godfrey resigns his position as butler. With a final act of gift giving, Godfrey assets his rank, and "flattens" his rivals, (the sadistic) Cornelia and (the irresponsible) Father. The scene begins when Father gathers Mother and Cornelia to announce his ruin: "You might as well all know point blank, we're about broke." Father then confesses to losing his own stock in Bullock Enterprises and embezzling stockholders' shares in an attempt to recoup.

At that point Godfrey intervenes, "I've known for a long time that the Bullock's interests were in a bad way." Consequently, Godfrey used his skill as a market trader to buy back most of Father's lost stock. He returns the stock to Father as a gift. Meanwhile, he explains how he raised the capital for his endeavor.

"You see, with the aide of Tommy Gray, I was able to transmute a certain trinket," he takes Cornelia's pearls from his pocket, "into gold and then into stock and then back into pearls again." He hands the pearls back to Cornelia.

Her response: "You win."

When she attempts to return the pearls to Godfrey, saying "these are rightfully yours," he responds:

"No thank you. I've repaid my debt and am grateful to all of you."

Cornelia says, "If anyone's indebted, we are, after the way some of us have treated you."

When Godfrey departs, Cornelia throws the pearls to the ground and begins to weep. The final shot of the scene, the last with the family, shows Cornelia and Mother in tears, while Father is almost literally flattened, seated on the sofa with his head in his hands.

Through this final exchange of gifts, Godfrey purchases his freedom from service. Despite the fact that, in an earlier scene, Father had refused Godfrey's offer of help in the market, the butler intervenes and saves the family fortune. Rather than expressing gratitude, Father rightly evinces his shame, flattened by Godfrey's power. At the same time, the pearls, Cornelia's unconscious gift to Godfrey, return to their point of origin, like the Maori *taonga* described in the first pages of Mauss' study (Mauss 1990: 11). Moreover, when her pearls return to her, they contain a surplus, Godfrey's gift of forgiveness for her deception. The force of the thing overwhelms. She attempts to reclaim some power by returning the pearls. When that doesn't work, she throws the symbol of Godfrey's power to the ground. But both her words and her tears signify his victory. And for the film's contemporary audience, Cornelia's acknowledgement of her debt to Godfrey produces the visual fantasy of a privileged family shamed for their irresponsibility and for their inability to repay what they owe. When she says, "If anyone's indebted, we are, after the way some of us have treated you," she's speaking directly to the audience, apologizing for the indifference of her class, satisfying the need for justice, even only in imagination.

At the same time, in this final revelation and exchange, Godfrey unveils his own almost mystical power as an alchemist who can make something from nothing. Indeed, it is this very skill that allows him both to save the Bullock family and rescue the Forgotten Men. While he does not produce commodities, he has the uncanny ability to create money. After all, he began with a pearl necklace, and ended with a pearl necklace and enough capital to buy Bullock's lost stock and finance the initial investment for "The Dump."

As if with the Marxian critique of capitalism in mind as target, the film produces what Marx would call a mystified vision of the source of profit: $P \rightarrow Cap \rightarrow S \rightarrow P + Cap$, where P represents the pearls, Cap represents capital, and S represents stocks. Moreover, Godfrey places himself at the center of this transformation, even referring to his quasi mystical power. "I was able to transmute a certain trinket..." Through this magical (mystifying) power, he is able to transform P into $P + Cap$.

Perhaps screenwriter Ryskind (1994), a one-time socialist on his way to becoming a Wilkie Republican, was offering his own refutation of Marx's claim that the capitalist contributes nothing to production. "The capitalist, it is true, pays [the worker] in money, but this money is merely the transmuted form of the product of his labor" (Marx 1967: 568). Marx demystifies the seemingly mystical power of the capitalists with the formula: $M \rightarrow C \rightarrow M^{\wedge}1$, where M represents money/capital, C represents the commodity, and $M^{\wedge}1$ represents surplus value, which is M + the surplus the worker invests in the commodity. The capitalist's contribution to this process is, from this point of view, quite literally mystical, in the sense that such a contribution is an illusion (Resnick and Wolff 1987). Like RIFFRAFF, but from a different point of view, MY MAN GODFREY contests the Marxian theory of exploitation. Against this theory, the film argues Godfrey, as a skilled Captain of Finance, has something to contribute to the social good. And this representation of Godfrey as the "moral investor" satisfies the fantasy desires of an audience battered by the market crash of 1929, the bank failures of the early 1930s, and bankers and investors who often seem to care for their own self-interest at the expense of the community.

Mask as Mark

MY MAN GODFREY is an "ideological fantasy," in Zizek's sense of the term. The function of such a fantasy is to mask the fact that the corporatist community represented does not exist, "and thus to compensate us for the failed identification" (Zizek 1989: 127). At an imaginary level, the film resolves a number of real social tensions and contradictions: It projects the fantasy of a reformed manhood and interdependent genders; it projects the fantasy of the wealthy family brought to shame; it projects the fantasy of the "moral" speculator who uses his financial wealth and social connections for the betterment of the poor. Finally, the film projects an explanation of the production of wealth that attempts to counter the Marxian notion of exploitation.

Yet, just as the "fantasy is precisely the way the antagonistic fissure is masked," and thus a "*means for an ideology to take its own failures into account in advance*," (Zizek 1989: 126, italics in original), such fantasies also *mark* those antagonistic fissures. In its demand for a "moral capitalism," the film implies that the capitalism of the world inhabited by its audience was immoral. And in its demand for a reformulated manhood, the film acknowledges the crisis in masculine domination brought, at least in part, by the economic forces of the Depression. While the interdependent vision of gender identification it projects may have been a fantasy, that fantasy underscores the insufficiency of traditional conceptions of masculinity to face the problems of the times. In both cases, the fantasy that sutures the fissure is also the mark of a persistent social tension. In both cases the *mask* of antagonisms is the *mark* of their existence.

Without a doubt, MY MAN GODFREY offers a critique of the conditions it represents, and, as Lary May persuasively argues, this critical demand for a moral capitalism was widespread in 1930s and 1940s cinema (May 1998). But May makes a categorical mistake when he calls these representations "radical." While critical, most cinematic demands for a moral capitalism tended to advocate reform and class compromise. On the other hand, this was not the only perspective offered by Hollywood cinema. As I will demonstrate below, John Ford's disillusioned corporatism drives him to a radical traditionalism that cinematically represents irreconcilable antagonisms between two classes (imperialists and colonized in THE HURRICANE (1937); capital and labor in THE GRAPES OF WRATH (1940) and HOW GREEN WAS MY VALLEY (1941)). In this sense, some of Ford's work from the late 1930s and early 1940s represents a radical rejection of the corporatist compromise advocated by METROPOLIS and GODFREY.

But it wasn't only "prestige" directors like Ford who indicted the corporatist compromise. In SWING TIME, Fred Astaire and Ginger Rogers represent the new "common" man and woman, and, as such, participate in a community radically opposed to the ruling "leisure class." As the next chapter argues, SWING TIME utilizes an overtly Veblenian rhetoric in order to indict the vested interests and the leisure class and celebrate a new proletarian mass culture.

CHAPTER 3

Swing Time (1936)[1]

SWING TIME is a simple song and dance picture with Fred Astaire and Ginger Rogers that offers a fiery indictment of the values of the leisure class, while, at the same time, portraying an oppositional working class community in the language of protest and the Popular Front. I begin this chapter by exploring the roots of SWING TIME's critique of vested forms of desire in Thorstein Veblen's *The Theory of the Leisure Class* (1994). I argue that SWING TIME offers an extension of Veblen's theory by analyzing the power of mass communication to re-shape social circuits of desire. I then explore the meaning of the stylistic realism and the language of protest operating in the film's narrative. SWING TIME offers a critique of capitalism precisely in order to affiliate itself with a new, working class oppositional culture. But in affiliating itself with this oppositional community, the film also accepts and reinforces the language of racial privilege circulating within the "white" working class. With a final critical act, however, SWING TIME reveals the invidious character of white privilege, as well as the fact that the cultural heritage of the (white) working class (swing music itself) comes from the theft and plunder of African American originality.

Hollywood cinema, or the producers and executives behind Hollywood, con-sciously attempted to promote a more or less classless kind of "common cultural ground" free from politics (Rogin 2002: 89), and free from the struggles of every-day life. But to the degree that writers and directors (often unintentionally) allowed history, and their audience's expectations, experiences, and desires to penetrate the cinematic object, a different kind of common ground was created, a common space for the expression of a new, oppositional "structures of feeling" (Williams 1977) and modes of desire.[2] SWING TIME was one of the most popu-lar films of 1936, just behind Charlie Chaplin's phenomenally successful MODERN TIMES (1936); and, like Chaplin's picture, it attempts to represent a new common world, to affiliate itself with an audience of laborers that stand in conscious opposition to the leisure classes. A seemingly generic musical, SWING

---

1   An earlier version of this chapter originally appeared in "Working Class Self Fashioning in 'SWING TIME' (1936)," *Critical Sociology*, May 2014.

2   Here I intentionally mean to play on the double entendre of "common world." The "common world" is both the world of common discourse, a community, and the "*common* world" inhab-ited by "common" (e.g. working class) Americans.

TIME builds its entire narrative upon a radical critique of desire under capital-ism. But in affiliating itself with this oppositional culture, SWING TIME also posits imaginary cultural boundaries. It represents a working class community that is, at the same time, a normatively "white" community in which immigrants are relegated to a secondary status, and African Americans are hidden from view even as their culture is pillaged and their cultural forms appropriated.

Although Allan Scott was a writer on both pictures, SWING TIME is quite different from Astaire and Rogers' breakthrough musical of the previous year, TOP HAT (1935). Many depression era musicals incorporated themes of pov-erty, hunger, and desperation, if only to romantically resolve those "social problems" in the final reel. The opening scene of GOLD DIGGERS OF 1933 (1933) is emblematic. The picture begins with Ginger Rogers, dressed in over-sized gold coins, dancing on a stage and singing "We're in the Money." The number comes to an end when the Sheriff closes down rehearsal because the producers hadn't paid the bills. Economic reality bites into the film's imaginary texture. TOP HAT, on the other hand, represents an almost clichéd version of the 1930s musical fantasy. The action takes place among the elite. The spaces of action, London and Venice, are self-consciously conjured dreams. While some early scenes in London include a few exterior shots that look as if they were taken from a tourist reel, most of the action takes place in a "Venice" magically imagined, surreal, utopian. True, at one point, Ginger Rogers threatens to leave a suitor, go back to America, and "go on the dole." The scarcity of such remarks, however, suggests history is somehow suspended within cinematic space, put under erasure. But even TOP HAT is not simply "escapism." Rather, it is a *cam-era obscura*, offering an inverted image of the world beyond the projector's lamp. Outside, hunger, depression, "the dole." Inside, a veritable "Heaven," as the film's recurring theme, "Cheek to Cheek," constantly reminds the viewer. ("Heaven, I'm in heaven...") The narrative concerns problems of identity, trust, and love, not of hunger, unemployment, and homelessness. TOP HAT became the most successful RKO picture of the 1930s (Balio 1995: 222). The film certainly seems to confirm Michael Rogin's (2002) thesis that labor and labor struggles were present mainly in their insistent absence from Depression and New Deal era cinema screens. While no other Astaire-Rogers collaboration equaled the success of TOP HAT, SWING TIME came closest. SWING TIME, however, is the reverse image of TOP HAT's *camera obscura*. It appropriates TOP HAT's themes, costumes, and scenarios, but puts them to new use. SWING TIME subverts the fantasy elements that make TOP HAT possible, and anchors its own narrative in a world where the stakes of struggle are more than heartstrings.

The film begins with an exchange that highlights its central theme, "fashion." After the credits, the screen goes black, strings give way to an arrangement that emphasizes horns syncopated to a high-hat's distinctly swing beat. Fade into a stage with John "Lucky" Garnett (Fred Astaire) dancing center, a men's chorus dancing behind. Cut backstage: a stagehand lounges, while "Pop" Cardetti (Victor Moore) performs a card trick. The stagehand ignores the old magician's sleight-of-hand, looking out, instead, at the dancing men. "When did you change the act, Pop?"

"I didn't. He did," nodding his head toward Lucky.
"He did?"
"Yeah, he says 'straight magic is too old fashioned.'"

This exchange foreshadows the argument of the film's first act. For its first 30 minutes or so, this musical confronts the power of fashion, of the mass media, of the leisure class, in a language that echoes Thorstein Veblen's *The Theory of the Leisure Class* (1994). SWING TIME begins with a Veblenian theory of desire. Lucky's desire for specific commodities, and for his fiancé, is shaped by his desire for recognition by America's ruling elite. And this desire for recognition by the leisure class is exemplified vividly in Lucky's fashion choices. To the extent that fashion, as an expression of desire, and desire as an expression of leisure class power, are central to the narrative, the film remains close to Veblen's original text. But the film offers an extension of Veblen's theory through its analysis of the relationship between fashion and mass communication.

In SWING TIME, representations of leisure class desire are mediated by mass communication. The film makes a two-fold argument: First, the mass media functions to inculcate hegemonic forms of desire, represented by dominant modes of fashion that affiliate the subject to the ruling desires of the leisure class. But, second, because the film posits the power of mass communication itself to re-shape social forms of desire, it represents mass media as potentially liberating forces that can free the subject from the yoke of leisure class sensibilities. In the place of the dominant desires of the leisure class, SWING TIME offers an oppositional "scheme of life," through the use of working class cultural forms. Thus, while for Veblen, "fashion" represents the dominance of leisure class desire; SWING TIME suggests that working class fashions (especially, swing music itself) can also represent affiliation with oppositional forms of desire.

Recognition and "Schemes of Life"

Thorstein Veblen lived long enough to witness the birth of sound pictures, but never wrote about this new cultural form. This is remarkable, especially given the fact that *The Theory of the Leisure Class* is about socialized paths of desire. But whatever the reasons for Veblen's silence on cinema, he articulates a theory of desire central to SWING TIME's argument. Veblen's work was notorious enough, and well enough known in the 1930s, it may have exercised a direct influence on SWING TIME's screenwriters and director. Kenneth Burke (1935), John Dos Passos, and New Deal economists were remembering the old man's name and recycling or revising his central ideas. And Diggins (1999) suggests that the years 1934 to 1936 were particularly important in the revival of Veblen's work and his "reputation among writers of the depression generation" (213). But whether the artisans behind the picture had a conscious intention of conveying Veblenian themes or not, the film's representations of the leisure class, the barbarian status of women, and the dialectic of social desire directly parallel Veblen's theories. Further, in Veblenian fashion, the film reflects upon its own power to shape the social dialectic of desire.

Veblen's best remembered phrase is "conspicuous consumption." But in *The Theory of the Leisure Class,* "conspicuous consumption" itself is driven by yet another social psychological force, the desire for "prestige" through recognition by the community.[3] This drive for recognition emerges from Veblen's conception of the interactive character of the "self." The "self" is a social structure, developed through communal interaction, and shaped by a multitude of others. Put another way, there is an other (representing the community) at the heart of every self. I come to know myself only through the gaze of this internalized other. If the other greets me with approbation, I have self-respect. If the other offers me scorn, I come to hate myself. Thus, in a society in which consumption and wealth are conventional markers for prestige, "Those members of the community who fall short of this...normal degree of prowess or property suffer in the esteem of their fellow-men; and consequently they suffer also in their own esteem, *since the usual basis of self-respect is the respect accorded by one's neighbor"* (1994: 20, emphasis added; Cassano 2009b).

Social norms are generated through this internalization of the other's desire. The other within demands respectable behavior. Otherwise, I lose my "good name" (Veblen 1994: 19). Using the theoretical foundation provided by this

---

3   It's important to highlight the drive behind "conspicuous consumption," because without understanding Veblen's theory of the human desire for recognition, the reader won't fully grasp the critical edge in his work. Veblen emphasizes that in contemporary society, property and consumption are the "conventional basis" for prestige and recognition. The key here is the term "conventional basis." Veblen's critique is not of the human drive for recognition, a drive, he argues, founded in the very social structure of the self; rather, he critiques the form this drive takes in his contemporary America (Cassano 2009a, 2009b).

"looking glass" theory of the self (Cooley 1922), Veblen constructs a model of social domination legitimated through desire. In the United States the conventional prestige awarded the leisure class is more than a motive for economic behavior. It is the means through which the normative ideals or "the scheme of life" promulgated by the leisure class becomes a force among those excluded from privilege. In other words, the desires of the leisure class shape the desires of the "common lot."[4] The values and ideals of the leisure classes are unserviceable for the majority of the population, who will live lives of "chronic dissatisfaction" because they can never achieve a reputable standard of consumption (1994: 20). Yet "among [the] highest leisure class...decorum finds its fullest and maturest expression...[and] serves as a canon of conduct for the classes beneath" (ibid.: 33). For Veblen, exploited industrious workers accept and endorse an unserviceable system of desire precisely in order to receive recognition from the powerful. This system of privileged desire is simultaneously a canon of conduct or "scheme of life." The "members of each stratum accept as their ideal of decency the *scheme of life* in vogue in the next higher stratum, and bend their energies to live up to that ideal" (1994: 52, emphasis added). Because of the power of the leisure class over the desires of other social strata, because to retain one's good name one needs recognition from these leisure classes, whatever social practices, commodities, ideals, and fashions, the privileged endorse are normative forces in society (Veblen 1998). And the "baseborn commoner delights to stoop and yield" (1994: 34) to the scheme of life offered by the leisure class because to "affiliate themselves by a system of dependence...to the great ones" provides an "increment of repute" (ibid.: 48). I retain my good name by endorsing the worldview, the system of desires, and the *scheme of life* produced by the leisure class. Thus, style and fashion are markers of allegiance to leisure class desire. Style is an emblem of power (Cassano 2009b, 2005b).

The Power of Fashion

As the number that opens the film comes to an end, Lucky rushes off stage, saying "I've got to get married." Pop tries to talk Lucky out of the wedding, and

---

4   Throughout this chapter, I employ Veblen's terminology for class. Against the "vested interests" that constitute the "leisure class," Veblen posited the "common lot" of working people. In this sense, Veblen's class rhetoric was somewhat more inclusive than the early Marxist language of the industrial proletariat conventionally employed by the left during much of the 20th century (Veblen 1964; Cassano 2009a, 2008, 2006).

out of leaving the troupe. But Lucky has his mind made up. "My talent is gambling, Pop. Hoofing is alright, but there's no future in it." The film sets Lucky's gaze firmly on the future. He represents the quintessential "modern man," and throughout, the film uses modernity as a trope, emphasizing the here and now of the narrative. Lucky may have a past, but he has no visible roots.

The film begins with abandonment as Lucky prepares to leave his co-workers to marry a wealthy woman. Lucky hungers for leisure class respectability. The mechanism through which this hunger reveals itself is his obsession with dress, with looking modern, and above all, with living a fashionable existence. The film plays on the multiple meanings of fashion: fashion as the latest style; and fashion as a kind of (self) construction. Lucky's self is fashioned, but, as the film begins, his self-fashioning remains subservient to the fashionable gaze of the leisure class.

A pivotal sequence that drives the rest of the narrative begins backstage, with Lucky, dressed in tails, but already late for his wedding. The "fellas" gather around. One finds a copy of *Squire*, "A Man's Magazine," on the dressing table. He opens to a fashion ad. A man, dressed in Lucky's same outfit, stands beside a chauffeured limousine, lighting a cigar. For the audience in 1936, the ad immediately evokes TOP HAT and its fantastic world of wealth. But SWING TIME subverts the fantasy promulgated both by the ad and by its own precursor, and dramatizes the consequences of TOP HAT's fantasy as a force in the material world.

Taking pencil in hand, the chorus dancer alters the magazine illustration, adding cuffs to the trousers. Meanwhile, Lucky literally evokes the prior film for the audience by donning his *top hat* and asking:

"How do I look?"
At first, murmurs of approval, then: "You're not going like that?"
"Why of course. Church wedding, first family, very social, whole town there." Lucky snaps and clicks his heels.
"I guess it doesn't matter..."
"What doesn't matter?" Lucky shows concern on his face.
"Last year's trousers...No cuffs."

The "fellas" convince Lucky he's wearing last year's trousers and when Pop takes the garment to the tailor, Lucky is left without his pants, thus delaying his wedding and setting the film's narrative in motion. In this game of deception and desire, the "fellas" play off Lucky's hunger to be the image, his desire for an imaginary other's approval. More than that, the "other" whose approval the film first posits comes from a world of wealth and privilege. Lucky wants to be a mirror image of the ad in order to please the leisure class gaze. His fiancé,

Margaret, and her family, are means for achieving the new identity he seeks. (Lucky hopes to marry into his hometown's "first family.") But, using a Veblenian rhetoric, the film argues the community to which Lucky aspires is decadent, and their gaze, corrupt and corrupting.

Lucky identifies with and aspires to the world of privilege painted in the imaginary pages of *Squire* and imagined in the real film TOP HAT. Thus SWING TIME also offers a theory of cinema: The mass media captivates the desires of its audience, shapes them, binds them to an imaginary community and set of social norms. While the film demonstrates the power of the mass media to disseminate leisure class desires, it says something else as well. When the chorus dancer takes his pencil to the ad in *Squire*, he re-purposes the artifact, transforming it into a weapon of opposition. The ad becomes a vehicle for subverting the system of class-based desire the film posits. In articulating this oppositional possibility, the film provides space for its own work as an oppositional commodity. Through this use of the ad to undermine Lucky's affiliation with wealth and power, the film represents the mass media as an arena of class struggle. In this sense, SWING TIME supplements Veblen's argument that style is an emblem of power. Style *can* serve such a function. But SWING TIME also argues that style and the mass media have the potential power to disrupt established norms, taken for granted schemes of life, and even vested circuits of social desire. More than simply a sign of power, style is an emblem of community affiliation; and the struggle between two communities plays out in a struggle over style.

SWING TIME dramatizes the ambivalence in Lucky's desire for recognition as a struggle between two identities. In fact, I've been wrong to call the Astaire character "Lucky." He is "Lucky" to Pops, to Penny, to the dancers in his troupe, but to Margaret and to her world of repute and wealth, he is "John." These two names represent two possible directions for the character's desire, two possible communities from which he craves recognition, and, ultimately, two possible schemes of life. It wouldn't be too much to say that Lucky's ambivalent desire signifies a class conflict between two radically different worldviews: one represented by the leisure class and Margaret, the other by jazz dance, blackface and Penny. By the end of the film, Lucky's original scheme of life is inverted and he surrenders his dreams of wealth and respectability for a cheap song (or penny carol) played to a SWING TIME beat.

The Political Economy of Desire

Having missed his wedding, John Garnett arrives at Margaret's family mansion. Father is yelling: "we'll be the laughing stock of this whole town." Clearly, like

Lucky/John, Father's concern is community esteem. What follows is an exchange between Father and John so remarkable that it bears reproduction in full.[5]

> "I wouldn't let you marry her for $10,000," says Father.
> "How 'bout 20?"
> "Not for $20,000."
> "25" says John, extending his hand in the motion of a bid.
> "Not for twenty-fi," Father breaks off, the briefest smile crossing his lips, "say young man, where could you get $25,000? By dancing? And there's another thing, coming back to your own hometown in a *dancing act.*"
> "I'm going into a new business. Why only this afternoon I made $200," John doesn't mention he made it gambling.
> "$200?"
> "Yes, that's why I was late for the wedding."
> "Well...that makes it a little different. Now I'm not consenting to your wedding, but I always admire any young man who can make money. It shows...Well it shows *character.*"...
> "Then Margaret and I can get married?"
> "Well, if you go to New York and work hard at your business and if you're successful you can come back here and ask me for my Margaret. And in all probability, I'll be very happy to give her to you."
> As he's leaving, Margaret asks John, "Come back soon, won't you?"
> "That all depends upon the stakes um the stocks uh the business," he answers as Father shakes his hand goodbye.

As in Veblen's *Leisure Class*, reputability (here "character") comes from property (here in the abstract form of money), but Lucky's work as a professional dancer brings disreputability. By the last reel, the film definitively associates dance with "blackness" and this association could be reason enough for Father's initial disapproval. At the same time, the film associates dance with work. As a dancer, *Lucky* is a common worker. As a gambler, however, *John* gains Father's admiration. In a slip of the tongue, Lucky calls gambling "stakes," "stocks," and so plays upon the popular idea that there is little difference between a stock speculator and a gambler. Both make something from nothing and live more by luck than hard work. The slip of the tongue hardly matters. Father admires "*any* young man who can make money."

---

5   Unfortunately, I cannot here reproduce the rhythm of the dialogue, which sounds every bit like an auction.

But the film's critique doesn't end with the fact that Father's admiration is calculated in dollar amounts. In a strikingly Veblenian vein, SWING TIME offers a picture of gender relations in which Father owns Margaret, but is willing to sell her to John for $25,000. The point of this sequence is to demonstrate, once more, the emptiness of the scheme of life offered by Father and his community. Even in its fragmentary form, however, this critical representation of gender relations raises fundamental questions about masculine domination as it intersects with class privilege.[6]

SWING TIME's narrative couldn't properly be called a "critique" were it not for the fact that the film goes beyond the pillory of the wealthy. Lucky's aspirations are initially anchored in the leisure class scheme of life. But Penny Carrol (Ginger Rogers) represents a different scheme of life. From her first appearance, she is located *as a worker*, and more than that, as *working class*, at least in terms of the treatment she receives from those with power. This representation offers a vivid contrast to the role she played in TOP HAT.

Swing Time's Realism

Stylistically, the first act of SWING TIME evokes cinematic realism. Compared to the leisure class life in a picture post-card London and a surreal Venice presented by TOP HAT, SWING TIME's portrayal of working women struggling in New York City is brutal. Again, it's worth recalling GOLDDIGGERS OF 1933, which also portrayed women workers in the entertainment industry who were unemployed, hungry, and cold. Echoing that earlier film, SWING TIME connects these themes to a political economy of desire that indicts the very leisure class portrayed so effectively in TOP HAT. And unlike GOLDDIGGERS, SWING TIME utilizes the rhetoric of labor and the left. True, Popular Front language

---

6   Veblen, of course, argued that private property began with the capture and enslavement of women. In a speculative pre-historical narrative, he argues that warriors in early human communities needed to provide evidence of their prowess in order to receive the esteem of the community. They did this in the form of "trophies" of war and of the hunt. Women, however, were particularly "useful as tropies" because they did the industrious labor that kept the community alive. To capture a woman was to capture her labor power. "From the ownership of women the concept of ownership extends itself to include the products of their industry, and so there arises the ownership of things as well as of persons" (1994: 16). Veblen makes this argument not because he believes it applies to the past, but because it offers a mirror on his present. Marriage, he argues, continues to be a form of ownership in which the wife becomes the symbolic representation of her husband's wealth, just as a daughter represents her father's wealth (Veblen 1998).

and imagery are deployed for comic effect. But viewed in the context of the times, this use of left ideology, even only as a kind of *fashion*, indicates a shift in the structures of feeling animating SWING TIME's audience. Speaking largely to a working class audience, SWING TIME builds a cinematic rhetoric from tropes familiar to workers engaged in labor struggles. At least for part of the narrative, this labor rhetoric intersects with a continued critique of gender relations; and the women characters enter the scene as *workers*.

In conventional social problem dramas like I am a FUGITIVE FROM a CHAIN GANG (1932), BLACK FURY (1935), or DEAD END (1937), cinematic "realism" is a trope, a stylistic device that attempts *evoke* reality, and not, of course, a direct representation of the struggles workers face. But SWING TIME's is a "realism" of the second order, a meta-realism meant to evoke not "reality," but the "realistic" style of social problem films, without actually entering their terrain. Consider Chaplin's great hit of the same year, MODERN TIMES. At first it would seem wrong to put Chaplin's film in the same stylistic category as Ford's THE GRAPES OF WRATH (1940). Scenes like the Tramp trapped by the automatic feeding machine, or the sequence where the machine operator becomes enmeshed in the gears of his own device, certainly seem more surreal than real. But when Chaplin portrays the suffering of Gamine (Paulette Goddard) or the labor struggles that hover about the edge of the narrative, he does so to mobilize his audience. Like THE GRAPES OF WRATH, MODERN TIMES is constructed with a self-conscious political intention to turn popular sentiment against the excesses of modern capitalism, even against capitalism itself. SWING TIME, on the other hand, uses the politics and language of the left almost as costuming, like one of the gowns Ginger Rogers wears. I might put it like this, whereas "realism" styles "reality," SWING TIME uses "realism" as a kind of designer label. Through its evocation of the style and subject matter of social problem films, it claims the allegiance of the "common lot" against a perverse ruling "leisure class." And while SWING TIME's "realism" might be called "mere fashion," the film has already taught its audience how to think about "mere fashion." Through the mass media, fashion itself has the power to re-fashion life.

SWING TIME's play with the social problem genre begins in a rail yard. After he loses everything but his gambler's talisman (a lucky quarter) in a bet with "the fellas" over whether he'd marry Margaret, Lucky, dressed in wedding tails and top hat, jumps a flatcar bound for New York, with Pop in tow. Poverty doesn't seem to touch Lucky, but the audience sees its own suffering in Pop's hunger for a cigarette as he walks the city streets. Once again, in striking contrast to TOP HAT, the New York represented in this sequence is crowded, loud, dirty, and, most importantly, unjust. Injustice appears in the form of a police force whose central purpose is to protect the wealthy from working people.

When Lucky chances upon Penny Carroll, he trades her his lucky quarter for two-bits so Pop can buy some cigarettes. While Lucky flirts with Penny, Pop steals the quarter back. Lucky doesn't realize the theft until Penny has already called a cop. The cop smiles and salutes the man dressed in a top hat. "Good morning, Sir"

> "Good morning," says Lucky.
> "This man stole a quarter from my purse," says Penny, "make him give it back."
> "Now does he look like a man who would go around stealing quarters?" asks the cop.
> ..."I don't care what you happen to think he looks like, I know he stole my quarter."
> The cop takes a couple of steps back and calls Penny away from the men.
> "Now you run along sister before I run you in for disturbing the peace."
> The cop forces her to "move along," but not before she retorts: "why you...*Cossack*."
> By this time, Pop has managed to tell Lucky about the theft.
> Lucky says: "Officer, you know you had no right to speak to that little girl that way."
> "Listen," says the cop, "*guys like you pay me to protect them from screwy dames....* Why you ought to thank me for what I done!"

Here the film continues its Veblenian critique of American society. It doesn't matter that Lucky is broke. His top hat and tails put wealth into evidence. In turn, the image of wealth provides access to power. Both the cop and Penny recognize the function of the police, to "protect" the wealthy from the common lot. As her name makes clear, Penny Carol represents the common lot, living in a world of work and workers. The film places its audience on Penny's side, by portraying wealth as empty desire, corruption and show; and by dramatizing the power the privileged wield through their "Cossack[s]." And the film *genders* inequality, demonstrating the intersection of class privilege and masculine domination. For the cop, Penny is just another "dame" after a rich man's pocket book.

When Penny storms into work at the Gordon Dancing Academy, still angry at the exchange with the cop, her boss, Mr Gordon (Eric Blore), says:

> "No wonder this school is losing money, everybody late every morning. Any more of this dilly-dallying and some of you are going to lose your jobs."
> Then to other passing instructors: "Yes, and that goes for you girls too."

This brief exchange brings into the cinema the arbitrary power of management, the condescending attitude managers often had toward women workers, and the constant fear of unemployment that affected so many depression era workers. These "realistic" elements have a dual function in SWING TIME: first, in contrast to TOP HAT, they locate SWING TIME in the here (New York) and the now (1936); second, they locate the film in the common world of a working class audience. Before Lucky and Penny join as lovers, they unite as *workers*. But first, they engage in collective bargaining.

The scene begins with a close shot of a man's feet as he walks a picket line. The camera pulls back to reveal Pop and Lucky wearing sandwich boards. "PENNY CARROL UNFAIR to JOHN GARNETT." Lucky's slouched fedora, his grim, determined expression, and even the lighting of the shot itself evokes the image of the striker in Joe Jones' canvas "We Demand" (1934). Penny's friend Mabel (Helen Broderick) sticks her head through the transom to say: "Keep up the good work boys, the public is with you."

> Penny says to Mabel: "How could I fall in love with a common gambler?"
> "Penny, when a man takes a little quarter and turns it into a bank roll that would choke a horse...I'd call him an *uncommon* gambler."
> Moments later, Mabel opens the door for the men, saying: "come in comrades." Then, "you're a big success. She's willing to arbitrate."

Once again, in utilizing the imagery and language of labor the film is not so much attempting to make a political statement as a *fashion statement*. But that statement of fashion is also a *claim to community* (and thus a kind of political claim after all). The audience it claims for itself is an audience that understands references like "come in, comrade," or "she's willing to arbitrate." True, it wasn't only among working people that these expressions would have currency, but the film has already clearly articulated its class allegiance. It stands with the common lot, in the common world of work, struggle and love.

Yet despite the imagery of protest, Lucky remains an *uncommon* gambler. SWING TIME's portrayal of gambling is free from the usual stigma. Lucky's gambling isn't a habit, it's a gift, access to money, and through money, to respect. Early on, Lucky connects gambling to stock speculation. And once Lucky earns twenty-five thousand dollars through his gambling, he's bound to go back home and marry Margaret. Through this mechanism, again, the film connects gambling to the decidedly uncommon world of wealth and privilege.[7]

---

7   Veblen, too, argued that gambling and the belief in luck are marks of leisure class desire (Veblen 1994: 169–179).

This connection is certified in the final shot of the film. Throwing away his lucky quarter for a mere Penny, Lucky breaks his attachment with a community of privilege in exchange for the solidarities of the common working life. SWING TIME is a film for and about working class communities of solidarity emerging out of the struggles of the mid-1930s. At the same time, in its final reel, the film also defines the boundaries of this new community. SWING TIME's common workers live in a world of unspoken white privilege.

Immigrants and The Shadows of Blackness

Midway through the second act, the critique of the leisure class and the colorful use of labor rhetoric fall into the background. Instead, a different set of issues of direct concern to SWING TIME's working class audience take center stage. These themes revolve around questions of ethnic identity, racial masquerade, and the social function of blackface for a new immigrant working class community. Through the use of blackface, the common world becomes the "white" world. But SWING TIME's whiteness has ambiguous contours. Some characters are on one side of the color line, some are on the other, and some are "in-between." And while the role of blackness seems at first simple and formulaic, SWING TIME devotes its final critique to the color line by figuring swing music itself as a cultural form stolen by a white community that unconsciously trumpets its own guilty conscience.

SWING TIME builds two separate worlds, one marked out by leisure class desire, the other by the desire for what is common (a Penny Carrol) and for a common world based in work. From the motto of the dance academy ("to know how to dance is to know how to control oneself") to Penny and Lucky's struggle to get and keep shows, dance becomes a trope for labor. Hardly surprising, then, that a film that locates itself within the common world of work, and claims the side of the working class against the leisure class, would take up themes of racial and ethnic belonging. The working class emerging during the age of the CIO was a community largely made up of immigrants (Gutman 1987; Barrett 1992; Denning 1998). And within that working class community was a "second generation" youth culture for whom the feeling of "inbetween-ness" made the question of racial identity burn (Roediger and Barrett 2002; Roediger, 2005: 177–198). In Hollywood, the psychological and social struggles of "second generation" immigrants caught in a white America were repeatedly dramatized. From the first sound picture, THE JAZZ SINGER (1927), analyzed so well by Michael Rogin (1998), to social problem films like BLACK FURY (1935), gangster pictures, especially SCARFACE (1932), to melodramas like Frank Borzage's

MANNEQUIN (1938), second generation immigrants were portrayed as caught between old and new worlds. Some films, like Michael Curtiz's BLACK FURY (1935) and Borzage's BIG CITY (1937), go much further, taking a stand for social justice by vividly portraying the racism experienced by Southern and Eastern European immigrant workers. While rarely exposed to the level of vicious racism experienced by African Americans, Asian Americans, and indigenous peoples, the racism, forms of exclusion, and racial domination these "new immigrants" did experience within the normatively "white" culture of the U.S. shaped their experience of assimilation and Americanization. For the new immigrant population, their children and grandchildren, assimilation meant accepting American values, and this Americanization simultaneously meant the acceptance of white supremacy and normative racism. As Roediger (1999, 2005), Rogin (1998), Barrett (1992), Mink (1996) and others have demonstrated, the Southern and Eastern European immigrant became "whiter" to the extent she or he acknowledged the socially constructed racial boundaries that made white supremacy possible.

Both David Roediger (1999) and Michael Rogin (1998) argue that blackface minstrel performances have sometimes played a unique role in the Americanization, and consequent whitening, of immigrant performers and their audience. By "blacking up," Irish American minstrel performers of the 19th century affirmed their often ambiguous whiteness. Every performance ended with the burnt cork wiped away, revealing a "white" face. Minstrel performance was thus an assertion of white supremacy (through its parody and attack on stereo-typed Black culture), and, simultaneously, an assertion of the "whiteness" of the performer. Through their attack on Blacks, nineteenth century Irish minstrels achieved some measure of recognition from the normatively "white" American community. (Roediger 1999: 133–163) Rogin finds this same process at work for second generation Southern and Eastern European immigrants in the early 20th century. THE JAZZ SINGER portrays a racial "other" (in this case, the Jewish son of a cantor) achieving fame and recognition through an attack on African Americans played out behind blackface. But if blackface performance was one element in the process of the whitening of non-white immigrants like the Irish and Eastern European Jews, it was never a simple racist parody. In fact, both Roediger and Rogin argue that blackface performances were shot through with ambiguities and ambivalence. Blackface performances attacked African Americans as stupid, lazy, ignorant, and wild, but at the same time celebrated the perceived excellence of African American cultural forms like music and dance. Precisely because African Americans were stereotyped as wild creatures of nature, black cultural forms came to represent the inversion of the bourgeois values of thrift, sobriety and self-discipline that shaped the lives of so many industrial workers. "Just as the minstrel stage held out the possibility that whites could be 'black' for awhile but nonetheless white, it offered the possibilities that, via blackface, preindustrial joys could survive among industrial discipline" (Roediger 1999: 118).

If for immigrant workers and their children, "whiteness" becomes a metaphor for industrial discipline, and the experience of social domination and exclusion, it is simultaneously an aspiration, a sign of acceptance. And while "blackness" represents rejection and exclusion, it also signifies freedom, pleasure and life. While the deep desire for success in a white supremacist culture pulled the second generation toward an idealized whiteness, the accoutrements of African American culture (swing music, tap dancing, the blues) represented freedom from the constraints of industrial discipline. In SWING TIME, this opposition plays out, but is also extended. Blackface performance is the inversion of industrial discipline. But it is represents the hidden heart whose beat makes white working class culture possible. As its very title suggests, SWING TIME posits swing as central to working class self-formation; and, at the same time, it symptomatically recognizes this "white" culture's debt to African American originality.

The racial subplot begins with a love triangle. Ricardo Romero, bandleader, crooner, and Mediterranean lothario with accented English, pursues Penny. Again, a contrast with TOP HAT: In the earlier film, there is an Italian suitor involved with the Ginger Rogers character. But the Italian character in is a European effete and fallen aristocrat, not, as in SWING TIME, an immigrant entertainer on the make. While Romero's motivations for pursuing Penny are never explicitly articulated, they parallel Lucky's desire for the common world and, simultaneously, resemble the racial dialectic of desire played out in so much 1930s cinema. Racial and ethnic "others" pursue white lovers precisely in order to gain access to that whiteness, to be allowed into the common world. And whatever Romero's motivations, one thing is clear: He stands below Lucky in the social hierarchy. This invidious comparison emerges from another remarkable scene.

Romero refuses to play for Lucky and Penny's dance number. But Lucky wins Romero's contract in a card game with the gambler and gangster "Dice" Raymond, another Mediterranean immigrant.

> "I wonder if you'd be kind enough to play something for Miss Carroll and myself?" asks Lucky, "If you don't mind?"
> "But I do," responds Romero.
> "Well, I'm afraid you'll have to, because, you see," says Lucky, "*I now own you.*"
> "What do you mean you 'own me'?"

"He just won you," responds Penny. "At the gambling table."

"Oh, I see. Congratulations on winning such a valuable piece of property," responds Romero.

"Now will you play your waltz for us?".

"Oh, no, no, no. If you read the contract, you'll see I don't have to play after this hour unless I want to."

What matters here is the language of contract and ownership. Romero is, by his own admission, a "valuable piece of property." He is a kind of commodity, bound to an owner. A bond (in bondage) symbolically connects Romero to blackness. But this comparison to blackness only goes so far. Romero, like other skilled immigrant workers, has some capacity to control and direct his labor (Barrett 1992). Through the use of popular stereotypes (the Latin lover, the dark skinned immigrant gangster), the film marks immigrants as unassimilated "others." But to mark them as unassimilated is not the same as to mark them as black. Indeed, the one African American character in the film is Romero's butler (Floyd Shackelford). And his step-and-fetchit portrayal whitens Romero through comparison.

Romero, the crooner, and Raymond, the gangster, are not the only "ethnics" portrayed in the film. Early on, Pop takes Lucky's trousers to an immigrant tailor for mending. But that scene, played for laughs, doesn't tell the viewer much about the films attitude toward the new immigrants. In fact, that attitude remains the most ambiguous aspect of the film's narrative; and it remains ambiguous precisely because Lucky's own ethnicity remains unmarked and ultimately ambiguous. This is part and parcel of his modernity. As the viewer learns from the early scene with the cop, Lucky becomes the part he plays. In this, could Lucky be the representation of a second or third generation Mediterranean immigrant? Consider, especially, Lucky's relationship with Pop. At the very least, Pop is a foster father, but the narrative suggests more.[8] The audience learns Pop's last name early on, Cardetti. Does this make Pop a second or third generation Italian immigrant? Not necessarily. Pop is a magician, and SWING TIME's audience would be familiar with the convention of magicians of all ethnicities adopting Italian stage names. But Pop calls himself "Cardetti" even though his career as a magician is apparently long over. The film never resolves these ambiguities, never explains Pop's name, never specifies the nature of his relationship with Lucky. But Lucky has multiple identities. For one community, he becomes

---

8   While there are homoerotic overtones to the relationship between Pop and Lucky, they don't contradict the equally strong paternal overtones.

Lucky; for another, John. In both cases, his moniker "Garnett" suggests a stage name. Like Penny, he's a *common* gem. But is there a genealogical line from *Cardetti* to *Garnett*? From the second generation immigrant to the third generation "American"? The names are similar enough to suggest an ambivalent inheritance. Perhaps Lucky altered his last name for the same reason he pursued the wrong trousers: He wants a "good name." These questions remain (centrally) obscure in the narrative, allowing the audience to imagine its own answers. At the very least, Pop's name suggests that an assimilated Mediterranean might, under the right conditions, become "white."

One thing is certain: John/Lucky stands between two communities. By the end of the film, his inbetween-ness will be resolved in favor of the common world. But only after Lucky's climatic "tribute" to Bill "Bojangles" Robinson danced in blackface. Before the dance sequence, Penny steals away to Lucky's dressing room, and out of camera shot, they kiss. The only evidence of this off-camera escapade, lipstick traces on Lucky's face. In a sense, the kiss is an initiation ritual: Through it, Lucky enters into a new community. His shift in identity is solidified by a mark, a ritual tattoo of sorts—the lipstick stain on his face. And with the stain still visible, Lucky sits down in front of his mirror, sings "old Bojangles of Harlem," and begins to apply the burnt cork. Penny's lipstick merges with the cork, establishing a kind of metonymy in which the entry into the common world marked by the lipstick traces becomes the entry into a white community marked by performance in blackface.

But the function of blackface in SWING TIME is more complex still. True, through this assumption of a racist disguise, Lucky affiliates with the common world (now an unambiguously "white" world) and rejects the leisure class. The dance sequence that follows, however, reveals another connection between the white world celebrated by SWING TIME and the blackness the film attacks. Without African American culture, without *swing music*, both the film and the community it imagines would be impossible. The culture celebrated by SWING TIME is working class culture, but also black culture, or at least a whitened version of black culture. And Lucky and Penny's own labor depends in turn upon a fundamental cultural appropriation, a dispossession, upon theft. Through his blackface dance, Lucky shows the audience that the common white world he's joined depends upon and exploits the shadows of blackness.

The number begins with a full orchestra playing, and two rows of dancers, half dressed in black, half in white, tapping and singing. The curtain opens to reveal a huge black face, with bowler hat, thick red lips, and a polka dot bow tie. The minstrel face then dissolves into huge shoes, and the women dancers take hold of enormous phallic legs, separating them to reveal Lucky in striped suit and blackface, with his arms extended in the classic minstrel pose. At first

Lucky dances to orchestral accompaniment with the chorus of women, but the orchestra fades and eventually the chorus line disappears. A solo stride piano plays as Lucky dances alone, with three huge shadows in the background. For most of the sequence, the huge shadows are mirrors, accurately reflecting Lucky's foreground dance. But at one point, the shadows break free and begin to dance on their own. A dance contest between Lucky and the shadows ensue. When Lucky seems to win the contest, the shadows wave him off in disgust and leave.

Following Marshall Berman, Dave Roediger shows the connection between the cinematic "shadow" and blackness in THE JAZZ SINGER.

> In the film, Yudelson the "kibitzer" from the ghetto falters on seeing Jakie in blackface. "Jakie, this ain't you," he begins, before turning to comment to the audience, "It talks like Jakie, but it looks like his shadow." In the shooting script, Yudelson's lines ended instead with, "but it looks like a nigger".
>
> ROEDIGER 2005: 184

Just as in THE JAZZ SINGER, the shadows here are blackness, the image of Bill Robinson transformed into a symbol of black culture itself. And while Lucky's dance celebrates white supremacy—after all, he beats his shadows—it also signifies a remarkable admission, an understanding that the cultural forms that make the common world possible are stolen. The shadows literally lose control, but in loss of control there is symbolic victory. When the shadows walk away in disgust, they walk away from the white world of industrial discipline symbolized by the Gordon's motto, "To Know How to Dance is to Know How to Control One's Self." This sequence illustrates the hollow ring of that motto. After all, these three parts of Lucky's "self" refuse his control and walk away. The blackness at the heart of swing is, indeed, the other of industrial discipline: that which refuses to be subjected to control. To the extent that the working class culture represented by the film refuses to be subjected to the scheme of life imposed by the leisure class in the first reels, cultural resistance (and class struggle) is figured as "black." Jazz becomes a symbol of a new working class culture. And, in his blackface, Lucky not only affirms white supremacy, but celebrates the resistance of new cultures of solidarity. In the 1930s, working class resistance played out to a swing beat.

Rather than overturning white supremacy, however, SWING TIME symptomatically reveals its own guilty conscience in one final sequence. After breaking his engagement to Margaret, Lucky learns that Penny plans to marry Romero. He and Pop manage to prevent the union through the same trick that set the narrative in motion. Finding a *Squire* magazine in Romero's dressing room, Lucky pencils in cuffs and convinces Romero that he's got the wrong trousers. Later, when Romero appears at the wedding, and after Lucky's already won his prized Penny, the crooner is wearing trousers two sizes too big. While Romero looks ridiculous, beside him stands his black manservant, wearing an overcoat, *but no trousers*. Everyone laughs at the situation, and at the black man. Romero may not have gotten Penny, but he is whitened by his servant's humiliation. Most importantly, when Romero appropriates his black worker's trousers, he echoes and amplifies the message of Lucky's blackface dance. A successful bandleader and composer of music in "Swing Time," Romero achieves status (becomes whiter) by exploiting African American culture.

Culture and Barbarism

In January of 1936, an item appeared on the front page of daily *Variety* under the heading: "Esquire's Show-Cause order in Astaire's $25,000 Damage Suit.": "'Esquire magazine has been given until Thursday to show cause why it should not be restrained from using the photo of Fred Astaire in a jewelry advertisement in the January issue." The ad, for "Top Hat Evening Jewelry as inspired by Fred Astaire," irritated the actor enough that he filed suit against *Esquire*, the jewelry manufacturer, and the advertising firm. Apparently understanding the power of the mass media to shape public perception and desire, he complained mainly of the poor quality of the ad, arguing "I am being exposed to public ridicule and contempt" (*Variety*, January 29, 1936). This event only has historical significance because George Stevens, Allan Scott, and Astaire take a kind of wry revenge on *Esquire* early in Swing Time. Lucky is captured by the image from *Squire* magazine, and his imagined insufficiency ("no cuffs") is nothing other than an imagined "public ridicule and contempt." Swing Time uses this reference to the world beyond the film as an anchor, directing the audience's attention outward, to the "real world." The joke is yet another meta-realistic marker, trumpeting the "relevance" of the picture that's about to unwind. And the joke focuses the audience upon the power of the image circulated through mass media.

Through the sequence involving *Squire* magazine, Swing Time reflects upon its cinema's social function. The unmistakable references to Top Hat in the ad further suggest the magazine, as one form of the mass media, represents the double of another form, cinema. Certainly, argues the film, they both function in similar ways to shape social desires and norms. At the same time, in narrative and thematic terms, SWING TIME sets itself in conscious opposition to TOP HAT.[9]

Yet the film also takes refuge in ambiguities, the most salient having to do with the "race question." By 1936, second and third generation immigrants made up much of the working class, and thus much of SWING TIME's audience. SWING TIME understands the power of the mass media image, and thus understands that through its representations of race, the film participates in generating dominant perceptions of immigrants and African Americans. At the same time, the film subverts the immigrant stereotypes it employs (the Gangster, the Lothario) by suggesting, through Pop Cardetti, that ethnic identity itself changes over time, that ethnics can "Americanize" and thus "whiten." The question of blackness is more complicated. But here the film goes beyond other portrayals of the period by inserting its minstrel routine within an ironic context. That irony begins with the picture's title itself. The film appropriates "swing" music to use as a symbol for (white) working class culture. But, as the audience understood, this cultural form came from black Americans. Thus the film addresses the central paradox at its heart, the absence of blackness in a movie about swing, with Astaire's "tribute" to Bojangles Robinson. The "tribute" announces swing's lineage and the film's debt. But when placed in context beside the final scene of the film, both the shadow dance and the stolen trousers signify an anxious acknowledgement of the crime at the heart of American culture. In cinematic language, the film prefigures Benjamin's 1940 remark: "There is no document of culture which is not at the same time a document of barbarism" (Benjamin 2003: 392).

Let me return to the "wrong trousers." From the beginning of the picture, these trousers are a figure for the power of mass media representations to shape perception. When the film ends with a black man standing without

---

9 Through its audacious critique of leisure class desire, its uneven critique of masculine domination, and its early focus upon class injustice and the language of the labor movement, SWING TIME suggests but never fully imagines an alternative set of values and desires. In an essay discussing the shadows of blackness in the film, Elizabeth Abel offers an assessment of the film's use of racial tropes: "SWING TIME ventures further than The Jazz Singer in imagining an outside to its sexual and racial plots, but although this exterior exerts greater pressure on the resolution, it has no more bearing on the racial status quo than did its predecessor" (Abel 2002: 186). For Abel, the shadows that dance with Astaire point toward the films exterior, toward the unspeakable. What Abel says of the film's attitudes toward African Americans can equally be applied to its attitude toward capitalism and class domination. It points to what is beyond itself as if to announce its own insufficiency. SWING TIME reflects upon the fact that it participates in history, that it is a contestant in a struggle, that it has to *take a side*.

his trousers, laughed at by the other characters in the film, "exposed to public ridicule and contempt," it offers an analysis of the representation of blackness in the media. SWING TIME both participates in the humiliation and subordination of African Americans, and critiques the very representations of blackness it puts on display. In this sense, both participating in racial domination and recognizing its injustice, perhaps SWING TIME approaches the experience of its working class audience, many of whom participated in white supremacy while understanding, perhaps from bitter experience, its injustice.

SWING TIME documents a recurrent theme in New Deal cinema: when radical representations appear, they are propelled by the energies of symbolic forms of traditional domination. The films that come closest to challenging traditional modes of domination, like RIFFRAFF and MY MAN GODFREY, take openly anti-left positions, even as they critique masculinity and male privilege. Again, with John Ford's radical indictment of colonial whiteness, THE HURRICANE (1937), radical critique depends upon a defense of community and traditional forms of domination. While THE HURRICANE (1937) deconstructs "whiteness" and critiques imperialism, Ford's radical critique of white supremacy abroad justifies an anti-black racism within the United States. This ambivalent radical traditionalism will shape Ford's cinema through the 1930s and 1940s, leading him, ultimately, to abandon his ambiguous radicalism in the name of a traditionalism that asserts white supremacy and represses the cries of the "world's afflicted races."

CHAPTER 4

The Hurricane (1937)[1]

In 1937, the filmmaker John Ford called himself "a definite socialistic democrat—*always* left."[2] And, indeed, between 1935 and 1941, John Ford directed a series of films that turned a critical eye toward capitalism, colonialism, and imperialism, sometimes with surprisingly radical results. Thus, in this chapter I will examine the collaboration between Ford and the Popular Front screenwriter Dudley Nichols on THE HURRICANE (1937). Drawing upon their common memory of Irish dispossession, Ford and Nichols produced one of the most startling critiques of western imperialism found in 1930s cinema.[3] That critique of imperialism was based upon a paradoxically "progressive" orientalism that posited a wild lust for freedom among South Pacific Islanders; yet, in 1934's JUDGE PRIEST, these same filmmakers represented African Americans as servile and dependent. This chapter argues that it was precisely the projected independence of colonized peoples that allowed Ford and Nichols to normalize black oppression in the United States.

Popular Front and Labor Affiliations

Ford's public sympathy for organized labor surfaced during the first New Deal. In 1933, when the wave of bank failures allowed Hollywood producers and executives to attempt to institute a series of wage and salary cutbacks (aimed

---

1 This chapter is an expanded and revised version of an article that originally appeared as "'The Last of the World's Afflicted Race of Humans Who Believe in Freedom': Race, Colonial Whiteness and Imperialism in John Ford's and Dudley Nichols' *The Hurricane* (1937)," *The Journal of American Studies*, 44:1, 2010: 117–133.

2 It must be noted, however, that Ford expressed his "socialistic" leanings in a private letter to his nephew who was at the time fighting the Fascists in Spain (McBride 2001: 271).

3 The common arguments that Ford's 1930s politics were somehow inauthentic because he viewed the dispossession of the Okies through the lens of the colonization of Ireland by the English, or that "his attraction to the Spanish Loyalists stemmed from his ability to generate an imaginative analogy that compared Franco's forces to British troops in Ireland and the Spanish Loyalists to the Irish Republican Army" need to be re-contextualized (Maland 2003: 57). The fact that Ford's identification with Irish dispossession by British imperialism allowed him to generate such imaginative analogies, thus re-casting both his own past and the political present, is precisely what needs to be emphasized (see also Eyman 1999: 186–188).

more at lower level production staff than at directors), Ford made an impassioned plea for collective solidarity. Arguing to his fellow directors that "we're not stupid enough to deny that the picture racket is controlled from Wall Street," that the "banking industry is going on a sitdown strike" in order to push wages "back to where they were in 1910," Ford rallied the others to "pitch in with our coworkers and try to find a way out of this mess." "I grant you," he said, "that the producers haven't recognized us, but for Christ's sake, and I say that with reverence, let's not get into a position where the workers of the industry don't recognize us" (quoted in McBride 2001: 193–194). At this point in his career, Ford was something more than a journeyman director; but it was not until the end of that decade that a combination of critical acclaim and popular success allowed him to accumulate significant symbolic capital and institutional power.

The Screen Directors Guild (SDG) formed in 1936, though the impetus for the group grew out of a meeting in King Vidor's living room in 1935 where Ford was present (Ross 1941: 208–209, McBride 2001: 191). At that time, Emanuel Eisenberg, in an article for *New Theater,* described Ford as one of the SDG's "most embattled members" (Eisenberg 2001: 258). Ford told his interviewer, "Do you know anything about the way they're trying to break directorial power now? To reduce the director to a man who just tells actors where to stand?" When Eisenberg asked if movies would now be made "like a Ford car," the director responded, "Not if the Screen Directors Guild can help it, boy. Hang around and watch some fireworks" (Eisenberg 2001: 258). Clearly, Ford thought the SDG and the various other Hollywood craft unions would help workers re-gain at least some control over the productive process.

A decade later, Dudley Nichols expressed some of the frustration that he and Ford felt over the Taylorized methods of conventional film production:

> For while it is neither a difficult nor a notable task to make a motion-picture by the customary assembly-line methods, it is another thing entirely to eschew these factory methods and attempt to make a film by individual effort.... The unthinking may believe that the assembly-line films of Hollywood...have a style, because they are so much alike in their photography and technical finish, as apart from content. Yet it is precisely because of this neat and sumptuous similarity that we can assert definitely that they have no style.
>
> NICHOLS 1947

In part, this frustration with Hollywood's "assembly-line methods," "controlled from Wall Street," by absentee owners and "autocratic money interests," drove

Ford into his pro-union sense of solidarity with other less privileged craft workers in the industry (Eisenberg 2001: 258).

On the one hand, like many activists and leaders in the emerging Congress of Industrial Organizations (CIO), Ford was also motivated by a sense of social justice derived from the Catholic corporatist tradition, as evidence by his exclamation "but for Christ's sake, and I say that with reverence, let's not get into a position where the workers of the industry don't recognize us." (On the Catholic social justice principles and the rise of the CIO, see Zieger 1997). At the same time, through Nichols, Ford was indirectly exposed to a broader array of Popular Front political ideas. Whether collaborating with Nichols, or another screenwriter, themes of labor solidarity, class struggle, and colonialism infuse Ford's cinematic productions during the 1930s and 1940s.

By suggesting that during the 1930s Ford evinced sympathy for Popular Front politics, I don't mean to argue that he was a Popular Front liberal or radical. Ford's personal politics were always mercurial. Even when he was closest to Nichols, "Ford, Ward Bond, John Wayne, and a number of other friends who often gathered to drink at the Hollywood Athletic Club set up a mock social club that they called the 'Young Men's Purity Total Abstinence and Yachting Association.' A running gag of the club was to repeatedly deny Nichol's membership because his liberal politics were judged 'socially reprehensible'" (Maland 2003: 57). Perhaps what C. Wright Mills said of labor leaders in 1948 could usefully be applied to Ford himself: "The American labor leader, like the politician and the big businessman, is now a public figure: different groups hold various images of him.... And, as a public actor and as a private man, the labor leader responds in various ways to the images others hold of him" (Mills 1948: 13). Like those labor leaders, Ford had a number of political personas. And his films took shape in relation to his perception of his audience and their expectations. All the more significant, then, is Ford's remark to Eisenberg, "there's a new kind of public that wants more honest pictures" (Eisenberg 2001: 258). For this "new kind of public," Ford produced a series of films that corresponded to a "labored" sensibility. Those films often transcended the usual liberal platitudes found in filmmakers like Frank Capra, sometimes offering fundamental challenges to western imperialism and class inequality (Stricker 1990).

THE HURRICANE is particularly interesting since it stages the dialectic of colonized desire and the emergence of a decolonizing "national" consciousness, cinematically anticipating several central themes from Frantz Fanon's *Black Skin, White Masks*. While Ford and Nichols offered an attack upon (colonial) whiteness that had few parallels in New Deal Cinema, that anti-colonial critique displaced and repressed any cinematic discussion of white supremacy within the United States. The mechanism of that displacement and repression was an orientalism that depicted exotic South Pacific "primitives" with an irrepressible and savage "love of freedom"; while, in other pictures made during the same period, Nichols and Ford represented African American "primitives" whose child-like dependence required constant shepherding. (On orientalism, see Said 1978: 1–110; for the application of Said's argument to classic Hollywood cinema, see Shoat and Stam 1994.) The tension between these various themes in their work reflected a shared radical traditionalism that paralleled broader forces in the American working class. The fact that THE HURRICANE was included in *Variety's* top ten grossing films for 1938 suggests that, at least to some degree, Ford and Nichols had found their "new kind of public" (Balio 1995: 405).

Colonial Order and Pacific Passions

In brief, THE HURRICANE tells the story of Terangi (Jon Hall), a Europeanized native who, after breaking the jaw of a white man, is unjustly imprisoned for six months. Because Terangi's wild heart cannot stand confinement, he continually attempts to escape his jailors, leading to a 16-year sentence. During his final escape, a hurricane destroys his home island, presumably as God's wrath for those injustices. In another director's and writer's hands, this film would probably have been an existential tale of dueling wills. But Ford and Nichols turn it into a story of two communities, both dominated by the unbending force of French colonial honor, embodied in the form of Governor De Laage (Raymond Massey). THE HURRICANE begins with a framing narrative. On a ship bound for a south sea island, a young woman tourist stands beside an unshaven Dr Kersaint. As the audience will soon learn, Kersaint, as both a cur and a saint, stands upon the boundary between French colonial honor and the native desire for liberation.

> "The south sea islands," she begins, "the last hiding place of beauty, and adventure."
> Dr Kersaint replies, "That's what all the travel folders say."

What follows is a flashback: ominous music plays and the scene of the wasted island dissolves into the past, the dunes now filled with palm trees and contented natives walking hand in hand. The ominous notes of the orchestra's horn section give way to melancholy violins and cellos evoking a vanished utopia. The camera pans along the coast: a small church, with the priest digging in its garden; native huts, fishing nets and hammocks hung from the palms; natives waist deep in the water, readying their vessels for work; children diving beside the docks and playing. Another dissolve: trumpets blowing martial music, a shot of the French flag waving in the wind. Then the camera takes us into an administrative office, with the Governor seated behind a desk; a native, bare-chest covered only by a garland of flowers, stands before him. "You've stolen a canoe," says Governor De Laage, with trumpets amplifying his dark verdict. "You must pay the penalty for breaking the law. You are sentenced to thirty days punishment."

The music and cinematography anticipate the narrative trajectory of the entire picture. Two communities stand against one another. On the one hand, the natives in their paradise, and here the Church and the priest are clearly marked as a part of the paradise that French law will disrupt and, ultimately, destroy. The shot of the French Tri-color billowing in the wind to the martial trumpet march marks the Governor and his minions as colonial intruders. Ford and Nichols imply that colonialism represents a specifically European malady, thereby distancing America—and their American audience—from the critique they will offer. And the first lines uttered (after the initial framing narrative) identify Governor De Laage as the embodiment of the Law. In fact, when the Governor first speaks, the same trumpet theme that played over the Tri-color plays again. Through music, Governor and the flag are metonymically bound to one another. He is almost literally wrapped in his country's colors. (On cinematic metonymy, see Jakobson 1954: 92).

What follows is a piece of dialogue worth noting in full because it anticipates and shapes the subsequent narrative. De Laage says to his native prisoner, "when you have finished those thirty days, you will know better than to break the law again." The native responds in his own tongue and De Laage says to his colonized collaborator, Chief Mehavre (Al Kikume), "I'm sorry, but I don't understand what he's saying." Before the Chief can translate, Dr Kersaint, invisible until now, speaks up:

"He's defending himself against the power of the French government, and very ably."
"Does he deny the theft?" asks De Laage.
"No. He offers in rebuttal that there was moonlight, an awful lot of it. And his lady love says she saw a gold fish in the sea." A shot of the native's "lady love" sitting at his feet serves to signify the sexual abandon of these wild primitives; whereas De Laage, the representative of colonial order, stands against sentiment, sexuality, and desire.
"My dear doctor, I am as sensitive to the whims of love as the next man. But as governor of these islands, I cannot afford to sit by admiring the quaint and the curious. Thirty days, my good fellow."

"It's not exactly my business, De Laage. You've only been here a year; whereas I, indolent wretch, have spent a pitifully long time in these islands. I know these people.... You'll [destroy] yourself if you try to govern these somewhat childish people according to your ideas instead of their's."

This exchange places the film squarely in a long tradition of western representation that figures the colonized as the seat of passion and the colonizers as the forces of order and restraint. Dr Kersaint stands on the border between colonizer and colonized. He speaks their language, and according to his own admission, is an "indolent wretch." While he doesn't fully indulge in the passions presented by the natives, he clearly lacks the restraint that holds De Laage's desires in check.

Precisely because of their childish ways (a typical orientalist justification for colonialism), the natives require western guidance and improvement. But here Ford and Nichols offer a rather sly critique of colonial self-importance. As the film proceeds, the audience discovers that the "childish" characteristics of the natives are actually products of colonialism itself; and, by the end of the story, they achieve a "mature" national consciousness irretrievably opposed to their colonial conquerors. In this affirmation of subaltern autonomy, the natives become architects of a community that manages to shake off the manacles of western colonial desire.

"I'm Just the same as a White Man"

In *Black Skin, White Masks,* Frantz Fanon mobilizes his autobiographical experience of colonized consciousness to sketch the dialectic of colonized desire. The colonizers seize the "native" world, appropriate it, a dispossession that takes a semiotic as well as a physical form. "To speak a language," he argues, "is to take on a world, a culture. The Antilles Negro who wants to be white will be the whiter as he gains greater mastery of the cultural tool that language is" (Fanon 1967: 38). In fact, the colonized cannot resist the draw of whiteness. Whiteness represents power and honor. By seizing the native's world, by imposing western values through the barrel of a gun, by annihilating the cultural originality of the colonized—and marking any residue as "savage," "primitive" and "bestial"—the colonizers remake native desire. At the same time, the "fact of blackness" means that no matter how much "whiter" the colonized subject becomes, she or he will never be fully white, never fully human. Because of the fact of his blackness, Fanon found that "the white world, *the only honorable one*, barred me from all participation" (Fanon 1967: 114. Emphasis added).

This semiotic bond—between "whiteness" and colonial honor—figures prominently in THE HURRICANE.

At the end of the opening scene where Kersaint pleads the case of the nameless native canoe thief, the church bell rings, announcing the return of a ship that carries both Terangi and De Laage's beloved. As a last ditch effort, Kersaint argues that the sentence should be commuted as a "homecoming gift" for Madam De Laage. De Laage responds: "I am ready to give my wife and my friends anything I own in the world, except my sense of honor and duty." Throughout, the film fuses the concept of colonial honor with imperial injustice.

Terangi serves as the pivot for this representation. At the beginning of the film, his is the mind colonized by whiteness. Unlike the nameless native in the earlier scene, Terangi mastered the European language. Again Fanon: "Rather more than a year ago in Lyon...in a lecture I had drawn a parallel between Negro and European poetry, and a French acquaintance told me enthusiastically, 'At bottom you are a white man.' The fact that I had been able to investigate so interesting a problem through the white man's language gave me honorary citizenship" (Fanon 1967: 38). Terangi, too, believes that his mastery of French gives him an "honorary citizenship" in the white world. Furthermore, Terangi has a position of status as the first mate of a European ship, *The Catapoa*. It is precisely this position of honor within the white man's world that deceives Terangi.

Terangi has returned to the island the marry Chief Mehavre's daughter, Marama (Dorothy Lamour). On their wedding night, Marama has a prophetic dream and she begs Terangi not to leave.

> What are you worried about, Marama...Where's my cap?" He looks into the mirror as he dons his uniform. "It's very funny what a difference a cap makes in the world, Marama. In Tahiti, when I wear this cap, everybody's my friend. You think I'm just Terangi, who used to swim with you when you were just a little fish. In Tahiti, when I sit down in the café with this cap on, *I'm just the same as a white man.*

Despite Marama's warnings, Terangi, armed with this signifier of his status as an honorary white man (his cap), and with his fluency in the colonizer's tongue, prepares for his voyage back to Tahiti. Marama stows away upon *The Catapoa*. When the Captain discovers her, he orders her back to the island. He says, "You have no reason to go to Tahiti." She replies:

> "Oh yes, I buy a dress with a ribbon on."
> "And red shoes with high heels," adds Terangi.

"And a hat with a feather on it and a petticoat," says Marama.

"And a doll that dances," says Terangi.

"Alright, alright, you stay on board," says the Captain, "but we'll take Terangi's cap away from him...I can't have a first mate with a bride hanging around his neck. He'll be an ordinary sailor from now on."

Like Terangi, Marama desires the symbolic accoutrements of white status. When the Captain tells her she has no reason to go to Tahiti, he is, in a sense, correct: Marama has no use for a dress with ribbons, red shoes with high heels, nor petticoats. Her usual attire is a native sari; her feet are always bare. She desires those things she does not "need" precisely because they signify the honorary whiteness that Terangi prizes. And when the Captain threatens to take away the symbolic emblem of Terangi's honorary citizenship, Marama returns home.

Entering the cabaret in Tahiti, Terangi and his shipmates are greeted by a woman singing "I Can't Give You Anything But Love" (Jimmy McHugh-Dorothy Fields). This is the only popular music present in the film. And it evokes the dialectic of colonized desire. While all the other actors speak English (represented as French), this song is performed in French, the only moment in the film where the European language is heard. Dorothy Fields' original English lyric is:

I can't give you anything but love, baby.
That's the only thing I've plenty of, baby.
Dream awhile. Scheme awhile.
We're sure to find,
Happiness, and I guess
all those things you've always pined for.

The happiness that Terangi pines for comes from his white colonizer's love, the love he thinks he has attained through his cap and fine words. But the fact of his "blackness" bars him from the white world. For Fanon, "the occasion arose when I had to meet the white man's eyes. An unfamiliar weight burdened me. The real world challenged my claims [to honorary whiteness]" (Fanon 1967: 110). Terangi begins to discover his blackness in the cabaret. Recall, "with this cap on, I'm just the same as a white man." But the burden of his blackness comes from the white colonizer's gaze.

Sitting at a table with other native shipmates, Terangi opens his present for Marama, a small doll with a grass skirt. He winds the doll, and as it gyrates, he and his comrades laugh and imitate the dancing. Quite literally, the colonized

sailors embody the corporeal "historico-racial schema" imposed by their masters, wearing the "livery that the white man has sewed" (Fanon 1967: 111, 34).
A white man comes to their table, yelling "get up!" His companions jump from
the table, but Terangi meets the white man's eyes with his own hard gaze.

"Get up when a white man tells ya!" The colonizer slaps Terangi across the
face. As the song ends, Terangi lays the man flat with a blow. The Captain
pleads Terangi's case to the Governor, "I've spent eight hours...trying to find out
why my first mate was sentenced to six months in jail, and for doing exactly as
you or I would do under the same circumstances."

The Governor: "Your boy hits too hard."

"The sentence is unjust...and you know it.... You don't know the Manakoora
natives. They're not like your Tahitians. They can't stand confinement....
A mere matter of maintaining European prestige? A native mustn't raise his
hand against a white man?"

Terangi "hit the wrong man," a man with "influence at home." Despite the
injustice of the sentence, an injustice repeatedly acknowledged by the colonial
authorities, European honor and prestige, fueled by colonial corruption,
demand satisfaction.

Behind barbed wire, Terangi watches his ship sail homeward. He jumps the
fence and swims for *The Catapoa*. Although the other native sailors, and perhaps the Captain, see their old mate's approach, they continue on. Struggling
back to the beach, he is swarmed by brutal guards. Through the lash, he discovers his blackness (Fanon 1967: 112).

Two Communities

Although in the footage that follows the audience sees various scenes of
Terangi resisting his imprisonment, this is not the existential story of a man's
survival, but of two communities, the tensions between and within them. Let
me begin this section of my study with an investigation into the colonizers'
community. Ford and Nichols mobilize a maternalist and quasi-Catholic symbolism to capture and shape the sentiments of their audience. Among the
colonizers, there are two distinct positions, one represented by Governor De
Laage, the other by three liminal figures: Dr Kersaint, Father Paul (C. Aubrey
Smith), and Madam De Laage (Mary Astor), who wears a prominent gold cross
around her neck. Again, as with many of Ford's films, women represent the
voice of sentimental reason, the voice of the heart; while Father Paul's sympathy for the natives demonstrates Ford's and Nichols' commitment to the
Catholic social justice tradition that fueled many of the activists in the CIO.

Before *The Catapoa* returns to the island, news has already spread of Terangi's imprisonment. Ford uses a series of close-ups focused upon native faces in order to evoke their desolation and incipient anger. At a breakfast that includes Kersaint, Father Paul, and Madam De Laage, the Captain asks Governor De Laage to intervene in Terangi's case. Kersaint adds that Terangi is the "best loved" of all the inhabitants of Manakoora, that this injustice will return to haunt the French colonial authorities. But De Laage refuses. To his companions: "I know you all mean well. But I am not the representative of well-meaning points of view. I represent a civilization that cannot afford to show confusion or conflict to the people it governs. The law has spoken in Tahiti. I must uphold that law." His interest is in law, and more importantly *order*, rather than justice. Law sides with white oppression, while justice—and *freedom*—must be fought for by the natives themselves. Over and again, Ford and Nichols demonstrate the impotence of those colonial voices whose sympathy sides with the natives. The Captain, Kersaint, Father Paul, and Madam De Laage are repeatedly shown to be powerless in the face of colonial rule.

> "Would it influence your sense of duty at all to know that Mrs Terangi is about to be a mother?" asks Kersaint.
> Madam De Laage immediately responds, "That's wonderful...that puts everything in a different light, dear."
> Then the Governor again, "No, that only puts me in a worse light. Now I'm not only Terangi's persecutor, I'm the oppressor of an unborn child."

De Laage appears "in a worse light" not only from the perspective of the island-ers, nor simply from the perspective of the sympathetic colonists, but from the perspective of the cinematic audience itself. Throughout the rest of the picture, Ford and Nichols associate Marama with the Madonna, and mobilize the audience's revulsion against the oppression of innocents in order to accomplish their work of critique.

Plagued by guilt at her husband's intransigence, Madam De Laage brings Marama Terangi's doll and asks her to stay at the Governor's mansion. But Marama, now transformed by melancholy, tells the woman to "go away...I don't go to your house." Despite the white woman's sympathy, Marama begins to perceive the connection between whiteness and oppression. Framed within a deep shadow close-up, tears in her eyes, Marama takes a defiant tone, "everybody will laugh at the jail that will try to hold Terangi." As she breaks into tears, a close-up of the grass-skirted doll, dancing. Here the filmmakers introduce the beginnings of a decolonized national consciousness. Through Terangi's

experience, mediated by the Madonna-like Marama, the natives will soon recognize white paternalism as colonial injustice and oppression.

"Look at them Dance. There's the Island's Answer to your Law"

What follows are more scenes of brutality and violence directed against
Terangi: guns shooting him down, white men with whips lashing him, sadistic
captors laughing. But Terangi never speaks a word during these scenes.
Whatever's happening in his mind, however his consciousness is being transformed by captivity, the audience never knows. Rather, the audience sees the
transformation of native consciousness on Manakoora.

Kersaint and Madam De Laage continue to plead for Terangi, all without
effect. During one such session, Chief Mahavre finally speaks his mind. Up to
this point in the film, Mahavre has been the ideal colonial subject, subjugating
his own people under the French flag.

> "Excellency," he begins, still deferent and obedient, "the people on my
> island were all happy before. Now they are very unhappy. This is not good
> law, or good justice."

But De Laage simply takes another puff on his cigarette and ignores the Chief's
plea. With that puff, De Laage destroys the last breath of French colonial legitimacy. "There is no Terangi," says De Laage, and "it is not a question of justice or
injustice to a human being. It is a question of upholding the law under which
these islands are governed." What happens next reveals the maturation of an
anti-colonial consciousness.

Until now, the escapes had been relatively non-violent. But upon this venture, Terangi kills one of his guards. This homicide is centrally significant
because once the natives hear the news, they celebrate not only the escape of
a national hero, but the death of white oppression. The music in the film
changes from melancholy to ominous as De Laage and his wife, playing chess
in their sitting room, hear native drums. They look to the village where they see
scenes of excess, dancing, hooting, and Kersaint lost in the orgy of freedom.
Marama sits beside the fire, the grass skirted doll in her hand. That doll has
been transformed from a sign of racial domination to a carnivalesque representation of native autonomy. As women dance before her, she holds the doll
before each one, comparing them, and laughing at the insufficiency of western
representations. Marama is not simply laughing for joy at Terangi's escape
and his revenge upon the white guard, she laughs at her former desires for

whiteness, now buried by a lust for freedom and a new consciousness as part of a nationalized, decolonizing people. The islanders are no longer simply what the white man had made them; through Terangi as a unifying symbol, they've broken the bonds imposed by the colonizer's gaze.

This scene of frenzy offers a revision of typical orientalist ideology. As Shoat and Stam argue, hegemonic colonialist "discourse operates between...two master tropes, alternately positing the colonized as blissfully ignorant, pure, and welcoming on the one hand, and on the other as uncontrollably wild, hysterical, and chaotic, requiring the disciplinary tutelage of the law" (Shohat and Stam 1994: 143; see also Koritz 1994: Locke 1998). While not escaping the exoticizing and eroticizing tendencies of orientalist discourse, Ford and Nichols set this chaotic hysteria against the injustice of colonial administration. It is the sexualized love for liberty that breaks the bonds of white desire. True, subaltern sexuality is figured as dangerous. But to whom? Governor De Laage evinces a palpable terror at the natives' symbolic uprising. But the audience does not identify with De Laage and his community. Rather, the entire narrative demonstrates the corrupt character of imperial whiteness and colonial honor. Perhaps Ford and Nichols imagine the audience standing in the liminal position of Kersaint; yet Kersaint is no longer on the boundary. His alcoholic frenzy, his own wild gyrations, as well as his words, place him in the natives' camp.

When the Governor appears, all fall silent, waiting. To Chief Mahavre he says, "what has given the people happiness?" To this point, Mahavre had dressed in the white man's colonial uniform, wearing a white jacket over his native garb. But now he's dressed wholly in native costume. He spits the word "Excellency" through his teeth like poison. "Terangi, Excellency...he has escaped, Excellency." Even Mahavre has broken with the white man's world.

> Slurring his words, Kersaint interjects, "is there any law against dancing and singing when the heart's happy?"
> "Is he on this island, have you seen him?"
> "You don't have to see him. He's a legend.... *He's the soul and symbol of all these good people...*No cage can hold him. They're the last of the world's afflicted race of humans who believe in freedom. Look at them dance! There's the island's answer to your law."

Again and again, Ford's cinema argues that community requires symbolic mediation. Just as Ford uses metonymy to stage his "realism," he continually returns to metonymic political representations of "peoplehood." Terangi, Tom Joad, and Colonel Thursday all become symbolic embodiments of the communities with which they are associated. At the end of THE GRAPES OF WRATH, Tom Joad becomes the symbol of Casy's "one big soul." Near the conclusion of FORT APACHE (1948), Thursday's ghostly image symbolizes a new multi-ethnic American community bound together by its opposition to those beyond the border. (See Chapter 6.) In THE HURRICANE, Terangi is the symbol of freedom and rebellion forging a new people. True, before Terangi, the islanders were a community, under the paternalistic protection of French authority. But now they've achieved a decolonized national consciousness. They've shaken off the shackles of white desire.

De-Colonized Independence and Enslaved Servility

In THE HURRICANE, Ford and Nichols associate "whiteness" with a corrupt political regime and a discourse of "honor" that represses social justice, sentiment, sexuality, and feeling. They evoke the genesis of a decolonizing national consciousness among the natives founded upon a fundamental rejection of European values and the forms of desire (for whiteness and status) imposed by a paternalistic European regime. The energies behind this critique came from their association (through Nichols' social networks) with Popular Front and (through Ford himself) labor politics.

At the same time, they base this critique upon a kind of orientalist ideology that celebrates the wild independence of the colonized people. And while THE HURRICANE bases its argument against colonial oppression on the wild love for freedom evinced by the natives, JUDGE PRIEST offers a conventionally racist depiction of African Americans as dependent, servile subjects, thereby justifying a white supremacist social order. From the first scene, with Stepin Fetchit as a lazy, eye-rolling, mumbling "negro," to the last, where Judge Priest (Will Rogers) brings Yankee and Rebel veterans together in (white) racial harmony, the film unrolls racist imagery long familiar to American filmgoers. True, Rogers, Ford and Nichols, play with racial stereotypes; true Ford himself seemed to believe the film provided an anti-racist argument; but the evidence of the picture makes it very hard to accept Lary May's (1998) claim that Will Rogers' cinema escaped and challenged the limitations of American racial ideology.[4]

---

4   Ford told Eisenberg, "I remember...with a Judge Priest picture, putting in an anti-lynching scene that was one of the most scorching things you ever heard. They...cut it..." (Eisenberg 2001: 259). Later, in 1953, and without Nichols as collaborator, Ford remade JUDGE PRIEST as THE SUN SHINES BRIGHT. The same racial characterizations dominate that picture, and, with complete creative control, Ford finally inserts his "anti-lynching" scene. The audience

The seeming conceptual discord between the critique of whiteness offered by THE HURRICANE and the overt white supremacy of JUDGE PRIEST is not surprising. As David Roediger points out, American racial ideology always treated its own colonial victims differently from the victims of its enslavement.

> Even on a mythic level...Native Americans served poorly as foils against which whites could measure themselves as workers. Comparisons with Black slaves or even Northern 'free' Blacks were tempting precisely because whites had defined these groups as servile.... But the mythic/historical Native American male was seen as *independent*... Any systematic social construction of the white worker's position that used the Native American as the 'other' would therefore have had to take people of color as a model rather than as a negative reference point.
>
> ROEDIGER 1999 22–23

Just as white settlers defined Native Americans as both fearful racial "others" and, simultaneously, as "independent," so too Ford and Nichols take the colonized islanders as independent models for counter-hegemonic community formation, rather than negative reference points. Indeed, while Ford and Nichols represent Indians as fearful "others" in STAGECOACH (1939), Ford's own cinematic and personal history shows evidence of a slow revision of his racial attitudes toward Native Americans. Beginning with FORT APACHE (1948), much of his later cinema explicitly indicts the imperial conquest of Native Americans (Slotkin 1998). In a famous remark to Peter Bogdanovich, Ford argues that his "sympathy was always with the Indians," comparing what he calls the "genocide" against Native Americans to the Black and Tan conquest of Ireland (Gallagher 1988: 254). Defining the Mankoora natives as unbreakably "independent," Ford and Nichols simultaneously preserve a Jim Crow white supremacy that allows for the disenfranchisement of African Americans precisely because of their "servility." It is the projected independence of the islanders—and, later in Ford's work, of the Indians—that sets the projected servility of African Americans in relief.

"You're all Guilty"

As the islanders become increasingly restive, the weather corresponds to their mood. For instance, the sequence detailing the celebration of Terangi's escape

---

sees eye-rolling "Negros" screaming and running for cover. On May's discussion of the Ford-Nichols-Will Rogers collaborations and their racial meanings, see (1998: 30–38).

discussed above begins with a rapidly swirling weather vane set atop the Governor's mansion. Ford and Nichols proceed through metonymy, connecting the elements to the increasingly elemental rage of the colonized population. Upon Terangi's final escape, a mighty wind begins to blow. Meanwhile, Governor De Laage realizes that everyone—white and native—has now turned against him, even his priest. When Father Paul secretly aids Terangi, De Laage confronts him. "You're all guilty. The whole island.... You helped Terangi. You, my own priest.... You helped a murderer."

"I aided a man whose heart is innocent," replies Father Paul.

"You've betrayed your own government...given aid to anarchy and bloodshed."

The priest casts his eyes skyward. "There are stronger things than governments in this world, De Laage. Something deeper. More real."

Set on a mad course of vengeance and colonial honor, and against the warnings of both Madam De Laage and Kersaint ("hear God howl and laugh at you"), Governor De Laage commandeers *The Catapoa*. In the midst of their escape, Terangi, Marama and their young child, return to Manakoora to save their people. Kersaint and some of the natives take to surfboats. Despite native warnings, Father Paul and Madam De Laage head for the church. Winds tear the Governor's mansion to pieces. As the Church is destroyed by a tsunami, Terangi pushes through the waves to the vestibule's doors. Father Paul gives Madam De Laage over to Terangi, and, as the priest and his last few parishioners sing, the walls crumbles atop them. Waves overwhelm the island. After the storm, De Laage returns to the ruins, believing his wife dead. But she's alive in a hidden cove, with Terangi and his family. As *The Catapoa* approaches, Madam De Laage helps launch Terangi's canoe. The Governor, overcome by the sentiment his honor can no longer hold in check, watches through binoculars as Terangi and family escape, and, although he clearly sees the natives, he tells his wife "it's only a floating log."

It is useful to compare this climax to the more conventionally orientalist BIRD OF PARADISE (1932) analyzed by Shohat and Stam. The story of a romance between a "white" sailor and a South Seas "native," King Vidor's film contains many similar narrative elements, but in the service of a substantially different narrative goal.

The South Seas native woman (Dolores del Rio) metaphorizes her land; she betokens the "natural" paradise untouched by "civilization." But the very same ecologically harmonious landscape which yields a cornucopia of food abruptly metamorphoses, during the course of the film, into a threatening volcanic universe, a disordered hysterical body, as pastoral nature is inundated by the lava which swallows and sucks into itself the very beauty to which it had given birth. In the traditional equation between nature and woman, the South Seas heroine mirrors these opposites of

Edenic pacificity and infernal danger.... If the initial images associate the
del Rio character with peaceful water, the final shots superimpose her
image over flames—an infernal punishment for the sexually hungry
subaltern as well as for the prescientific natives.

SHOHAT AND STAM 1994: 143

Like BIRD OF PARADISE, THE HURRICANE sexualizes the native population,
inscribing them as the other of European colonial honor and repression. But
while del Rio represents temptation and sinfulness, there is a paradoxical
innocence about the sexuality of Manokoora's population. Like Terangi, they
may be guilty in the eyes of the law, but in their hearts are innocent. It is the
law itself that imposes and provokes guilt. While the Volcano in the earlier film
destroys the dangerous subalterns, here the hurricane symbolizes de-coloniza-
tion. Most of the natives are destroyed during this symbolic uprising. But
Terangi preserves the new national consciousness forged through struggle.
After all, as the film argued throughout, *Terangi is his people*. He is their symbolic embodiment, and the hope of all the world's "races" afflicted by the
scourge of European imperialism.

   Nonetheless, faced with a stark recognition of the contradictions and corruption of imperial racism, Ford and Nichols cannot provide a political resolution. Rather than staging a more literally figured native uprising against
colonial oppression, they take flight into allegory. In a scene that anticipates
the final sequence of STAGECOACH, where the outlaw and the prostitute ride
off to liberty *across the border*, it is only by fleeing the white man's gaze, out
across the open sea, that Terangi's people find freedom.

Contradictions and Paradoxes

John Ford worked with a number of screenwriters during the 1930s and 1940s.
But, at least through 1948, he had a special relationship with Nichols and
"working with Nichols seems to have been much more of a marriage between
equals than working with Frank Nugent or Laurence Stallings...." (Eyman 1999:
320). In 1936, on the eve of making THE HURRICANE, Ford expressed this to
Eisenberg: "Combination of author and director running the works: that's the
ideal. Like Dudley Nichols and me. Or Riskin and Capra" (Eisenberg 2001: 258).
Between 1934 and 1948, the pair produced a series of pictures for a "new kind
of public" that demanded a new kind of socially relevant and politically
engaged cinema. Ford and Nichols took typical genre pictures and shaped
them into political allegories made possible by the New Deal, Age of the CIO,

and the Popular Front. Throughout his career, the political labels applied to John Ford ranged from "reactionary" to "socialistic democrat" to an "old fashioned anarchist" (Eyman 1994: 187, 497). He was a strong supporter of Roosevelt, and, later, a committed anti-communist critic of the civil rights movement (Peary 2001: 140). He was an architect of the Cold War imaginary and the hand behind one of the most radically pro-labor films in the history of classic Hollywood. His close collaboration with D.W. Griffith not only shaped his cinematic style but his representation of African Americans (McBride 2001: 77–91). Different cinematic projects, at different historical moments, brought different elements of Ford's complex political identity to the fore. During the period of his collaboration with Nichols, it was Ford the socialistic democrat, the angry Irish critic of colonialism and (European) imperialism.

Yet it is equally significant that their collaboration ended in 1949, at the dawn of the anti-communist crusades in the United States, with two failed projects. The first was THE FUGITIVE (1947), a political allegory with Henry Fonda as a priest persecuted by a totalitarian Latin American regime. In that box-office failure, the same orientalist attitude toward colonized people found in THE HURRICANE serves as the narrative's backdrop. While in their earlier film, Nichols and Ford mobilize the Catholic social justice tradition in the service of a critique of imperialism, THE FUGITIVE uses Catholic traditionalism to support a vision of totalitarianism that assimilates communism and fascism (Eyman 1994: 320–326; Chapter 6 below).

In their final collaboration, PINKY (1949), Nichols demonstrates an evolution of his racial attitudes. The story of a young woman who passes as white, and her Black grandmother, played by Ethel Waters, this film directly confronts American racial attitudes in a cinematic language that largely rejects the racial paternalism found in JUDGE PRIEST. But Ford didn't like the politics of Nichols' representation. He and Daryl Zanuck, the producer, called in screenwriter Philip Dunne as a fixer. When Nichols objected, Ford said "Well, Dudley always was a sort of white nigger, anyway" (McBride 2001: 489). The irony of this utterance could hardly be lost on Ford, the self-consciously Irish filmmaker, since it echoes the typical 19th and early 20th century racist description of the Irish. "Nativist folk wisdom held that an Irishman was a 'nigger', inside out" (Roediger 1999: 133). With the rewritten screenplay, Ford still could not complete the picture, primarily because Waters refused to play the "Mammy" that Ford wanted on the screen. Zanuck recalled that "Ford's Negroes were like Aunt Jemima. Caricatures.... Ford had old-fashioned race views." Zanuck gave the picture to Elia Kazan (McBride 2001: 489; Eyman 1994: 361).

Yet, during this same period, Ford's attitudes toward American colonialism and the genocide against Native Americans showed a profound alteration. In many ways, FORT APACHE (1948) is a virtual remake of THE HURRICANE, with Colonel Thursday (Henry Fonda) and his unbending sense of imperial honor standing in for De Laage, while Captain York (John Wayne) represents the liminal figure speaking for the colonized peoples conquered by the United States. Unlike the earlier picture, however, this film turns a critical eye on *American* imperialism. And its ambivalent ending, where York consciously falsifies history in the name of national unity, marks the movie as both the last of Ford's Popular Front films and the first of his Cold War allegories. When seen in context with THE FUGITIVE, the ironic compromise that concludes the narrative represents an acceptance of imperialism and genocide as an answer to the totalitarian anti-Catholicism Ford perceived in the Soviet Bloc (see Wood 2001, Slotkin 1998, 332–349). The elements that shaped Ford's Cold War liberalism, and the Cold War politics of his public(s), were found already in his Popular Front collaborations with Nichols: a racial paternalism toward African Americans, a "progressive" orientalism toward colonized, "wild" natives. This dyadic racial perspective allowed Ford's cinema to normalize white supremacy at home, while justifying American military adventures abroad in the name of freedom for the world's afflicted races.[5]

In Chapter 6, I will more fully document Ford's transformation from a Popular Front critic to a Cold War white nationalist. In order to contextualize that transformation, however, I turn first to Ginger Rogers as she exemplified the Hollywood proletarian imaginary of the late 1930s and early 1940s. Left writers like Dalton Trumbo and Paul Jarrico created overtly political roles for Rogers. And although their politics were circumscribed by the Hollywood apparatus and the Hays Office, radical representations penetrated Rogers' most popular films. KITTY FOYLE (1940), her most successful film during this period, offers an uncompromisingly radical depiction of the opposition between the wealthy classes and the common classes. BACHELOR MOTHER (1939) is premised upon a sly critique of the masculine gaze and male fantasies about women. And Jarrico's TOM, DICK AND HARRY (1940) contains a fragmentary but powerful argument against Hollywood fictions of cross class romance. In short, Rogers' films during this period represent a kind of highwater mark for proletarian themes and proletarian writers in Hollywood cinema, and signify the brief emergence a new doxic order with a relative openness to critiques of economic inequality.

---

5 During the late 1960s, Ford produced the propaganda picture for the United States Information Agency, VIETNAM! VIETNAM! Although not directed by Ford himself, that film still shares characteristics first developed in THE HURRICANE. According to McBride, Ford romanticizes "the pastoral life of the Vietnamese before the coming of the war" (McBride 2001: 694; Eyman 1994: 534).

CHAPTER 5

Ginger Rogers and the (Hollywood) Proletarian Imaginary, 1939–1941

Ginger Rogers was one of the most popular stars of New Deal Cinema. From 1935 to 1939, Rogers' film persona was firmly linked with her dancing partner, Fred Astaire. However, after THE STORY OF VERNON AND IRENE CASTLE (1939), Ginger Rogers returned exclusively to solo work (at least until 1949, when she teamed with Astaire one last time for THE BARKLEYS OF BROADWAY). And, by 1940, Rogers had established an independent cinematic identity, and her films "were money in the bank for [her studio] RKO" (Schatz 1999: 57). "While Astaire's career temporarily flagged, Rogers scored in romantic dramas like KITTY FOYLE (1940), winning an Oscar for best actress, and in light romantic comedies like TOM, DICK AND HARRY (1941)" (Schatz 1999: 103). Between her split with Astaire in 1939 and the U.S. entry into the Second World War late in 1941, Ginger Rogers made six films. While the films fall into different Hollywood genres, a consistent character emerges from the roles, a proletarian hero, but a hero whose strength and independence is ultimately tempered by her dependence upon men and her "natural" desire for motherhood.

This chapter explores the contours of this gendered proletarian trope through reading four of the six films Rogers made between 1939 and 1941. The films selected are her four most popular (in terms of domestic box office gross) of the period, with KITTY FOYLE and BACHELOR MOTHER being among the top grossing and most profitable RKO films of the decade between 1931 and 1941 (Sedgwick 1994; Jewell 1994). In addition, the films I have chosen all emerge from an engagement with the Popular Front politics of the late 1930s. The architects behind Rogers's image include future blacklisted writers and directors like Dalton Trumbo, Donald Ogden Stewart, and Paul Jarrico, as well as sympathetic progressives like Garson Kanin and Allan Scott. This chapter begins with an examination of the collaboration between screenwriter Scott and director Gregory La Cava, 5th AVENUE GIRL (1939), followed by a brief examination of one of Rogers' more successful efforts of the period, BACHELOR MOTHER (1939). I then look at two products of Popular Front screenwriters, Rogers's top grossing film of the period, KITTY FOYLE, written by Trumbo, and Jarrico's TOM, DICK AND HARRY. Each of the films I examine casts a critical eye on some elements of American society, and often on capitalism itself, but in doing so tends to reinforce the gendered version of left politics criticized by the screenwriters behind RIFFRAFF. This depiction of gender, and especially women's dependence upon men, becomes a basis for social critique, but also disrupts the vision of social equality the films sometimes advocate.

Ginger Rogers may seem an unlikely choice to represent the *proletarian imaginary* of late 1930s, early 1940s. For instance, Buhle and Wagner describe TENDER COMRADE (1944) as "a great romantic-sloppy favorite with the pairing of real-life reactionary Ginger Rogers and real-life progressive Robert Ryan" (Buhle and Wagner 202: 231). And this characterization as a "real-life reactionary" was cultivated by Rogers herself after 1947, most notably in her autobiography (1991). Rogers' mother, Lela Emogene Rogers, was a founding member of the anti-left Motion Picture Alliance for the Preservation of American Ideals, and testified as a friendly witness during the May 1947 HUAC hearings, precursor to the October 1947 hearings that produced the blacklists (Rogers 1991: 334–335; Ceplair and Englund 2003: 255). Whatever the case with Rogers "real life" politics, the screen image she cultivated during the late 1930s and early 1940s was as a New Deal supporter of Roosevelt, often with a class consciousness, and sometimes with left sympathies. And it was precisely this screen persona as a class conscious, left leaning hero, that made Ginger Rogers one of the few RKO women "in 1940–1941 who definitely could carry a picture" (Schatz 1999: 103). In this sense, the popularity of Rogers' screen persona signifies the high-water mark of the politicized proletarian imaginary in Depression era cinematic culture, but a proletarian imaginary that continued to police and enforce the normative boundaries of traditional conceptions of gender.

In the previous chapters, I presented careful analyses of entire films. In this chapter I proceed somewhat differently, concentrating, for the most part, on important film fragments. KITTY FOYLE receives most extensive attention, and this because the film is both among the more radical of the group, and the highest grossing of Rogers' films during the period. Thus, in order to contextualize the fragments I examine, I have provided a brief plot synopsis at the beginning of each discussion to provide context and help ensure clarity.

5th Avenue Girl (1939)

5th AVENUE GIRL, Rogers' first film after separating from Astaire, comes closest to violating the normative taboos surrounding masculinity and femininity, even as it expresses an obviously ambivalent attitude toward the left and left politics. Directed by La Cava in a bid to recapture the success of MY MAN GODFREY, the later film has considerably more political and narrative complexity. The writer behind the picture, Allan Scott, had been a long-time collaborator with Rogers, writing or co-writing most of her pictures with Astaire, including TOP HAT (1935) and SWING TIME (1936). Scott himself stood on the liberal edge of the Popular Front. Although not remembered as an activist during the 1930s and 1940s, he was elder brother to Popular Front producer Adrian Scott, whose work, CROSSFIRE (1947), became such an important target during the early days of the blacklist (Langdon 2008). Further, in 1948, Allan Scott composed an attack upon HUAC and the anti-Communist hysteria in the form a stage play, "Joy to the World," directed by another blacklist victim, Jules Dassin (*New York Times*, March 19, 1948; Ceplair and Englund 2003: 399). And, of course, Allan Scott wrote a scathing and radical critique of leisure class values in SWING TIME. 5th AVENUE GIRL, however, not only takes aim at the leisure class, but critiques conventional trade unionism and the pretensions of left politics. Yet even as Scott critiques some elements of the left, a broader Popular Front language and vision are at work in the picture. In a sense, Scott's critique of the left is from the inside, as if in a missive to a friend, or a brother.

Synopsis: Timothy Borden (Walter Connolly) is the head of *Amalgamated Pump*. A responsible capitalist who cares for his workers' welfare, Borden, like the millionaire in GODFREY, has been forgotten by his family. His wife dates other men; his daughter is a debutante in love with the family's Communist chauffeur; his son spends more time on polo than his work at the family firm. Alone on his birthday, Borden meets Mary Grey (Ginger Rogers) in the park. She is an unemployed, and apparently carefree, working class woman. As the story unfolds, Mary performs two functions. First, she helps Borden reconnect with his working class sensibility. Second, she plays the part of his mistress in front of the family, causing his wife once again to notice Borden exists. After Mary helps Borden restore his marriage, the ruse is revealed and the film ends with Mary literally carried away by Borden's son, the polo playing playboy now turned responsible capitalist and potential husband. Along the way, Borden's daughter, Katherine, marries the chauffeur, Michael, who in turn resigns to open his own repair shop. "Doesn't that make you a capitalist?" asks Borden. "I shall never forget my proletarian beginnings," says Michael, as he puffs out his fedora, and says to his wife, "come on babe," strutting away jazz style. Notably Michael does not become a "capitalistic parasite" (Katherine's words), but a repairman, a kind of engineer.

While on the one hand, 5th AVENUE GIRL can be seen as an allegorical demand for a moral capitalism, this seeming corporatist argument is undercut by a deeper Veblenian validation of the engineer's "instinct of workmanship" (Veblen 1994). In this sense, the film shares the anti-capitalism of Marx's depression era adherents, but it is an anti-capitalism founded upon a cultural celebration of the engineer as the common man, and the unskilled worker as the common woman. Indeed, the contrast with MY MAN GODFREY is striking. Unlike in the prior La Cava effort, the capitalist character in 5th AVENUE GIRL is the epitome of the socially responsible business man. His great merit, in fact, is that he is a business man by necessity, but an engineer by vocation. If anything, his skill at engineering hampers his effectiveness as a businessman. Business talk leaves him "bewildered." Bewildered and invisible, Borden comes back to sense and visibility through the mediation provided by Mary Grey. Mary gives Borden back both his sense and his sensibility, and that sensibility is marked, explicitly, as working class.

The gaze: On the advice of his butler, Borden goes to the park to watch the spring buds bloom. When he arrives, he stands in front of a tree, directing his vision at the buds. A crowd gathers, also looking in the direction of his gaze.

A passing boy says, "What's he looking at?"

Mother responds, "Oh never mind. Come along."

Borden leaves the tree and goes on to meet Mary Grey. And when, some minutes later, the two leave the park together, a larger crowd of gawkers has gathered.

Mary says, "What are they looking at?"

"I don't know," says Borden.

This little visual joke illustrates the work of cinema. Vision, like consciousness itself, requires direction. In the theatre, the camera's focus on a scene, a character, an aspect of life, trains the vision of the audience on that same reality, brings it into focus in a new way. At the same time, in order to win his wife and family, Borden needs to be seen in a new way. As Rogers did for Astaire, Mary Grey provides Borden's sex appeal by pretending desire. Her gaze, directed not toward Borden himself, but toward an illusion (she doesn't desire him), makes his wife see him in anew. "What are they looking at?" It doesn't matter. They are looking.

Four years before this scene was shot, Popular Front playwright and screenwriter, Albert Maltz, published his response to BLACK FURY (1935) in the *New York Times*. According to Maltz, filmmakers direct the viewer's gaze and construct a "generalized" meaning and (political) sensibility (see the Introduction above).

> An author is a propagandist by what he [sic] says or fails to say. He is a propagandist for one cause or another, directly or indirectly, by the very nature of the "slice of life" he selects or fails to select (Maltz 1935).

Whether Scott had Maltz's editorial in mind or not, his joke makes the same argument. Just as Mary Grey's gaze will invest Borden with desirability, so the filmmakers' representation of the common world as opposed to the pretenses of the leisure class, valorizes working class life, even as it undermines that valorization with its fairy tale conclusion.

The Burdens of Wealth: The opening credit montage situates the film in a New York City bursting with the traffic of commerce, the final dissolve leading to a skyscraper and then a plaque on the building, "Amalgamated Pump Inc." In the next shot, the camera follows a secretary through a door marked "Private," into a meeting between Borden, his unions, and his company advisors. It's worth noting that the film begins with a conflict familiar to much of its audience, a fight between CIO and AFL unions. Borden, seated behind his desk, the rest of the men in a semi-circle around him, pounds his fist:

> "All I know is we're facing bankruptcy. I spent a week going through the factory, talking to the men, and none of them want to strike, if they can help it. That's true, isn't Joe?" Borden turns to a factory worker seated beside him.
> "They don't want to, but they got to unless the unions get together."
> Union Man #1 speaks first, "We're not going to let Stanton's outfit put anything over on us," he says, indicating the second union man.
> The second man, Stanton, a stand-in look alike for John L. Lewis himself, responds, "If you think we're putting anything over on you, why don't you put it to a vote."
> "We were there before you were," says the first man.
> "You'd get licked," says Stanton.
> The problem, it seems, is that Stanton, the CIO representative, wants the same deal the company gives the AFL, a 44 hour week. Borden's CFO says that it's impossible. "We won't have any operating capital."
> "Not our problem," responds the first Union Man.
> After several more moments of such conversation, Borden waves his hand, "Gentlemen, I'm tired and bewildered."
> The encounter ends with the CIO stand-in saying, "we don't want you to think we want to run your business."
> Borden responds, "You don't want to run it and you won't let me run it. So good day gentlemen."

Although the union conflict does not appear again in the film's narrative, several elements of this short exchange deserve highlight. At the very least, the exchange underscores the importance of the industrial labor movement to ordinary Americans. The principal characters, AFL leader and insurgent CIO leader, are familiar enough to the audience through work experience, through the mass media, and through contemporary legend, that the screenplay need not explicitly identify the organizations, nor the nature of the conflict. The line "We were there before you," clearly situates the first Union Man as an AFL representative. While the line "You'd get licked" signifies the (obvious to the audience) popularity of the new insurgent movement led by the CIO. But just as significant, at the very moment that the CIO begins to achieve a certain cultural currency, the film takes a lukewarm attitude toward unionization itself. The unions seem to care more about their own internal struggle than about the workers and it's Borden who really wants to keep the factory open ("some of those men have been with him for 20 years," says an aide). This caricature of union leaders could be seen as part of a wider initial disillusionment with the promise of the CIO. After all, Capra offers an even more sinister representation in MEET JOHN DOE (1941), where the union leader actually sits at the table of the Capitalist-fascist villain of the picture (see Cassano and Rondinone 2010).

But since 5th AVENUE GIRL doesn't press the point, or resolve the conflict, this opening scene hardly amounts to an attack upon unions or the industrial union movement. Rather, Allan Scott, perhaps again influenced by Thorstein Veblen's work, depicts unions as vested interests, with the primary aim of achieving some advantage for their members (over and against other members of the working class) (Veblen 1964; Cassano 2006). In any case, the scene situates Borden's sympathies with his workers, and, ultimately, with the working class. Thus, as I've suggested, Borden is the inversion of the irresponsible and criminal millionaire at the head of Godfrey's family. Indeed, throughout the picture, a fantasy of working class life is valorized and presented as free of care and responsibility, while Borden is literally burdened.

> Higgins (Franklin Pangborn), his butler, remarks, again in a Veblenian vein, "I find my work here very pleasant."
> "Why?" asks Borden.
> "We servants enjoy the luxuries of the rich and have none of the responsibilities."

Again, a comparison with MY MAN GODFREY seems in order. Godfrey rediscovered responsibility through work as a butler, but Borden's butler frees himself from responsibilities through service. And, once again, the later film sets itself against GODFREY by figuring Borden as responsible to a fault. His success as a capitalist has become his burden. Indeed, not long after this scene, Borden explains to Mary Grey, "I'm not a capitalist, I'm a victim of the capitalistic system. I never wanted all this. It isn't my fault I invented a pump." Precisely because his success as an engineer led, unexpectedly, to his success in business, he lost his connection to what he originally wanted, "fun" and "family."

In order to win back what he's lost through success, Borden must return to a working class sensibility. This valorization of working class culture figures wealth as a trap, and business as a prison. But more than that, because the film identifies working class values with "American" values, there is something faintly un-American about wealth and the wealthy (Cassano and Rondinone 2010).

Miss America: When Ginger Rogers appears, more than 10 minutes into the picture, she is introduced as aggressively working class, with a sharp class consciousness. Borden meets her in the park, where she's eating a meager dinner of apples and crackers.

> "Haven't you got a job?" he asks.
> "Who has?" she responds.
> "It doesn't seem to worry you very much."
> "It doesn't. I'm alive and kicking. I have five dollars in my pocket book and my room rent's paid for another week."

It is this independence that attracts Borden. Mary Grey is not a spendthrift. She worries when Borden pays too much for dinner and drinks. But, at the same time, she won't let her life be ruled by money. If she can't have steak and champagne, she'll be happy with apples and crackers. In short, she is a fantasy projection of working class independence, and functions, in the narrative, as the counterweight to the projected burdens of the responsible capitalist.

At the same time, Mary expresses her class consciousness by expressing her opposition to "those 5th avenue cadavers."

> "How do they sound," asks Borden.
> "Oh, they're always squawking. You'd think the country were going to the dogs."

Later, drinking with Borden in the upscale Flamingo Club, Mary overhears a conversation at the next Table.

A man with a Park Avenue accent and tuxedo says, "It's a question of either too much government interference in business or too much business interference in government."

Mary Grey, a little worse for the champagne, turns to him: "Hey you! Lay off the government!" then to the waiter, "Would you tell that wax dummy to lay off the government."

Class consciousness for Mary means support of the New Deal. This association does not necessarily make her a New Deal liberal, but rather marks her working class belief that Roosevelt and the New Deal were on the side of the working class. Whatever the reality of the New Deal, workers all over industrial American perceived Roosevelt as an ally in their class struggle. Through fireside chats and policies perceived as pro-worker, Roosevelt became "The People's President" (Roscigno and Danaher 2004: 32–45). Thus, Mary's allegiance "to the government" becomes a marker of her class sensibility, signifying that she is one of the "dogs" reclaiming her nation. And her class sensibility expresses itself in her opposition to the un-American attitude that the "country were going to the dogs."

In fact, Mary Grey's class consciousness is her strength. The film makes this explicit in a third act scene. Mary and Borden are in the back of the limousine, riding through the park, while Borden's family thinks the two out drinking and dancing. With the Communist chauffeur whisper singing a Russian song, Borden and Mary discuss their plot. Borden notes how nice his family has been recently. Mary explains:

> "Pretty simple. You take something from somebody they don't want and they want it more than ever."
> "You've got a lot of common sense," says Borden.
> "You've lost yours, but it'll come back," she replies.
> "You've got something more than common sense."
> "You've got to have common sense on my side of the fence."
> "We'll there's a lot of nice people on your side of the fence.... Does my side of the fence look any different to you now?"
> "You can have it."
> "You're beginning to feel sorry for the rich, eh?"
> "I guess rich people are just poor people with money."

Mary has "common sense," the kind that comes from "her side of the fence." And she makes it clear there are only two sides of the fence. In other words, she provides a class analysis that conceives of unskilled workers, industrial laborers, as well as engineers, as part of the "common lot" (Veblen 1964), on the same side of the fence. Their commonality lies precisely in their opposition to the un-American leisure class, and that opposition signifies their common sensibility. Borden has lost his common sense, but it will come back once he recovers his "proletarian beginnings." The film clearly opposes two communities, and valorizes the life of one (the common lot) as more compatible with happiness, family, fun. Mary does acknowledge the humanity of the other class ("I guess rich people are just poor people with money"), but with sarcasm reminiscent of Hemingway's famous retort to Fitzgerald.

On the one hand, this cinematic fantasy can be seen as a way of reconciling a working class audience with their necessary economic destiny in a capitalist society. At the same time, however, this valorization of working class culture, even in a fantastic, sublimated form, signifies the film's attempt to claim its audience by projecting a proletarian sensibility. Common sense is the sensibility of common Americans.

In fact, early in the picture, a drunken Borden refers to Mary Grey as "Miss America." He seems to understand that her sensibility is the American sensibility, a sensibility he needs to recover. 5th AVENUE GIRL offers a representation of a specifically working class sensibility that is, at the same time, a celebration of that sensibility. In cinematic terms, Mary Grey provides the contours for an idealized cinematic vision of independent proletarian womanhood during the Age of the CIO (Denning 1998).

Proletarian versus Communist: While 5th AVENUE GIRL celebrates working class culture and sensibility, it both connects working class sensibility to Communist theory and sets that working class common sense in opposition to Communist dogma. But while it plays Communist ideology for laughs, the film is never overtly anti-Communist. Michael, the Communist chauffeur, is young, overly earnest, a bit narcissistic, chauvinistic, and perhaps a little hypocritical. But he's neither sinister, nor irresponsible, nor violent, nor deceptive. In short, the film is free from the conventional anti-Communist associations that dominated American cinema throughout most of the twentieth century. Moreover, the film makes no attempt to deny the social problems that the young Communist is constantly identifying. The worst that can be said of Michael comes from the old immigrant cook, "He talks too much."

Mary Grey's sensibility is connected to Michael's, but freed of the rhetoric and the weight of dogma. This connection is revealed through parallel discussions about champagne. In the Flamingo Club with Borden, Mary is overwhelmed by the cost of the champagne. She says:

> "Every time I take a sip of this it's like drinking six pair of silk stockings."
> "You can't drink silk stockings," laughs Borden.

But, of course, what Mary's sensibility reveals is that you can drink six pair of silk stockings. Her working class sense understands the generalizable equality of commodities through money, that cash wasted on champagne or stockings could be spent upon food, rent or medicine.

Later, Michael makes this implied suggestion explicit, but in "talking too much," he weakens the argument. When the debutante daughter comes to retrieve two bottles of champagne from the kitchen, she says:

> "These aren't for me. They're medicine for Skippy. He swallowed two goldfish."
> "Medicine," barks Michael, "do you realize there are 40 million people in this country whose annual income is less than 12 cases of that, 78% of the population have less than 25 cases, and 67% of the 78% cannot afford medicine without depriving themselves of the necessities of life?"

Both Mary and Michael understand the connection between capital expended upon champagne and its other potential uses. But while Mary's comments reveal her working class sense, Michael's words become empty rhetoric. Later in the film, when Mary challenges Michael, she doesn't attack his politics as much as his authenticity. "You try to get people to believe things that you don't even believe." Mary's not necessarily opposed to Communism, but she does have her suspicions about Michael himself.

While Michael is not a sinister character, Allan Scott's treatment of his commitment to ideology, and his near inability to communicate with common working people (the kitchen staff), suggests a certain disillusionment with Party radicals, perhaps the result of the Communist Party's abandonment of the Popular Front during the Hitler-Stalin Pact (Ceplair and Englund 2003). Like so many left leaning artists of the period, it is possible that Scott was disillusioned and angered by the positions taken by Party members during this period.

Nonetheless, Allan Scott's treatment of Communists and Communist ideology is ultimately rather gentle. And given Adrian Scott's deep involvement in the Party, perhaps it isn't surprising to find his brother poking fun at Communists rather than attacking radicalism (Langdon 2008). And while Mary Grey's class consciousness has a distinctly non-Communist relation to dogma, her common sense represents a radical rejection of the life led by 5th Avenue cadavers.

Valorization and Abdication: Thus, 5th AVENUE GIRL valorizes a certain fantasy of working class culture, vesting it with the glamour of Ginger Rogers. When Mary Grey evokes the dialectic of desire ("you take something from somebody they don't want and they want it more than ever"), she is, of course, referring to her own work, making Borden desirable by seeming to desire him.

At the same time, she refers to the work of cinema itself. Like Borden looking at the buds on the tree, film directs the audience's gaze, and, like Mary communicating her sensibility through her desire, it attempts to teach the audience how to desire, to communicate its own cinematic sensibility. And what the film desires is a common American sensibility, independent and class conscious. It is precisely Mary's projected independence, her freedom from desire (even as she bows to necessity), that makes her an object of desire. And, yet, in a pattern that will recur in Rogers' films of this short period, the story resolves with an abdication of that very independence.

Throughout her solo career, Rogers plays with the image first established in GOLD DIGGERS OF 1933 (1933), where she portrays a sexually independent, strong willed character. The wanton sexuality of that persona becomes a ghostly memory in 5th AVENUE GIRL, BACHELOR MOTHER, and later films. Rogers is perpetually associated with the fallen woman, even if, sometimes, only as a mistake in identity. And these representations become twisted synonyms for a dangerous, sexualized freedom. Each film thus establishes Rogers's dangerous (and attractive) independence, only to normalize and repress the danger with the final reel (Jacobs 1997).

Throughout 5th AVENUE GIRL, Mary plays the part of a "5th Avenue girl," another expression for "gold digger." And although the audience recognizes her artifice, the part isn't very far from her life. Independence, including some control over her sexuality, marks her character. In order to reduce this danger, the film introduces a subplot in the third act, when Borden's son (Tim Holt) begins to court Mary. Not much of the courtship is shown, and there's no clear basis for Mary's decision to wed young Borden. In the final scene of the film, after all has been revealed, the suitor swings Mary over his shoulder, cave-man style, and carries her inside the mansion. A passing cop hears Mary's protests and asks if she needs help. "Why don't you mind your own business!" she says as the mansion door slams closed. There has been almost no narrative preparation for this moment. In terms of the logic of character and plot, it comes out of some prepackaged Hollywood nowhere.

But what's most notable about this final restoration of masculine domination and the subjugation of an independent woman is that it takes place almost entirely off stage. During the action of the picture, Mary remained independent, free, single, and class conscious. She repeatedly distanced herself from the culture of the wealthy and explicitly rejected any desire to affiliate herself with the "5th avenue cadavers." Yet the final scene erases her class consciousness, her independence, and everything that made her desirable. By restoring the gendered order and, in so doing, erasing the class divide, the film represses Mary's sensibility and makes her life as invisible as Borden's had been.

Bachelor Mother (1939)

Garson Kanin worked closely with a number of Popular Front Hollywood artists, even staging a production of the left-wing play *Sticks and Stones* in the
1930s, along with Herbert Biberman, a member of the Hollywood Ten who
would eventually work as director for the blacklisted film SALT OF THE EARTH
(1954) (McGilligan and Buhle 1997: 240). But, at first glance, Kanin's BACHELOR
MOTHER seems distant from a Popular Front aesthetic. Nonetheless, it merits
discussion primarily for its portrayal of Rogers as a working mother. It reinforces the previous film's image of Rogers as a proletarian hero; and it repeats
the same resolution. While BACHELOR MOTHER's Polly Parish (Rogers) does
not evince the class consciousness found in Mary Grey, this fantasy of working
class life sometimes comes uncomfortably close to reality, especially in the
representation of the difficulties of a single working mother. Just as important,
however, the film disrupts the image of the "fallen woman" by suggesting that
the trope itself is the fictional product of male fantasy.

Synopsis: Polly Parish works in the toy department of Merlin's Department
Store. The holiday season ends and she receives notice. On her way back to her
flat after being fired, she comes upon a woman leaving a baby on the steps of a
"foundling home." Polly stops and brings the orphan inside the home. When
she tries to leave the baby, however, the social workers suspect she is the
mother and they contact Merlin's Department Store. Polly gets her job back
and a raise, but on condition she keep the baby. Meanwhile, the Department
Store heir, David Merlin (David Niven), takes an interest in Polly, even though
he believes Polly to be a single mother. Eventually, David's father, J.B. Merlin
(Charles Coburn), comes to believe that David is the father of Polly's child.
David accepts paternity and the film concludes with his proposal to Polly.

> "And you still think I'm the mother of that baby?" she asks.
> "Of course."
> Her last line is "ha ha."

Fallen Women/Working Mothers: Like 5th AVENUE GIRL, BACHELOR MOTHER
plays upon Rogers' prior image as the gold digging, sexually aggressive woman.
But it subverts that very image by portraying it as a masculine projection. Every
man seems willing and eager to believe that Polly is a fallen woman (a single
mother) despite her perpetual protests and her honesty. This eager projection
results from the masculine desire to perceive Polly as sexually available.
Projected desire deflowers her, transforming her into the "bachelor mother."

With her concluding laughter, the film offers subversive commentary about the power of controlling, gendered fictions over the reality of women's lives.

Perhaps to counter the weight of these projected fictions, some of the most powerful scenes in the picture attempt to depict the reality of a working mother's life. In one scene Polly comes to Merlin's hardly able to keep her eyes open. The baby had her awake all night. After the manager criticizes her and demands a speed-up, David strolls by. She explains her last few sleepless nights.

> "Don't any mothers sleep?" asks David.
> "I'm beginning to think they don't."
> "Well there can't be very much to it. After all, everyone here was a baby once and they all got through it alright [laughs].... Oh it's just a pose that all mothers put on, that it's so difficult to raise a child. I saw through that when I was six years old."

David may believe he sees through Polly's pose, but the audience has already seen Polly at work with the baby. David's words are as empty as they are ignorant.

Although BACHELOR MOTHER doesn't attempt to criticize the class divide, it recognizes that divide, and genders it. Polly Parish's life is represented as "normal," both her life as proletarian worker, and then her life as a working mother. And the men around her are portrayed as self-deceived fools, all of whom attempt to control her through their fantastic projections, as well as through their wealth, influence and power. Of course, the film participates in the very fantasy it critiques, with its titillating title and off color suggestions. Whatever the fantasies that made BACHELOR MOTHER such a success at the box office, however, they were intercut with representations of the realities of women's working class life, realities that were, in turn, represented as normal. This figuration of Rogers as proletarian woman, at a time when normative representations of working class life were overwhelming masculine, was more pronounced still in KITTY FOYLE.

Kitty Foyle (1940)

Less than a decade after making one of RKO's most successful pictures, the two primary architects behind KITTY FOYLE, the director and the writer, would both appear before the House Un-American Activities Committee. The director, Sam Wood, would testify as a "friendly witness," while the writer, Dalton Trumbo, refused to name names and became one of the blacklisted Hollywood Ten

(Ceplair and Englund 2003: 449–450). But whatever Wood's later reservations and revisions, KITTY FOYLE, written by Trumbo and another eventual member of the Hollywood Ten, Donald Ogden Stewart, projects a kind of (conservative) Popular Front sensibility. From the first scene to the last, the film utilizes a reactionary gender politics in an attempt to provide a critique of class relations. Mobilizing the rhetoric of labor's "radical paternalism," Trumbo uses gendered rhetoric to represent the wealthy as corrupt and corrupting (Stansell 1987). Although the film imagines women as workers, that work itself is potentially sexually corrupting. And Kitty's attempt to claim independence through her work becomes a kind of fall from grace. Finally, in line with both Popular Front "pronatalist" politics as well as the directives of Joseph Breen and the Production Code, the film figures motherhood as the ultimate goal and purpose of a woman's life (Rabinowitz 1991; Jacobs 1995: 138–146). Yet the film also offers an uncompromising class critique. Centrally important to that critique, it represents class conflict by demonstrating the impossibility of the kind of cross-class Hollywood romance found in 5th AVENUE GIRL and BACHELOR MOTHER.

Synopsis: Kitty Foyle, the daughter of a working class Irish alcoholic, grew up in the shadow of the Philadelphia elite (the Mainline) and their yearly gathering, the Assembly. Although she has a strong sense of working class identity, signified by her bond with her father, she also desires class advancement and privilege. She meets a member of the Philadelphia upper class, Wyn Strafford (Dennis Morgan) and, after a brief romance, they separate. Now living in a new city, she meets Mark, a doctor interested in helping the poor. Although she's ready to marry Mark, Wyn comes back into her life. Wyn proposes and they marry. But when Kitty meets Wyn's wealthy family, and finds they want to school her in the ways of their culture, she divorces Wyn. Kitty discovers she is pregnant and decides to be a single mother. But the child dies at birth. Years later, Wyn comes back into her life, now with a wife and family. He tells her how unhappy he is. They agree to go away together. Alone in her room, Kitty's mirror image comes to life and reminds her of her past and her father. As the film ends, she decides to marry Mark.

Despite the deceptively simple story line, Trumbo introduces narrative complexity by telling the story through a series of temporally fragmented flashbacks. But before any of the action proper begins, just after the credits, a film-within-a-film unreels.

Romantic Prologue: For the film-within-a-film that serves as prologue to the narrative proper, Trumbo offers a tribute to silent movies. The choice seems appropriate, since here he offers a misogynistic and romanticized vision of the past, not unlike Griffith's romanticized antebellum vision of slavery in BIRTH OF A NATION (1915). In the title card that opens this prologue, the film establishes its interest in proletarian women. *"This is the story of a white collar girl. Because she is a comparative newcomer to the American scene, it is fitting that we briefly consider her as she was in 1900."* Trumbo's language is deceptive. "White collar girl," suggests an office worker, but as the narrative demonstrates, the term also applies to "shop girls" and clerks. In short, it is a synonym for "working class woman." Nonetheless, as the romantic prologue unfolds, Trumbo begins with a mythic vision of *middle class* life.

A well-dressed woman enters a trolley car. The men rise, remove their hats, offer her a seat. A ukulele courtship comes next, with the suitor sitting on the steps of a middle class house. The suitor proposes. Cut to a well-furnished middle class living room, Victrola prominent in the foreground (as a demonstration of class position). The wife is on the sofa doing needlepoint. The husband comes home and (in a particularly atrocious piece of fiction) hands his wife his pay envelope. In short, all is peaceful and lovely in the home. The next title card read, *"But this was not enough."* The next shot shows the same woman at a suffrage rally, holding a placard. Next title card: *"And so—the battle was won. Women got their equal rights..."* The next shot is the same woman, now riding a street car, standing, being jostled by men, and generally disrespected. In short, the achievement of suffrage, and "equal rights," is figured as a fall, corruption, and the disfiguration of a happy, content home.

But the prologue ends with a remarkable sequence that highlights the very issue the film hopes to repress. Another title card appears, *"Thus woman climbed down from her pedestal and worked shoulder to shoulder with men..."* Cut to an exterior shot of a perfume shop, "Delphine Detaille," then an elevator filled with women workers.

One says: "Got a date tonight Jane?"
"Yeah, the same date I have every night, with the *Saturday Evening Post.*" All laugh.
Another speaks up, "Don't you girls ever think of anything but men? The idea of spending your whole life flattering the egos of some tobacco smelling males. I can think of a thousand better ways of being happy."
Yet another woman, "Well me, I wanna man and I don't care who knows it."
The skeptic speaks again, "Well isn't independence worth anything to you? After all, what's the difference between men bachelors and girl bachelors?"
Then Kitty Foyle (Ginger Rogers) appears, leaving the elevator with the other women. She responds: "Men bachelors are that way on purpose."

The elevator skeptic raises two questions that haunt this narrative: 1) Don't you girls think of anything but men? And 2) Isn't independence worth anything to you? The film's narrative is meant to answer both questions. To the first, it shows Kitty's thoughts as structured throughout by male desire. The desire structuring her thought isn't simply associated with her two suitors, but far more importantly, with her father. And it is precisely her identification with her father's desire that causes Kitty to value her independence. Yet, since she is unable to express that independence as a worker (because of the pre-given gendered role her father wants her to play), she expresses it through her class identity. Thus the narrative is built upon a central paradox: It is because Kitty must repress her independence as a woman worker that she holds all the more vehemently to her independence as a *working class* woman.

Frames and Mirrors: The prologue dissolves into the framing narrative that begins and ends the picture. In the present day (1940), Kitty leaves the elevator, then *Delphines*, and meets Mark in a taxi. He has to make a house call and she helps him deliver a poor woman's baby. With the baby in Kitty's arms, Mark proposes. She accepts. But back in her room, she finds Wyn waiting. He asks her to run away to South America. Despite the fact that he has a wife and family, she agrees. After Wyn leaves and Kitty begins to pack her bags, she lifts an old snow globe in her hand. She shakes it and watches the snow fall on a girl riding a sled. As the snow falls, her voice speaks from the mirror, "You're making a mistake, you know." Then, while she packs her clothing, she has a conversation with a second Kitty, this one inside the mirror.

> Mirror-Kitty says, "It's a pretty unsatisfactory role you're preparing to play. Even under the best of circumstances.... How do you imagine you'll be described? As Wyn's girlfriend?...His woman? That's getting warmer. That woman Wyn's mixed up with. Oh you have no idea how often you're going to get that one. ... Married people face things together. But you won't be married.... You better take a little time to think, sister, because forever is a long, long time and it never hurts to check with the conductor to see if you're on the right train."
> "Well marriage isn't everything? What is it any way? Just a piece of paper like any other legal document. I don't need a piece of paper to prove that I love Wyn. Or that he loves me."
> "You'd be a lot happier with Mark and that little piece of paper than you ever could be with Wyn and a snug little apartment. With a key for him. And a key for you."
> "I think you're wrong."
> "I remember you using those same words before..."

A close-up of the snow globe dissolves to the first flashback, the story of when she told her father he was wrong about Wyn.

As the film proceeds, it will become clear that the person in the mirror represents Kitty's identification with her father. Evidence for this identification lies in the conversation itself. The mirror is the voice of normative tradition, reinforcing satisfactory gender roles by underscoring the "unsatisfactory role" Kitty's about to play. In this sense, Mirror Kitty is the Lacanian name-of-the-father, enforcing the symbolic and normative order (Lacan 1985: 74–85). And two other pieces of evidence suggest this connection between Mirror Kitty and Kitty's dead father. First, the line "I think you're wrong," was the same line Kitty used on her father years earlier. But more than that, the entire flashback begins when Kitty gazes into the snow globe. The audience will soon learn that the globe is a gift from her father, and it returns in the narrative, repeatedly, as a symbol of her debt to him. This metonymic connection turns the globe into a kind of "transitional object," the mediating symbol that unites Kitty and her asymptotic reflection (Winnicott 1971: 1–25).

This relationship between Kitty's reflection and her "Pop" is fully explained at the end of the second act. Returning home from breaking her relationship with Wyn, Kitty stands before an entry way mirror. Through the looking glass she can see both her own face reflected and, in the background, the image of her father in a rocking chair. At that moment she says, "You were right, Pop." But as she turns toward him, she discovers his body motionless, dead, the snow globe at his feet. With her father's death, and his dead reflection together with hers in the mirror, the mirror becomes irrevocably linked to her father's image, his perspective ("You were right"), his voice (Lacan 1977: 1–7).

Thus, the work of the narrative will be to unite Kitty with her dissonant reflection. In the process, Kitty solidifies her identification with her father and his traditionalism. But Trumbo also reveals that traditionalism has a radical edge. By identifying with her father, Kitty assumes his radical class analysis. At the same time, this identification with the working class is cross-cut by a desire for status, and, especially Kitty's desire to dance at the Assembly of the Mainline Philadelphia leisure class. Thus, Kitty's two suitors represent her conflicting desires for working class solidarity and for social status advancement. When, at the end of the picture, she chooses Mark, with his commitment to the poor and downtrodden, she also chooses her father and the working class and thus is finally fused with her asymptotic reflection.

Wealth, Work and Corruption: Trumbo's radical traditionalism appears in his representation of the corrupting power of the wealthy and of wealth itself, as well as the corrupting influence of work upon young women. In the framing narrative, when Wyn first appears Kitty asks:

> "How did you get in? Men aren't allowed in this hotel."
> "The operator on the back elevator's corrupt."

Of course this line also means that the back elevator operator was *corrupted* by Wyn's bribe. This initial association between Wyn and corruption continues throughout the film. After he first meets Kitty, he offers her a job. With Kitty working as his secretary, Wyn seduces her. When his magazine goes out of business, Wyn offers to keep Kitty on the payroll even without work. (She refuses.) As if the recurrent representations of Wyn's corruption weren't enough, Trumbo goes further still. When Wyn proposes, the engagement ring he offers (his grandmother's) is a golden snake eating its own tail. He calls it a symbol of eternal life and family. But, as the context makes clear, the ring represents Wyn himself, the corrupting snake in the garden. Finally, after Wyn and Kitty marry, they cannot establish their independence because Wyn remains a hostage to the family money. Their divorce shows even marriage is corrupted by wealth.

Trumbo's tropes follow the contours of a radical paternalism more than a century old (Stansell 1987: 106–154). He represents women's work outside the household as corrupting, and working women as sexually available, for seduction or harassment. Further, Trumbo represents the wealthy not only as corrupt and corrupting but as incapable slaves to their wealth. Kitty's first disillusionment with Wyn comes when his magazine folds and he decides to go back into the family business, banking, rather than strike out on his own.

"They can't make a banker out of you," she says, "you're too sweet."

Class Consciousness: The roots of Kitty's class consciousness begin to appear in a scene with her ailing father. Prone on the couch, coughing occasionally, he picks up the snow globe.

"You remember when I gave you this thing?" holding out the globe. "Well I think you got me wrong. I didn't mean that you should be a little girl on a sleigh ride.... I mean Wyn Strafford.... Has he ever asked you to meet his family?"

"Well I've never worried much about his family because I've always had a funny idea that I'm just as good as they are."

"Just as good? You're so far above them that they can't touch you with a ten foot pole. You got good Irish eyes Kitty and they're looking into the future. The 'Mainline', they haven't even caught up with the present. Your grandpa was a Mainliner you know?"

"Grandpa Foyle?"

"Yes, he helped lay the tracks. That was real Mainlining, because those tracks were going somewhere. Oh Kitty, why can't you fall in love with a man that's going somewhere?"

This conversation explicitly identifies her father's class background, as well as his allegiance. His father had been an Irish immigrant railroad worker, part of the real Mainline builders of America. In relation to the Philadelphia elite, the old Mainline, Kitty shows her own incipient sense of class pride, "I'm just as good as they are." But while Pop wants Kitty to identify with working class values, the values of his father who laid the tracks, he doesn't want Kitty to lay the tracks herself. Instead, she needs to *find a man* "that's going somewhere."

Earlier in the picture, Mirror-Kitty says "It never hurts to check with the conductor to see if you're on the right train." Kitty won't be allowed to lay the tracks, nor to conduct, but she can ride the right train. And her mirror image, a simulacrum of her father's desire, conducts.

This identification with her father's desire emerges most clearly when she visits Wyn's family after the elopement. Her costuming during this encounter is important. Surrounded by the trappings of wealth and pre-colonial furniture in the family mansion, Kitty wears a stylized three corner hat and a dress modeled on a revolutionary war uniform. In the language of American republicanism, her very attire announces that she intends to make revolution against the family.

Kitty and Wyn visit the family, she presumes, to inform them of their desire for independence. Instead, the family announces a plan for Kitty's re-education and cultural preparation, so she can become a proper wife for a leisure class husband.

Wyn says Mother plans to "take you under her wing and, well, prepare you."

"Prepare me? Prepare me for what?"

The family then explains Wyn can't leave the family, because his trust and all his wealth depend upon his taking a position in the family bank and residence in Philadelphia.

"You mean all those people who are dead can tell us what to do? You mean that Wyn can't live his own life?"

Trumbo seems to be offering an almost Marxist representation of history in this sequence. Wyn's family tradition, his wealth itself, weighs upon him, a historical burden from which he cannot free himself. Kitty doesn't care.

"I didn't marry Wyn for his money," she says. "Let's get a few things straight around here. I didn't ask to marry a Strafford. A Strafford asked to marry me. I married a man, not an institution or a trust fund or a bank! Oh I've got a fine idea of your family conference here. All the Straffords trying to figure out how to take the curse off Kitty Foyle. Buy the girl an education and polish off the rough edges and make a Mainline doll out of her! You oughtta know better than that. It takes six generations to make a bunch of people like you and by Judas Priest I haven't got that much time."

When confronted with the corrupting elite of Philadelphia, Kitty realizes that she does not want to be a Mainline doll. This is the beginning of the transformation that will eventually lead her back to Mark, and through him, back her working class identity (Mirror-Kitty).

Asserting Whiteness: While an explicit discussion of race is almost entirely absent from KITTY FOYLE, as in so many Hollywood productions of the period, racial questions however about the borderlines of the narrative. In particular, the film indirectly addresses the racial status of the Irish. Recall, the film begins in 1900, with the prologue film-within-a-film. And, as Trumbo probably knew, in 1900 it was by no means clear that the Irish were white. Yet, Kitty repeatedly refers to her whiteness. Indeed, in one pivotal moment, she asserts independence not as a worker, but as a *white* citizen. These repetitions of her racial status all come in conversation with Wyn, suggesting that Kitty is trying to convince Wyn, as well as herself, of her racial suitability.

When Wyn offers to take care of her during unemployment, Kitty replies:

"I'm free, white and twenty-one, or almost...Nobody owes a thing to Kitty Foyle, except Kitty Foyle."

Although "free, white and twenty-one," was a common idiomatic expression in the early 20th century, coming in the context of her impending job search, this overt assertion of whiteness becomes a way of claiming independence. Even if she is not allowed to find independence as a working woman, she claims a racialized independence (Roediger 1999).

Later in the film, when Kitty refuses Wyn's first marriage proposal, she tells him it's because of his family and Philadelphia, where she'd never be anything but a "sassy Mic."

"Is that all?" he asks.
She replies: "Well we're both the same color, if that's what you mean."

Again, at a key moment, Kitty asserts her suitability by asserting her whiteness. But the very need to assert whiteness suggests that she remains somewhat uncertain about her own racial status. After all, in Philadelphia Kitty will never be anything but a "sassy Mic." Thus the film conflates Kitty's uncertain racial status and her class position. Both mark out the boundary that separates her from the Assembly.

Motherhood as Penis Envy: Near the end, the film returns to the question "Don't you girls think of anything but men?" and offers an explicit answer. After her marriage with Wyn dissolves, Kitty finds herself a bachelor mother.

> I'm going to have this baby...And I know what I'm going to name him, too. The doctor called me Mrs. Foyle. So I'm going to call the baby Foyle. I'll call him Tom Foyle after my Pop. He'll grow up to be proud of his name. And proud of his mother! And by Judas Priest he'll be a fighter, too.... Tom Foyle, the toughest kid in the block.

Here, Kitty recovers her independence, her self-respect, by having Tom Foyle (her father) inside of her (and "proud of his mother"). Since she's already named him, Kitty quite literally carries Tom Foyle's penis within her womb. As if this implication weren't enough, Trumbo goes further. In the next shot, a close up of the snow globe, with Kitty in voice-over:

> This is what women want. It isn't men, not really. It's something down inside them that's the future. That was it, the future. In the year 2000 AD, your son will be only 65 years old.... Your candidate for the year 2000. Your sweet, tough little candidate.

Doane (1987) argues: "Kitty in fact states explicitly that what women really want is babies, not men" (120). But that's not quite what Kitty says. Instead, she claims that what she wants is not men, but "the future." And here, the future is mediated by men, or, at least by an idealized masculinity in the form of the literal name of the father, Tom Foyle. What Kitty can't achieve on her own, she achieves through her tough little candidate, her father within her. Again, the mirror image returns. Here, Tom Foyle, whether child or reflection, represents Kitty's "ego ideal." And she attempts to reunite herself with that reflection precisely in order to claim, in imagination, the independence denied her in reality. As Freud says of the idealized love object that becomes ego ideal, "We love it on account of the perfections which we have striven to reach for our own ego, and which we should now like to procure in this roundabout way as a means of satisfying our narcissism" (Freud 1989b: 56). Thus Trumbo makes Kitty's failed pregnancy into another attempt to capture her asymptotic reflection, and to achieve through her father the perfection (e.g. independence) denied her by gendered expectations.

If Trumbo reduces women's class solidarity to a kind of penis envy, suggests that women in work are liable to be corrupted and seduced, and that a woman's ultimate role is as mother, and wife-helpmate, KITTY FOYLE nonetheless celebrates working class solidarity and portrays the wealthy as corrupt and corrupting. In this celebration and valorization of working class life, it marks out the boundaries of the Hollywood Popular Front aesthetic. And in its misogynistic portrayal of working women, it participates in the left's radical paternalism, making an argument against capitalism, for the sake of traditional forms of social status and domination. Yet for all its orthodox Freudianism and misogyny, KITTY FOYLE accomplishes a notable task: It subverts the archetypal Hollywood fairytale of cross-class romance. Here, the prince is revealed in all his corruption, and the peasant girl recognizes the strength of her own community.

While KITTY FOYLE manages to evade the conventional demands of corporatist romance narrative, the deconstruction of the Hollywood cross-class romance cliché becomes the central concern of the next film I consider, Paul Jarrico's TOM, DICK AND HARRY.

Tom, Dick, and Harry (1941)

Even more than KITTY FOYLE, Garson Kanin and Paul Jarrico's TOM, DICK AND HARRY is an overt product of pre-war Popular Front aesthetics. Writer Paul Jarrico, who would go on to produce the blacklisted film SALT OF THE EARTH (1954), intended his screenplay to be a cinematic critique of Hollywood archetypes. And although, as he later admits, the critique partially fails, TOM, DICK AND HARRY once again situates Rogers as proletarian hero, celebrates and valorizes working class culture, and offers a fragmented, class based critique of Hollywood narrative conventions (Ceplair 2007: 49–52).

Synopsis: Janie (Ginger Rogers), a telephone operator, has three suitors, each from a different class background. Tom (George Murphy) is a middle class car salesman headed for success. Harry (Burgess Meredith) is a working class repairman with egalitarian left politics. And Dick (Alan Marshal) is a rich man's son. Each suitor courts Janie in turn, and after each courtship Janie has a dream or reverie suggesting her future expectations of life with her potential husband. At the end of the picture, Janie must choose between the three suitors. Saying "you're what I always dreamed of," she chooses Dick, the rich man's son. But after a goodbye kiss with Harry, during which she hears bells, she changes her mind. The film ends with Janie and Harry riding his motor scooter to their working class destiny.

Popular Front Imagery: The imagery of the Popular Front hovers everywhere about the edges of the picture. Appropriately enough, the film opens with Tom and Janie at the movies. After the picture ends, the newsreel runs. Adolph Hitler appears, the audience hisses. Tom and Janie both make sure to hiss before leaving the theatre. Released in June 1941, the film's antifascism was not a part of a wartime propaganda machine, but the product of Popular Front sensibilities (AFI Film Catalog). This becomes more obvious in one of the fantasy sequences. After Janie marries the wealthy heir Dick, a newspaper front page appears. The banner headline reads, "JANIE GETS MARRIED!," the lines beneath read "LOCAL GIRL MAKES GOOD" and "Luckiest Girl in the World tells of Whirlwind Romance." But as the camera closes in on the newspaper, other headlines appear prominently: "Adolph Hitler Assassinated" and under that line, "WORLD WAR END EXPECTED AS HITLER SLAIN," and, finally, to emphasize the link with the Popular Front and the Communist Party, "Nazi Dictator Struck Down in Moscow." True, these images are fleeting, but they establish the background, the taken for granted doxa, against which the picture operates (Bourdieu 1992: 164–171). In a later scene, Dick takes Janie to the Theatre Guild's production of "The Taming of the Shrew." Again, a Popular Front institution serves as a kind of backdrop, almost costuming. But the costume matters and serves as the cultural context, the Popular Front doxa, in which the action (and meaning) of the picture unfolds.

Class analysis: While TOM, DICK AND HARRY remains anchored in an androcentric world in which women's lives become meaningful through men, the film nonetheless attempts to criticize the typical Hollywood cross-class fairy tale romance. It does this by presenting a class analysis. Apparently, Jarrico's original idea for the story was more consistently critical than the final result. As Larry Ceplair writes, the original Janie

> is looking for her prince charming among the three eligible suitors...She finally chooses the mechanic because "he offers her dignity as a human being." In a memo to producer Pandro Berman, Jarrico explained his theme: "There have been so many Success Stories, so many Cinderella Stories. But actually there are as few rich men available to the millions of romantic girls as there are places at the top of the economic ladder for the millions of ambitious boys. These millions are in the theaters, they

are the audience. This story glorifies *them*, the failures and the frustrated ones. It tells them that their lives too have importance and meaning. And I think this is well worth saying".

CEPLAIR 2007: 49–50

So Jarrico's story itself is based upon his class analysis of his audience. He is writing for the "millions," the "failures" (according to the standards of capitalist enterprise), the "frustrated ones." And, as such, he sets himself the task to "glorify *them*," to tell the story of ordinary working Americans. On the one hand, the artistic ambition to capture the common is at least as old as Walt Whitman and has been a perennial desire for American artists. But, in 1941, it was also a key element of the Popular Front aesthetic (Denning 1998).

Further, Jarrico clearly hoped to deconstruct the Cinderella Story, and, by demonstrating that there are "as few rich men available to the millions of romantic girls as there are places at the top of the economic ladder for the millions of ambitious boys," use his critique of conventional narrative to make a larger argument about class inequality. But, as contemporary critics recognized, this was a class analysis that remains firmly rooted in women's economic and social dependence upon men. In *The New Massess*, Joy Davidman argued the film "never made any suggestion that the heroine might have something to offer the world" (quoted in Ceplair 2007: 52).

Even in its own terms, the film fails in its attempt to provide a consistent class critique of Hollywood narrative. Nonetheless, the fragment of critique that did survive the editorial and revision process is interesting enough to deserve some attention. As I've already noted, the film begins in a movie theatre. In the next scene, Tom and Janie sip sodas in a diner. Tom says:

"What are you thinking about?"
"The picture," she responds, almost literally swooning as she sips from her spoon.
"Did you think it was true to life? I mean, do you think a rich guy like that would marry a poor girl like that?" Tom asks.
"Of course he would. He loved her didn't he?…Well, of course."

From the beginning, the film situates itself as a film about film. More than that, the first question the film introduces, "Was it true to life?," becomes the guiding question for nearly half the picture. And then it simply disappears.

The class critique of the Cinderella narrative is most powerfully stated during Harry's working class courtship scenes. In a montage of working class locales (a record store, a coffee shop, a bowling alley), Harry explains why

Hollywood clichés are fantasies, impossible dreams for most Americans. The two dancing for free in a record store listening booth, Janie says:

> "Why can't a girl like me marry a millionaire?"
> "How many millionaires do you think there are?"
> "Oh, about a million..."
> "9,653 and most of them are already married...And do you know how many girls there are like you?"
> "One."
> "There's eleven million, six hundred and five thousand, five hundred and fifty-two. At least."

The conversation continues in the automat, now with an audience of familiar working class types (the ethnic counter worker, the sailor, the shop girl, the cop, etc.).

> "You gotta figure the odds, see," says Harry as he chews.
> "The odds are against any two people meeting...If a girl meets any fella, it's an accident. ...There's no reason the accident can't be a rich fella rather than a poor fella," Janie responds.
> "She's got a point there," says the counter worker.
> Harry, talking to the other man, tells him the reason it can't be a "rich fella, see, is that the rich don't move in the same circles."
> "What circles?" asks Janie.
> "Your circles..."
> "Well, why can't I move in their circles?" she asks.
> "You know the Hamiltons? Suppose they give a party, do they invite you?"
> "No," she says.
> Then Harry points to the other automat patrons, now gathered in a circle around him and Janie. He asks if any of them get invited to the Hamilton parties. "No," each says.
> "You're darn right they don't. They invite people from their own circle. And if they run out of 'em in this town, say, they import 'em from other towns, right?"
> "Right," yells the gathered crowd in unison.
> The scene shifts to a bowling alley. Harry continues, "You see you never get to move in their circles. You got one chance in a million."
> "I never heard such reasoning in all my life," protests Janie, "it just doesn't make sense. ...Every day you read about girls marrying rich fellas. Every day. It's in all the books. It's in all the magazines and it's in all the

newspapers and it's in all the books.... It's just as natural for a girl to want to make a good marriage as for a fella to want to get ahead."

Janie, who seems to know the world primarily through film, magazines and books, has "never heard such reasoning in all [her] life." Indeed, from the perspective of most Hollywood cinema, such an explanation of class barriers and class boundaries "just doesn't make sense." And it is Janie herself who connects this critique of Cinderella Stories with a general perspective on class, when she argues that the desire for a "good" marriage is as natural as a man's desire to "get ahead," and, by implication, the latter desire is just as unrealistic. But Jarrico does not draw out the implications of this analysis. While he has Harry say that he "doesn't believe in success," at that point the class analysis ends. Harry explains his lack of desire for success as an aspect of his general humanist outlook on the world, not as the realistic perspective of a working class man.

More important still, as seems to happen so often with Hollywood cinema, all the critical work of the first half of the narrative is erased by the second half of the story. After Harry offers his compelling (and rather long) explanation of class boundaries, he nonetheless manages to introduce Janie to wealthy customer Dick Hamilton. For reasons never explained to the audience, Dick asks Janie to marry. And while this fulfills her fantasy, at the last moment she returns to Harry, not because "he offers her dignity as a human being," but because she hears bells. Years later, Jarrico acknowledged the failure of the second half of the film. "Essentially, the girl marries the poor fellow not because his ideology is more persuasive, but because when they kiss they ring bells. So I found the picture propagating the very basic notions of love conquering all that I had set out, if not to subvert, at least to provide a substitute for" (quoted in Ceplair 2007: 52).

Motherhood as drudgery: One final element of the film deserves some attention. As I've mentioned, each courtship scene is followed by a dream or reverie in which Janie imagines her future. After the salesman Tom proposes, Janie dreams of a home and family in which she works and he succeeds. Each day he comes home with a new promotion. And each day she has another crying child. When he's finally promoted to President of the United States, she's still in the kitchen, taking care of the children. After Harry's date, she imagines a life of poverty and failure. But again, after each of Harry's failures, she has another child and another task to perform. Her only relief from the burdens of motherhood come in her fantasy of life with Dick, all banquets, gowns, nannies, and glamour. The significance of these fantasy scenes is two-fold: First, the fantasy of wealth and privilege make Janie's choice of Harry all the more difficult to understand. But, more important still, even in her fantasy life (at least with Tom and Harry), Janie imagines motherhood as drudgery. In a sense, the difference between Tom's class position and Harry's class position doesn't really matter, at least not as far as Janie's labor is concerned. In either case, she imagines herself as little more than a servant. Masculine domination penetrates even her deepest dreams.

In one sense, TOM, DICK AND HARRY participates in the same masculinist discourse that structures all of Rogers' pictures her RKO period. Meaning, independence and fulfillment come through a woman's ability to choose the appropriate suitor. While, at least in the fantasy sequences, the film comes closer to undermining the traditionalist vision of femininity than Rogers's previous effort, it ultimately remains bound by the same conventions of romance and gender. But, like KITTY FOYLE, TOM, DICK AND HARRY attempts to provide an antidote to the popular presentation of romantic relationships between working class Cinderellas and wealthy princes. While the latter part of the story ignores Harry's class analysis, the power of that analysis remains. Even if only in fragmentary form, the film achieves some of the subversive intention behind its origin. This narrative critique, together with the Popular Front imagery and the working class doxa that imagery establishes, makes TOM, DICK AND HARRY an exemplar of pre-war Popular Front ideology, at least in its Hollywood version, and the film further solidified Ginger Rogers's screen image as Popular Front proletarian hero.

Gingers Rogers career as a solo star at RKO was short lived. After KITTY FOYLE's success, and Rogers's Oscar for the role, "she too demanded—and received—a limited, nonexclusive deal" in 1941 (Schatz 1999: 57). But in that short time she established herself as a star and made some of the most successful RKO films of the decade. In these films, Ginger Rogers creates the persona of an independent working class woman. And despite the off-stage marriage that ends each picture, during the space of the narrative itself the audience sees Ginger Rogers as an office worker, a shop girl, a telephone operator. Later, with TENDER COMRADE (1944), she's on a factory floor. But in each case, a new reality has penetrated cinematic fantasy. Women workers are represented. This trope of women at work reflects the new doxa that shaped the consciousness of the working class cinema audience. Women were at work. And although this new contested reality could be resolved in fantasy, its perpetual presence in the films marks its presence as a reality in workers' lives.

Ginger Rogers' woman worker is independent, sometimes Irish, and critical of the wealthy and economic inequality. While her characters only occasionally voice that critique (as in 5th AVENUE GIRL and KITTY FOYLE), many of her films during this period take an overtly critical perspective toward class inequality. As I've suggested, part of the reason for this attention to class comes from the architects behind the camera. Hollywood in the late 1930s and early 1940s was remarkably open to Popular Front themes and ideas, and this relative openness also led to a willingness on the part of some screenwriters and directors to make more overtly "political" pictures. Evidence of Popular Front imagery and ideology appears most obviously in KITTY FOYLE and TOM, DICK AND HARRY. But it also appears to be part of doxic attitude behind 5th AVENUE GIRL. At the very least, Allan Scott was familiar enough with the language of the left to make it an integral part of the script. But with the language of the left and the rhetoric of the Popular Front comes a radical paternalism that normalizes gender relations by confining Rogers' own range of choice and freedom to the freedom to choose the proper mate. Motherhood is held up as a constant ideal and goal, with the expectation that her character will leave the proletarian workforce once she finds a good husband.

Rather than conflicting with dominant left notions of femininity, the maternal trope that haunts Rogers' characters is perfectly coincident with the new image of woman celebrated by elements of the Popular Front. Rabinowtiz (1991) argues that the "new rhetoric" of the Popular Front "found a place for the feminine, but that place was motherhood" (56). In order to make common cause with liberals, Communists and the left turned to a traditional "pronatalist rhetoric" in which it was "only as mothers that women could find expression as historical subjects" (Rabinowitz 1991: 58).

So, in KITTY FOYLE, Dalton Trumbo attempts to mobilize what he takes to be the audience's traditional attitudes toward gender and women's work in order to create sympathies for a left critique of class inequality. This radical paternalism is clearest in Trumbo's work (and especially in the later TENDER COMRADE (1944)), but exists to some extent in every Rogers's picture of the period. The films that come closest to subverting this ideal are 5th AVENUE GIRL and TOM, DICK AND HARRY. 5th AVENUE GIRL does so by investing audience desire in Mary Grey's independence; and when she relinquishes that independence at the end of the picture, the conclusion appears to be tacked on, a false "Hollywood ending" as the audience might say. TOM, DICK AND HARRY critiques Hollywood narrative itself, but is at its most critical when it represents Janie's fantasies of motherhood and matrimony as drudgery and servitude.

On the one hand, the popularity of Ginger Rogers' proletarian persona represents the strength of a new kind of audience and Hollywood's attempt to serve that audience. As working class concerns became American concerns, the left found a voice in mainstream cinema. On the other, when the left articulated a political vision, its class politics were based upon a radical paternalism and pronatalist rhetoric that confined women to the household and marriage. Moreover, while both KITTY FOYLE and TOM, DICK AND HARRY offer overt analyses of class inequality, neither explore the Marxist analysis of class and capitalist exploitation. Both are stories of social closure and class immobility. But neither represents the economic causes of that immobility. When a radical critique of capitalist processes of exploitation and expropriation does appear in a mainstream, successful Hollywood picture, the analysis does not come from a Marxist like Trumbo or Jarrico. Rather, it comes from John Ford.

CHAPTER 6

John Ford, From Radical Critique to the White Garrison State, 1940–1948[1]

At the end of THE HURRICANE (1937), the sympathetic Catholic priest is crushed by the walls of his own cathedral. This powerful image suggests John Ford's own increasing dissatisfaction with corporatist solutions to the social and economic contradictions amplified by the Great Depression. First with THE HURRICANE, as well as some other films of the period like STAGECOACH (1938), then with THE GRAPES OF WRATH (1940), and HOW GREEN WAS My VALLEY (1941), John Ford depicts the social and the economic systems as irredeemably corrupt. In fact, as I will argue in this chapter, THE GRAPES OF WRATH offers a singularly radical analysis of capital dispossession and ultimately rejects corporatist solutions to class conflict. HOW GREEN WAS My VALLEY is still more politically daring, one of the few moments in cinematic history where a sympathetic character is allowed to explicitly advocate socialism. Yet, with FORT APACHE (1948), John Ford seemed to abandon his Popular Front sympathies for a genocidal Cold War nationalism.

This chapter studies the symbolic energies that fuel Ford's cinema. In the late 1930s and early 1940s, those energies came from a radical traditionalism that attacked capitalism in the search for restored male authority; by the late 1940s, however, Ford's traditionalism shed its radical edge, and focused, instead, upon preserving the nation against the dangers of secular Communism. These changes in Ford's cinematic politics refract broader transformations in American politics and society; and the melancholy white nationalism of his late work reveals a constrained compromise that abandons social justice in the name of racialized security within a garrison state.

Radical Traditionalism in *The Grapes of Wrath*

Given the lack of consensus concerning the interpretation of classical cinematic artifacts, it is worth remarking upon the widespread agreement that

---

1   This chapter represents a much expanded and revised version of research that appeared in the following journal articles: "The Corporate Imaginary in John Ford's New Deal Cinema," *Rethinking Marxism* 21:4, October 2009: 480–497; "Radical Critique and Progressive Traditionalism in John Ford's *The Grapes of Wrath*," *Critical Sociology*, 34:1, January 2008: 99–116; "Race-making and the Garrison State," *Critical Sociology* 35:5, September 2009: 651–658.

John Ford's version of THE GRAPES OF WRATH constitutes something of a Hollywood monstrosity, the most unabashedly critical Hollywood production of the period (Rogin 2002, Slotkin 1998: 303, McBride 2001: 309, Denning 1998: 268). Consider the final scene for *THE GRAPES OF WRATH* (1940) that Ford directed himself, when Tom Joad (Henry Fonda) offers his mother some little comfort as he prepares to leave the family and pursue his life as a political organizer:

> Well, maybe it's like Casy says. A fella ain't got a soul of his own, just a little piece of a big soul. The one big soul that belongs to everybody... Then it don't matter. I'll be all around in the dark. I'll be everywhere. Wherever you can look. Wherever there's a fight so hungry people can't eat, I'll be there. Wherever a cop's beatin' up a guy, I'll be there. I'll be in the way guys yell when they're mad. I'll be in the way kids laugh when they're hungry and they know supper's ready. And when people are eatin' the stuff they raise and livin' in the houses they build, I'll be there too.

While hardly revolutionary, these lines support Joseph McBride's claim that "THE GRAPES OF WRATH represents the climax of Ford's Popular Front period" (McBride 2001: 309). In fact, I will argue that THE GRAPES OF WRATH offers a fundamentally radical critique of capitalism. However, Ford finds the ground for that critique not in a projected vision of a future socialism, but in energies animated by an almost reactionary, labor oriented traditionalism. In 1940, John Ford's cinematic politics represent a radical traditionalism that attacks capitalism while sustaining laborite myths of benevolent patriarchy.

Nonetheless, Ford's was a necessarily fluid and ambivalent "traditionalism." Although THE GRAPES OF WRATH's narrative relies upon an uncritical attitude toward structures of masculine domination, its attitude toward race is far more complex. Indeed, the Joads are depicted as simultaneously white and not white enough. Thomas Flanagan is one of a number of critics who point to the "Irish" character of Ford's version of the Joads' dispossession (quoted in McBride 2001: 308–309). And, like the Irish in 19th and early 20th century America, the Joads inhabit a nether region between social exclusion and normative inclusion. Thus, while Ford never explicitly articulates a racial argument within the film, through implication and allegory, THE GRAPES OF WRATH continues THE HURRICANE's critique of "whiteness." In the film, Ford argues for an expanded white working class community that includes new immigrants (but, notably, not African Americans).

If some significant number of social actors during the early twentieth century identified with a counter-hegemonic vision of restructured social relationships, such identification did not necessarily lead to an unambiguous "radicalism." A radical critique of capitalism cannot be separated from the cultural context of solidarity in which it emerges. "Nor is the social identity of many working people unambiguous. One can often detect within the same individual alternating identities, one deferential, the other rebellious" (Thompson 1993: 10). For E.P. Thompson, this alternation between deference and rebellion does not amount to an opposition between conservatism and radicalism. Rather, he finds a fundamental paradox in 18th century plebian discourse: "we have a *rebellious* traditional culture. The conservative culture of the plebs as often as not resists, in the name of custom, those economic rationalizations and innovations...which rulers, dealers, or employers seeks to impose" (ibid.: 9). Like Thompson's English "plebs," John Ford's cinematic rhetoric builds a radical critique of capitalism using symbolic energies fueled by the loss of traditional customs and prerogatives (on radical traditionalism, see Thompson 1993; Calhoun 1983; Fantasia 1988: 226–245; Stansell 1987).

In THE GRAPES OF WRATH, John Ford posits an expanded and expansive conception of social class and the American community that coincides with the ideological productions that shook the age of the CIO. But, like many of the cultural laborers in and around the new union movements, Ford used the language of patriarchy and tradition to radicalize his audience (Gerstle 2002, 153–195; Faue 1991, 69–99; Melosh 1991).

Symbolic Domination as Traditional Compensation

An example from another context will help illustrate the social function this progressive traditionalism may have had for Ford, as well as some of his working class audience. In his study of Woonsocket labor struggles during the 1930s and 1940s, Gary Gerstle documents the ideological clash between the secular radical leadership of the Independent Textile Union (ITU) and the largely Catholic, French-Canadian rank and file. Despite the fact that the radical leadership was very much influenced by the new industrial unionism of the CIO, as well as by various socialist currents, from Belgian social democracy to Popular Front Marxism, this secular leadership was, for a time, able to build a common ground with the traditionalist and religious membership. In building this common ground, the radical leadership probably did not recognize and certainly did not acknowledge the extent to which "moral traditionalism could easily lend itself to militant, even radical attacks on capitalism" (Gerstle 2002: 194). Although the radical leadership used the language of class conflict, revised through the symbolism of the American republican tradition, the workers often experienced this so-called "class struggle" as an assault upon their *cultural community*. "Many French-Canadian workers believed...that capital and community stood in opposition to each other.... It followed from such an analysis that workers would have to resort to unprecedented measures *to ensure the safety of family and community*" (ibid.: 194, emphasis added). For many of the workers in Gerstle's study, the "objective" forces of class conflict subjectively manifested themselves as the experience of an assault upon family and community. And, in their attempt to route this assault, workers used the symbolic and ideological resources most readily available, the resources of patriarchy and communal Catholic traditionalism.

The paradoxical complexity of this sort of response to capitalist development emerges from an illustration Gerstle offers. When, in 1938, Woonsocket industrialists attempted to hire women to operate spinning frames, the all-male, skilled mulespinners walked off the job. The job action represented "male indignation at the employers' unreasonable attack on the breadwinning and family provider roles of male mulespinners" (Gerstle 2002: 205). This intrusion of capitalist imperatives into community values (hiring women workers at a lower wage than skilled male mulespinners) helped radicalize white male workers in the struggle against capital. Class struggle became a struggle for community, with "French-Canadian workers insisting that their community values shape the practices of industrial relations in their city" (ibid.: 207). This demand had the paradoxical effect of simultaneously strengthening working-class unity and solidifying the conservative traditionalism already in the community. "On the one hand such insistence intensified conservative aspects of their community life, most notably the commitment to patriarchy; on the other hand, the very defense of community and patriarchy in a time of economic crisis required ethnic workers to intrude on the prerogatives of capitalist institutions to a degree they had never previously contemplated" (ibid.: 207). Consciously or not, the male workers used their sense of dispossession and patriarchal entitlement as an ideological weapon mobilized against the forces of capitalist exploitation.

In Gerstle's example, the threat to the community was, at the same time, a threat to male authority, both within the household and within the workplace. As we've seen, Cohen (1990) also documents the manner in which the economic and communal disruptions caused by the Great Depression were experienced in the family as a crisis in traditional modes of the exercise of authority. Prerogatives of authority were one of the symbolic compensations that white workers received in exchange for their labor. When those prerogatives were disrupted, the community was perceived by some as threatened (Cohen 1990: 246–249).

I've cited these examples from labor history because I believe they bring into focus the kind of ideological and symbolic warfare that Ford wages in his film. The fact that Ford equates community displacement with the dispersal of male authority emerges quite clearly in the scenes where the workers finally do begin to build their own community (sheltered by the government camp), with only men demonstrating any political agency or communal authority. In short, John Ford builds his critique of capitalism by mobilizing the symbolic energies produced by the disruption of traditional modes of masculine symbolic domination (Bourdieu 2001).

The Language of Patriarchy

Ford focused his cinematic rhetoric upon Ma's displacement in order to mobilize the critical energies that drive the work's critique of capitalism. In part, Ford accomplishes this task through his minimal use of music. The central melodic motif that runs sparingly through the film, "Red River Valley," becomes, simultaneously, Ma's theme, and the thematic representation of "home." Ford first introduces the motif in the last scene within the Joads' homestead. Ma sits alone, her features framed in an almost holy aura provided by a small fire in the stove. With a box of papers in her lap, she burns the material remains of her past. Ford uses this memory box to locate Ma Joad as an iconic American mother. In the heart of the home, beside the hearth, the memories she burns (a post-card Pa sent her—addressed to the "Oklahoma Territory"—"Greetings from New York," a news clipping, "Joad Gets Seven Years," etc.) are not abstractions, but representations of her American identity, binding her to the past as it binds her to the nation. And, though in a real and visceral sense the nation has betrayed her family, when Ma pockets that little porcelain dog, with the markings "Souvenir of Louisiana Purchase Exposition—St. Louis 1904," she symbolically signifies her continued allegiance to her own identity as an American mother. The scene is brief, but Ford's quasi-sacred composition techniques, along with his use of music in a film almost bereft of an artificial soundtrack, assures its centrality to the narrative. The Joads' dispossession becomes the story of Ma's loss and capital's assault upon the family.

Of course, all the Joads have been displaced. But there's a distinct difference in the modes of response to that displacement that Ford allows. While Casey and Tom are able to mobilize their sense of injustice and transform it into political agency, no such option appears before Ma or the other women lost to the migration. Ma can have little effect on the world around her. At best, she can find a "decent" place, like the government camp, a place that will shield her from the ravages of unbridled capitalism. And, as we will see, that camp is managed, run, and ruled by men. In John Ford's world, the plight of Ma and the children drive the critique of capitalism, but it is the men of the community who forge a new world.

Allegories of Race

Questions of racial identity are explicitly addressed in at least two important moments within the film. The first is a brief montage.

As the Joads cross the country, Ford visually elaborates the narrative by showing state boundary markers, followed by a vista that in some way illustrates the "sense" of the region. On the one hand, Ford does this to amplify the American character of the Joads' exodus. At the same time, his concentration on the fluidity of boundary markers reinforces the Joads' loss of place, their loss of a boundary for their experience, their loss of home and community. In one of these American tableaus, the shot begins with a highway marker, "Arizona US 66," and under that "Will Rogers Highway." Ford frames the next shot from within an Indian household. As a Native American blacksmith hammers at his anvil, the Joads' truck ambles past, only to be blocked by a herd of sheep driven by another Indian. Despite Ford's great affection for faces and close-ups, the Native Americans in this sequence are very nearly faceless. Rather, we see their hands working, and their sheep running. The sheep become metonymically associated with the Indians. This symbolism has a dual significance. On the one hand, the sheep are the Okies, driven across the highway. At the same time, through the sheep, the Joads are metonymically linked to the Indians as well. Here Ford connects the Native American experience of dispossession with the Joads loss of boundary. In a sense, the Joads are dispossessed "native" Americans.

But a more overt argument concerning racial boundaries comes a later in the film. The sequence where the Joads arrive as unknowing strikebreakers at the Keene Ranch is pivotal in the narrative. Here Tom's own labor consciousness will emerge. After an earlier separation, he finds Preacher Casy, now a strike organizer. And, as I will discuss below, when Casy is murdered, Tom receives the blow across his face that will mark his conversion to the preacher's vision. But for now I want to concentrate upon another aspect of the Keene Ranch segment, and the way in which it marks out the boundaries of the working class community.

The Joads drive through a picket line outside the ranch, guarded by company security, strikers yelling "scabs!" as they pass. Puzzled, Tom says:

"I don't know what these cops have to do with it, but I don't like it. These are our own people, too, all of 'em. I don't like this."

With these lines, Tom explicitly marks the boundaries of his community: Those boundaries coincide with the dispossessed, the strikers, the exploited. At the same time, the Keene Ranch gives this symbolic solidarity a physical boundary as well. "Our people" are the workers at the Keene Ranch, both the strikers and the scabs ("all of 'em"). This boundary marking matters because near the end of the sequence Ford makes the argument that "our people" includes new immigrants, otherwise so often situated as non-white strangers in Hollywood cinema (Roediger 2005).

After Casy's murder, and Tom's revenge for the killing, he and the family need to flee the Keene Ranch. As the Joads pack, another migrant family moves into camp, taking their place. An old man dressed like an Okie talks to the foreman. But the old man doesn't have an Oklahoma accent, nor a southern drawl. Rather, his speech reveals him to be an immigrant from Southern Europe. Tom overhears the conversation from inside his cabin.

"How many?" asks the foreman.
"Ten of us."
"House 25. The number's on the door."
"OK mister. What's ya payin'?"
"2 ½ cents"
"2 ½? Say a man can't make his dinner on that."
"Take it or leave it, there are 200 men coming in from the south that'll be glad to get it."
"But how we gonna eat?"
"Look I didn't set the price. If you want it OK. If you don't, turn around and beat it."
"Which way house 25?" (the line emphasizing the Southern European accent).
"Straight up the street."
The camera cuts inside the cabin, where Tom says: "That Casy! He may have been a preacher, but he seen things clear. He was like a lantern. He helped me to see things too."

The exchange between the new arrivals and the foreman confirmed Casy's argument. Once the strike was broken, pay dropped from 5 cents a bushel to 2½ cents a bushel. But more than that, Casy was a lantern who transformed Tom's vision of the world. Casy solidified Tom's new sense of solidarity with the exploited, his sense of "one big soul." And, notably, Tom's symbolic identification with "our people" is extended to everyone at Keene Ranch, including the new immigrants. At a time when racial boundaries were in flux, THE GRAPES OF WRATH, like BLACK FURY (1935), argues for an expanded definition of "our people." But this boundary also has limits. While BLACK FURY doesn't allow black actors any speaking parts, they appear within the film, and are projected as (clearly subordinated) members of the miner's community. But THE GRAPES OF WRATH represents "our people" through a transformed trope of whiteness. The boundaries of racial identity might be shifting to include new immigrants, but blacks remain excluded from the social compact.

Ford continues this allegory of racialized dispossession with his depiction of the treatment the Joads receive from other (more privileged) members of the working class. In the scene with Tom hiding in the shack after he takes revenge for Casy's murder, Ma tells him that there's talk he'll be "lynched." The Okies are forced into shanty town ghettos, they face vigilante violence, and are constantly looked upon as a threat to the community and its order. Theirs is a Jim Crow America. Indeed, in one scene Ward Bond plays a California police officer who is an Okie, but wants to keep that fact quiet. In short, he passes for white. Like Irish immigrants in an earlier America, the Joads appear "white" but are treated as less than fully human (Roediger 1999).

Consider the scene at the filling station before the Joads cross Death Valley. While Tom fills the tank for the crossing, in the back of the truck Grandma dies in Ma's arms. Meanwhile, the station attendant stands beside Tom, warning him of the dangers of the passage. "Takes more nerve than I got."

Tom responds: "Don't take no nerve to do somethin', nothin' else you can do."

As the truck pulls off, the two station attendants, dressed in pure white, comment on the Joads.

> "Holy Moses, what a hard lookin' outfit."
> "All those Okies are hard lookin'."
> "Ah, but I'd hate to hit the desert in a jalopy like that," handing the other a stick of gum.
> "You and me got sense. Them Okies got no sense and no feeling," he says as he casts the wrapper to the ground. "They ain't human. No, a human being wouldn't live the way they do. A human being couldn't stand to be so miserable."
> "Just don't know any better, I guess."

The Joads are marked by the attendants as racial others: "They ain't human." But the audience knows differently. Throughout the first hour of the film, the audience learns that the Joads are indeed human, and more than that, that they are familiar American types. And the audience knows that the Joads "know better," that they've been forcibly dispossessed, and that it doesn't signify a loss of sense to do something when there's "nothin' else you can do." The disdain of the station attendants, symbolically amplified by the cast off gum wrapper, attempts to produce indignation in the audience. In that moment, and throughout the film, the Okies become allegorical figures for America's dispossessed. They are the symbolic representation of the common effects of the Great Depression. And by staging their exodus, Ford implicitly demands a redefinition of the American working class, and the American community in general. Through both an identification with the Joads, and, at the same time, with the station attendant, the audience takes a critical position toward its own limiting and limited racialized class attitudes. By calling out the spectator's self-critique, Ford opens the path to a broader definition of the "white" working class community.

Despite his traditionalist orientation, John Ford was remade by his times, by his audience, and entered the public sphere as a contestant in the struggle over some of the central political and social problems facing the nation during the Great Depression. In particular, he fought for a heterodox re-definition of "American-ness," one that attempted to refashion notions of race, class and nation. Ford's version of THE GRAPES OF WRATH was both informed by a kind of labor consciousness, and, at the same time, attempted to leave its own mark upon the laboring classes. At least to some significant extent, his cinema participated in what Michael Denning has called the "laboring of culture" that characterized the age of the CIO (Denning, 1998).

Narrating Trauma as Radical Critique

Twentieth Century Fox's THE GRAPES OF WRATH was an overwhelming popular success, one of *Variety*'s top earning films for 1940, garnering the praise of Woody Guthrie, and even of Steinbeck himself (Schatz 1997: 466; McBride 2001: 314–315; Denning 1998: 270). "However," writes Denning, "despite its popular success, THE GRAPES OF WRATH is not a true exemplar of the cultural politics and aesthetic ideologies of the Popular Front" (Denning 1998: 259). Denning bases his judgment, in part, upon his claim that "none of the key figures involved in its production were Popular Front radicals," and, in part, upon the argument that the film portrayed a version of "New Deal populism" based in "sentimental and conservative" values (ibid.:267–268). While Denning is undoubtedly correct in underscoring the fact that "Steinbeck's racial populism" (ibid.: 267) becomes a major aesthetic element in the film, it is a racial populism that challenges the boundaries of normative whiteness. And Denning's argument concerning the film's "conservative and sentimental" ethos, seems to miss the radical, anticapitalist potential of that 'sentimentality'.

If Denning's judgments concerning the film are somewhat one-sided, nonetheless he asks the right questions when he writes: "Why did the story of the 'Okie exodus' have this mythic power? Why did it become the story by which Americans narrated the depression?" (Denning 1998: 262). Ford's film was precisely such a myth; and it functioned as a kind of imaginary resolution for the fundamental economic trauma of the age. In telling the Joads' story, Ford was giving the emerging American laboring classes a language for comprehending their own past. True, most workers were not literal migrants, like the Joads. But migration, disconnection, dispersal, served as privileged tropes in an age of social and economic anxiety. And, as Denning notes, "the representation of mass migration became one of the fundamental forms of the Popular Front" (ibid.: 264). While the sentimental elements in Ford's film can hardly be ignored, they need to be understood in terms of this unfolding migratory narrative. And, significantly, Ford situated this sentimental migratory narrative with the context of a systemic and radical critique of capitalism's economic imperatives.

Early in the film Tom and Casy meet Mulely hiding in the Joads' abandoned farmhouse. Just out of prison, Tom is anxious and confused by the absence of his folks. He presses Mulely for an explanation.

"Who done it?" says Tom.

"Listen," responds Mulely, as the wind whistles outside, "that's the one that done it. The dusters."

At first it seems that Mulely will repeat the common refrain that the great migration, like the Depression itself, resulted from a kind of natural disaster. But Mulely continues, "that's what started it, anyway."

"You crazy?" asks Tom.

"Some say I am," responds Mulely, and then offers the double entendre, "you want to know how it happened?," with "it" presumably referring both to the migration and to Mulely's own madness.

In the flashback sequence that follows Mulely offers a story that can be simultaneously read as an evasion and as an explanation. "The way it happens...the way it happened to me...a man come one day..." Ford then stages Mulely's memory, opening the sequence with a company man sitting in a convertible, talking.

"The fact of the matter, Mulely, after what them dusters did to the land, the tenant system don't work no more. They don't even break even, much less show a profit. Why one man with a tractor can handle twelve or fourteen of these places. You just pay him a wage, and take all the crop." Then the man tells the family they have to get off.

> "Get off my own land?" asks Mulely.
> "Now don't blame me," says the company man, "it aint my fault."
> "Well, whose fault is it?" ask Mulely's son.
> "You know who owns the land. The Shawnee Land and Cattle Company."
> Then Mulely again, "well who is the Shawnee Land and Cattle Company?"
> "It aint nobody. It's a company."
> "They got a president, aint they?" says Mulely's son, "they got somebody who knows what a shotgun's for, aint they?"
> "Oh son, it aint his fault, cause the bank tells him what to do."
> "Alright, then where's the bank?"
> "Tulsa, but it aint no use blaming him. He's just the manager. And he's half crazy hisself tryin' to keep up with the orders from the east."
> "Then who do we shoot?" asks Mulely.
> "Brother, I don't know. If I did, I'd tell ya."

On the surface, this moment in the film seems to be a kind of political evasion. No one is responsible for the migrants' plight. Disembodied, quasi-natural forces seem to be conspiring to drive them off the land. But a closer look at the dialogue reveals another possible reading. True, the discourse evades assignment of personal responsibility. Instead, Ford stages a radical explanation based in political economy.

Neither natural forces, nor bad actors, stand at the back of this drama of dispersal and loss. The windstorms are the immediate occasion for the transformation of the tenant system into a system based upon wage labor and pecuniary efficiency. But this transformation in the economy had significance for American workers that reached far beyond the dust battered plains. The systemic imperatives of market expansion inherent in a capitalist economic formation transform and colonize Mulely's world. It is not ill-will, or even an ill-wind, but the ever present and systematic demand for renewed *profit* and more efficient *productivity* that disperses the Okies.

As the company man drives off, Mulely, in tearful gasps, lays his own claim to the land in the "conservative" language of tradition and blood. He says his grandfather worked this land seventy years ago. His father was born on it.

"We was all born on it…. That's what makes it our'n. Bein born on it, workin' on it, and dyin' on it. And not no piece of paper with writin' on it."

Blood becomes the symbolic device that binds the people to the land. Through blood, labor, birth and death, Mulely and his family are metonymically attached to a particular space; and, although Mulely doesn't technically "own" the land, this metonymic bond provides the symbolic energy that makes his claim resonate with the film's audience. His "sentimental and conservative" ethos fuels a radical critique of capitalist imperatives.

Back with Tom and Casy in shadows, Mulely finishes the tale with his memory of the "Cats." In the only self-consciously modernist moment of the film, Ford produces a montage. With the rolling tread of a Caterpillar tractor as the frame, we see lines of the machines rolling over barren soil, driven by masked, anonymous men.

"And for every one of them," says Mulely, "there was ten, fifteen families thrown right out of their homes."

Mulely ends his tale with the story of the "one that got me." A tractor rolls toward his shack and Mulely stands with a shotgun, facing the driver. The driver removes his mask, revealing the face of a neighbor and fellow farmer.

"What are you doing a thing like this for, against your own people?" asks Mulely.

"Three dollars a day. That's what I'm doing it for.... First and only, I think about my own folks. What happens to other people...that's their own look out."

The bonds of community are broken. Market imperatives, capital expansion, and wage labor destroy the structures of solidarity that held the farmers together.

While THE GRAPES OF WRATH is, indeed, a "migratory epic," it is, simultaneously a saga of dispossession and "lawful" capitalist expropriation. When seen in these terms, perhaps we can begin to understand the enormous appeal the film had for its largely *metropolitan* working class audience. For this emerging industrial workforce, the two decades preceding the Great Depression represented a period of transition and disruptive re-composition that had a decisive effect on their anxieties and predispositions (Barrett 1992; Fraser 1989; Lichtenstein 2002; Gerstle 2002). Taylorism, and rationalized factory production, began to threaten the livelihood of skilled craft workers. But this threat to the workers' wage was simultaneously an assault upon their place in the social order. A new industrial order was emerging and this "order promised the social extermination of a whole social species" (Fraser 1989: 63). For these skilled workers, this new mass industrial society meant precisely dispossession and expropriation. Furthermore, new generations of rural immigrants, arriving from "decomposing peasant societies" (in Europe or in the United States itself), could perhaps achieve a more literal identification with the Joads' plight (ibid.: 63). In both cases, the expropriation involves a kind of material seizure. The peasants lose their land. The craft worker loses a privileged wage. At the same time, however, the dispossession involves more "immaterial" realities, including, especially, the social solidarity that traditional forms of life ensured. With the loss of both economic and communal security, anxiety takes root. And the Depression itself amplified anxieties, exposing workers to a perpetual sense of insecurity and loss (Cohen 1990: 213–249; Klein 2003: 78–115).

Now we can begin to see that although Ford sets his drama of the working class in a traditional, rural setting, the process he narrates potentially resonates with the entire American working class. He's not simply talking about the dispossession of a few thousand "Okies" from their farmland, but about an economic order in which traditional communal structures are systematically displaced by market imperatives and wage labor. Mulely's response is madness. Grandpa Joads' is death. These were "conservative" answers to the radical changes taking place across the industrial and agricultural landscape. But the age of the CIO generated another set of possibilities. This new age demanded new principles of solidarity.

Capital, Class and the Charmed Circle of the State

In order to understand the symbolic "resolution" Ford posits to the cultural trauma he dramatizes, we need to consider the final sequences of his film. For many critics, Ford's revision of Steinbeck's dark finale disperses and dissipates the narrative's political impact. Denning summarizes much of the frustration that critics have found in the film's final cut.

> In the Zanuck film of *The Grapes of Wrath*, this New Deal utopia becomes the happy ending. Whereas the novel ends with the killing of Preacher Casy, the defeat of the strikers, and the controversial scene in which Rose of Sharon breast-feeds a starving stranger, the film ends with the episode in the government camp, with its showers, toilets, and Saturday night dances. When the Joads drive off from the camp in the film's final scene, Jane Darwell delivers the famous ending: "We're the People".
>
> DENNING 1998: 266

Two aspects of the conclusion trouble Denning: first, the "happy ending" in the government camp; and, second, Ma Joad's final speech. It is worth noting that the "We're the People" speech was a post-production revision, stapled onto the film by Zanuck, and with Ford's only nominal and probably ironic approval. "This scene appeared in the shooting script as an addendum dated November

1, 1939, when Ford was still involved in principle photography. But the story goes that when Zanuck asked Ford what he thought about the new ending, Ford said it sounded fine and told Zanuck to direct it himself" (McBride 2001: 313). On the other hand, it was important, even essential, for Ford to end the film in the government camp. This ending allowed Ford to posit an alternative social and political economy, one that seemed within grasp during the height of the age of New Deal and the CIO.

While working as an unwitting scab in the California fruit groves, Tom re-encounters Casy as a union organizer. As Casy and Tom talk, vigilantes attack. They club Casy to death, and Tom, seizing the club, kills a deputy. Through Casy's self-sacrifice, Tom is transformed; and marked by the scar he receives upon his face from another vigilante's blow. Tom's scarlet letter excludes him from his maternal community while binding him to Casy's grand metaphor, "one big soul." The next morning, hiding in the Joads' shack, Tom tells Ma that he plans to leave the family. Ma Joad responds with a speech that's notable because in many ways it seems the model for Zanuck's "We're the People" sequence; and yet with some subtle and important differences.

> Tom, there's a whole lot I don't understand. But goin' away ain't gonna ease us. There was a time we was on the land. There was a boundary to us then. Old folks died off and little fellers come. We was always one thing. We was the family. Kinda whole and clear. But now we ain't clear no more. There ain't nothin' that keeps us clear. ...We're crackin' up, Tom. There ain't no family now. ...Got nothing to trust. Don't go, Tom. Stay and help. Help me.

Once again Ford illustrates the collective trauma of dispossession, the loss of boundaries, limits, and unity. But notice that while Zanuck has Ma Joad say that the people will endure, despite injustice and hardship, the case that Ford makes for the family is much more precarious. "We're crackin' up," says Ma, appealing to Tom to hold the family together. Although Tom reluctantly acquiesces, very soon he's forced to break this last bond and leave the disintegrating family to its fate. Zanuck's "people" may endure, but the traditional bonds that hold the family to the land, and, thus, together, remain in peril.

The government camp the Joads discover is no utopia, only a respite from this process of expropriation and dispossession. Through a series of metonymic associations, Ford establishes the fact that this rest depends upon the beneficence of the New Deal state apparatus. The first shot of this sequence shows the sign hanging over the entrance to this new civilization, "Farmworkers' Wheat Patch." The camera then moves in for a close shot of the shingle hanging just below the arch, *"Department of Agriculture."* The first authority figure the Joads encounter is a father like figure "made up to look remarkably similar to FDR" (McBride 2001: 311). When the camp superintendent explains the social structure of the community, a place where "people elect their own cops" and workers cooperatively run the schools, the sanitation, and the social life of the camp, Ma looks at the man with disbelief.

Says Tom to the superintendent, "You meanin' to tell me the fellas runnin' the camp are just fellas? Just campin' here?" Then Tom asks again: "Who runs this place?"

"The government."

There's a willful ambiguity in this dialogue. On the one hand, the "fellas runnin' the camp are just fellas," on the other, the camp is run by the "government." Ford uses this ambiguity to establish a metaphorical connection between the metonymically related "fellas" and the collective signifier, "the government." The serially related "fellas" need a common principle to transform them into a group. In a sense, the government becomes the metaphorical principle that binds these "just fellas" into a single social entity, a community. The scene continues:

> "Why aren't there more like it?"
> "You find out. I can't."
> "Is there anything like work around here?"
> "Well, I can't promise you that. But there'll be a licensed agent here later if you want to talk to him."

This last exchange underscores the limits of the community Ford envisions. True, the state, as protector and benefactor, mediates between the workers and the economic system. But, at the same time, this state apparatus has definite limits that its power cannot transgress. First and foremost, it cannot promise Tom and his family work. While the charmed circle of the state protects the Joads from the violence all around them, *it cannot answer the fundamental trauma animating their journey.* The state treats the symptoms, but the cancer remains. Still, Tom ends his conversation with the remark: "Ma's gonna like it here. She ain't been treated decent in a long while." The government camp doesn't solve the Joads' problems; but it represents a "decent" place, a site that contains both the promise of industrial democracy and, at the same moment, depends upon the structures of patriarchy and masculine privilege.

Workers' Control

This sense of partial resolution finds further amplification in the social relations that structure camp ritual life. Ford uses a worker run dance to illustrate both the promise and the limits of the participatory, social democracy he envisions. The sequence begins with Tom and two other workers, one "head of the central committee," digging ditches together. Their sympathetic employer warns them that county vigilantes have threatened to start a riot at the dance. In the next shot, the migrants, dressed in cowboy finery, dance across the improvised outdoor floor. Meanwhile, at the entrance of the dance, workers stand, holding a chain. This chain, however, rather than locking the community in bondage, protects an almost syndicalist social order from outside encroachment. The workers have quite literally seized their chains and turned them against their erstwhile masters. During the course of the sequence, Ford stages various dramas of family life, domesticity, and courtship, all in the traditional language of the dispossessed migrants. Throughout most of the scene, Ma sits beside Rose, protecting her from the advances of various young men. Although Ma is not exactly passive, her activity is decisively circumscribed by her traditional role as family protector and caregiver. Once again, Ford mobilizes the symbolic energies of his audience by appealing to their traditionalistic or "sentimental" vision of an ideal motherhood, sheltered and sheltering.

This elicitation of the audience's sentiment in the service of Ford's narrative goal climaxes in Tom's serenade. Tom takes Ma in his arms and sings the words of "Red River Valley." Just as the tune ends the vigilantes attempt their riot, disrupting Tom's momentary connection with his mother and invading the charmed circle of decency that surrounds her. But the workers in turn surround the thugs, who vanish into the mass of women and men; and, as the deputies arrive, the dance guards raise their chains and block the entrance. With law on his side, the camp superintendent intervenes and refuses the deputies and the thugs. In the final shot, the fiddles play for the dancers in the background, while in the foreground a group of children dance in a circle, hand in hand. These child-dancers become allegorical figures for the charmed circle of the state as a site of respite on the workers' interminable journey toward justice.

The government camp offers this symbolically isolated community as partial compensation for all that the migrants have lost. But Ford's film *does not* offer an unambiguously "happy ending." In the government camp, it's true, Ma finds a "decent" community, upholding more or less "traditional" values, while, at the same time, offering (male) workers an unprecedented degree of control over their lives. But Ford makes it clear that this compensation is not a resolution. In fact, the bonds of family have been broken. And the final crack that shatters this fragile enamel comes with Tom's enforced departure.

Tom can no longer accept the piecemeal provisions provided by the government camp. "And when people are eatin' the stuff they raise and livin' in the houses they build, I'll be there too." His ideal is a world no longer controlled by vested industrial interests, but run by, as well as for, common working people. Even with Zanuck's revised ending, this radical edge couldn't be wholly repressed. The last shot Ford directs has Tom Joad walking off, alone, in a scene that McBride rightly sees as a more or less conscious echo of the final moments of Ford's earlier YOUNG Mr LINCOLN (1939) (McBride 2001:312). Tom walks upon Lincoln's path with the hope of finishing the radical work of reconstruction that his predecessor could not. Tom's task will be to turn the republic into an industrial democracy.

The Paradoxes of Radical Representation

John Ford's film of THE GRAPES OF WRATH participated in the overall laboring of culture that characterized the age of the CIO by generating a system of identifications that had a potentially transformational affect upon the imagined possibilities of working class unity. In his depiction of collective traumatic dispossession, Ford taps into the predilections and sentiments of an insecure and desperate working population and constructs three distinctly "radical" representations. The first is Mulely's story, with its almost Marxian critique of capitalism's disembodied systematic imperatives that necessarily and unceasingly dislodge any community. There is nothing particularly new in Mulely's tale. The history of capitalism is the history of this perpetually repeated traumatic loss on the part of workers. What matters is the fact that Ford manages to insert a representation of this trauma into a mainstream product of the cultural apparatus. Through Ford's film, the dispossessed recovered their reality, now represented in the socially sanctioned language of cinematic "realism." In other words, THE GRAPES OF WRATH attempts to become a kind of "definitive" document (Mills 1959: 407), solidifying and authorizing the mass experience of dispossession. Then there is Ford's projection of the government camp, in which male workers have taken hold of the means of social reproduction. And, importantly, in Ford's vision of this camp, capital remains an ever-present threat, just beyond the boundaries of the State's charmed circle. Finally, there is Tom Joad's necessary rejection of the partial and social democratic solution to capitalism's fundamental contradictions.

At the same time, Ford works with a language of traditional patriarchy based in the metonymically derived symbolic compensations formerly provided to dispossessed men in the working class. The formation of a kind of class consciousness in Ford's work cannot be severed from the consciousness of a *gendered* class identity. Agency remains the province of male workers. Women become objects of nearly sacred adulation, and that holy, maternal aura provides the symbolic energies driving the critique forward. At the same time, Ford implicitly challenges normative racial categories by arguing for the inclusion of new immigrants in the class community, and by depicting the Joads' experience of dispossession in racialized terms. Finally, while the paternal racism present in Ford's usual depiction of black Americans is absent from THE GRAPES OF WRATH (see Chapter 4 above), this is primarily because black Americans are absent from the film. Though the racialized boundaries of the community Ford imagined had expanded, during this era of Jim Crow in America they remained "white only."

Two Voices

In his next film, HOW GREEN WAS My VALLEY (1941), Ford pushes the boundaries of acceptable political discourse in cinema by openly addressing "socialism." Often the radical edge of this picture has been lost on critics because of its nostalgic representation of a Welsh coal mining community. While it cannot be doubted that Ford's vision of the past depends upon more than a grain of wish-fulfillment, those fantastic elements do not wholly subdue the radical critique of capitalism that the film figures. Nor could the many script revisions demanded by producer Darryl Zanuck entirely dull the political edge of the picture (Puette 1992:18). HOW GREEN WAS My VALLEY centers its narrative on young Huw Morgan (Roddy McDowall) and his perception of labor strife in the mining town. Perhaps because of its historical setting, Ford felt free to make a more overtly political film. While THE GRAPES OF WRATH challenges capitalism, it never proposes an overt solution, and consistently avoids any mention of "socialism." In Ford's later film, however, "socialism" is directly invoked by the local parish minister as a solution to the miners' difficulties. While the representation of the union struggle in this film is fascinating, however, Ford also offers a critical perspective on the Hollywood fantasy of cross-class romance.

Huw's sister is Angharad (Maureen O'Hara), a working class beauty in love with the socialist parish minister (Walter Pidgeon). But, through a series of miscommunications and deflections, she loses hope that he will return her affection. At the same time, the mine owner's son falls in love with Angharad.

This is a remarkable piece of cinema for the period—given the proliferation of love stories portraying cross-class romances—since Ford makes no effort to dramatize the young industrialist's love for the working class girl. There is a brief introductory scene in which the mine owner comes to Huw's father's house and, obviously ill at ease in his worker's presence, asks permission for his son to court Angharad. The courtship takes place off stage and, soon after, we see Angharad in gown and veil.

When we recall METROPOLIS, this section of the film becomes quite significant. While in Lang's work the industrialist's son becomes the mediator between head and heart, capital and labor, Ford allows no such mediation. In fact, rather than mediating between the community and the mine owner, Angharad becomes a class traitor, at home nowhere. She rejects the mine owner's son, his world and class; but, at the same time, she cannot find her way back to her home culture. She is lost between worlds. For Ford there is an absolute abyss that separates the mine owner from the workers he exploits, and no mediation is possible. The film's bleak ending, with an adult Huw abandoning the wasted remains of the coal town, leaves little hope for the future. Ford's films during this period represented an increasingly radical departure from the comforting vision of an integrated corporatist totality. And this increasingly radical edge in Ford's work corresponded to an increasingly restive working class, as the New Deal raised working class expectations without satisfying their demands.

At the same time, Ford built his radical economic critique using the symbolic resources of patriarchy and racial exclusion. In THE GRAPES OF WRATH, Ford focuses upon Ma Joad's displacement, using the cultural construction of an idealized mother in order to elicit his audiences' identification. At the same time, at the end of the film, when Ford presents his ideal vision of a working class utopia, it is a utopia built and maintained by men. Later, in HOW GREEN WAS MY VALLEY, Ford continues to use these resources of symbolic traditionalism to construct his radical critique. The film presents two spokesmen for a working class politics. On the one hand, the socialist parish minister is clearly a sympathetic character and his calls for a "responsible unionism" combined with class solidarity resonate with the audience. On the other hand, the family patriarch opposes unionization and fears socialism. Again, this patriarch is presented in a wholly sympathetic light and there is no "conversion experience" that transforms him into a socialist or unionist. In other words, Ford uses these two figures, the socialist minister and the family patriarch, and their incommensurate political positions, to dramatize his own suspension between a radical or progressive modernism and a conservative traditionalism. This tension, so politically and cinematically productive for Ford in the late 1930s and 1940s, becomes repressed in his later work. And, in FORT APACHE, Ford will dramatize the very process of repression that transformed him from Popular Front progressive to Cold War liberal.

From Class Conflict (Back) to Corporate Community

By the time HOW GREEN WAS MY VALLEY entered theatres, the United States was at war. Ford, Capra, and other "Americanist" filmmakers were willingly drafted into the war effort. What's fascinating in this context is the way Ford based his nationalist rhetoric upon the cinematic foundation he had built as a Popular Front filmmaker. First, in his documentary short, THE BATTLE OF MIDWAY (1942), Ford utilized the voice talents of Henry Fonda (Tom Joad in THE GRAPES OF WRATH), Jane Darwell (Ma Joad), and Donald Crisp (the Morgan patriarch in HOW GREEN WAS MY VALLEY), in order to make the case for the war. Clearly trading on the images he had created in the popular imagination, through these actors, Ford meant to evoke and invoke the common sense of working people. At the same time, emphasizing a corporatism that was nearly eclipsed in his prior films, Ford argues for a unified national community, not a society divided by class, wealth, status, and race.

In a sense, these transformations in Ford's aesthetic are hardly surprising. The fact that notions of class conflict during this period were supplanted by the necessity of national unity might best be symbolized by the CIO's wartime "no strike" pledge. On a more personal level, however, Ford's transformation had much to do with the new social circles he inhabited and the acceptance they offered to an Irish American always somewhat unsure of his status in an Anglo republic. During the 1930s, Ford participated in union and Popular Front agitation, marching in demonstrations and giving speeches in support of Roosevelt and against Fascism. But during the 1940s, as he became one of America's foremost propaganda filmmakers, he cultivated new friendships with rightwing members of the American elite like fellow-Irish Catholic and radical anti-Communist "Wild Bill" Donovan, head of the OSS, and the anti-labor Senator Robert Taft. While these new relationships were a consequence of Ford's engagement in the war effort, their effects on his personal political positions also influenced his cinematic productions (McBride 2001).

The most remarkable document in this revisionary process is Ford's 1945 war picture, THEY WERE EXPENDABLE. Based upon the "true" story of a PT crew left behind after the retreat from the Philippines, this film again utilizes the extensive rhetorical apparatus that Ford had created during his Popular Front period. For the most part, it's a typical war film, in which social divisions of class, race, and culture are elided as the "men" pull together and fight off the "Japs." But there's one particular moment in the film that deserves special attention. On an island in the pacific, the PT crew works with an American expatriate shipbuilder called "Dad," played by Russell Simpson, the actor who portrayed Pa Joad five years earlier. This casting is no accident. Dad is Pa Joad remade as a nationalist hero. While Pa Joad had lost his home, Dad is determined to stay on the island and fight off the Japanese invaders. Lt. Ryan (John Wayne) is preparing to abandon the position.

"Why don't you come along with me?" he asks.

Sitting on his front porch, smoking a pipe, a shot gun on his lap, Dad replies "I worked forty years for this, son" pointing at the shipyard, "If I leave it, they'll have to carry me out."

As Ryan walks away, and Dad empties his pipe, the theme "Red River Valley" plays. In THE GRAPES OF WRATH, Ford used the tune to aurally elaborate the Joads' longing for a home. Now home has been found. Despite the fact that he's thousands of miles from Oklahoma, Pa Joad has his place in the sun. And, once again, John Ford evokes a kind of value theory. But rather than justifying the laborer's right to his product, this value theory justifies the colonialist's claim to his nation's imperial domain. Like Mulely, Dad lays claim to his homestead through an appeal to the work of his hands. His labor made this place home. Thus value theory returns in the service of nationalist hegemony. It was, after all, not Dad's labor alone that produced his claim to the land. As Ford makes clear visually, *home is where the flag is planted*. With this scene, Ford exhibits his transition from a Popular Front filmmaker attuned to the contradictions of capital and community to the great poet of American imperialism. All the fissures, divisions and conflicts in the corporate community evaporate beneath the flag.

In a private letter to his nephew fighting the fascists in Spain, John Ford called himself "a definite socialistic democrat—*always* left" (McBride 2001: 271). But, less than a decade later, speaking before the Screen Directors' Guild, Ford identified himself quite differently, as a "state of Maine Republican" (McBride 2001: 371, 477). The significance of this transition becomes clear when we consider the parallel scenes that close two films bracketing this period, THE GRAPES OF WRATH (1940) and FORT APACHE (1948). Both films end with the portrait of a collective soul, an American identity. But the structure of that soul shifts decisively in the eight years that separate the films. Tom's argument for community pivots on his transformed identity as a class warrior; that is, he argues for a class community in permanent opposition to the systematic processes of capitalist development. This (perhaps sentimental) radicalism clearly opposed the allegories of corporatist class collaboration Hollywood produced in the mid-thirties. But in FORT APACHE (1948), only fragments of Ford's Popular Front radicalism survive, in the film's discontinuously repressed critique of colonialism, and in its markedly ambivalent conclusion.

All I can See is the Flags

Released the same year that Mills published *The New Men of Power* (1948), John Ford's FORT APACHE is the fictionalized re-telling of the Little Big Horn "massacre." But in Ford's version, the "Indians" are the "heroes" of this conflict, while Custer, renamed Colonel Owen Thursday (Henry Fonda), is a complex, yet, ultimately, villainous figure who sacrifices his men to a lust for glory and power. He is a racist and a class bigot. He hates the Irish far more than the Apache, regarding the latter with a kind of casual disdain as nothing more than a tribe of childish "digger Indians." On the other hand, Thursday's adjutant, Captain York (John Wayne) not only respects the Apache as warriors, but through much of the narrative also sympathizes with their plight as a colonized people. York bargains with Thursday on behalf of the Apache; and, when that fails, he attempts to warn Thursday against the fatal charge. As Richard Slotkin says, "the colonel of the regiment is the fanatic and tyrant who breaks the code of warrior honor, women's values stand equal to men's, the Indians are victims and honorable fighters rather than savage rebels or aggressors, and the film's last stand is less a glorification of Western civilization than the culmination of a subtle critique of American democratic pretenses" (1998: 335). For most of the film, this configuration dominates the narrative: Thursday as enemy of the Apache, the Fort, and of his own troopers. But then there is the fascinating finale that Ford attaches to the film.

After the Apache "massacre" Thursday and most of his men, Cochise rides to the supply train where York has circled the wagons waiting for the final blow. Instead of attacking the last remaining troopers, Cochise drives a spear decorated with the company's banner into the ground before York. Then, in a moment of remarkable cinematic repression, a dust cloud envelops the mounted Apache. When the dust clears the Apache are gone. The next scene finds York, now Colonel, seated before a grand portrait of Thursday, and describing the "heroic" deeds of his former commander to a group of newspapermen.

In the last minutes of FORT APACHE, Ford depicts York consciously falsifying history as he praises the dead Thursday for his service to the nation and to the regiment.

One of the newspaper writers asks, "But what of the men who died with him? What of Collingworth?"

York immediately corrects him, "Colling*wood*." Then another reporter continues:

"That's the ironic part of it. We always remember the Thursdays. But the others are forgotten."

At this point, York walks to the window, and, as "The Battle Hymn of the Republic" plays in the background, he watches an imaginary line of soldiers ride by, reflected in the window's glass.

> You're wrong there. They aren't forgotten because they haven't died. They're living right out there, Collingwood and the rest. And they'll keep on living as long as the regiment lives..... The faces may change, the names. But they're there. The regiment. The regular army. Now and 50 years from now. They're better men than they used to be. Thursday did that. He made it a command to be proud of.

Now dressed in a costume that echoes Thursday's own attire, York ends the story by preparing for yet another foray against the enemy. Nearly the entire narrative of the film seems to have been somehow washed away, disappearing in the dust that gathered about the Apache. Colonel York uses the regiment as a figure for a collectivity that preserves personal identity even as it ensures community. The members of the troop become "one big soul" beneath the flag. Ford posits a militarized notion of community, with the soldiers' identities metonymically related to the image of the flags that pass across the window's pane. This transformation is solidified by the music, "The Battle Hymn of the Republic," a tune perhaps familiar to his audience as "Solidarity Forever," now reclaimed and reinvigorated by nationalism.

This association between flag and community is solidified in a scene focusing upon the women of the Fort, just before the confrontation between Thursday and the Apache. As "She Wore a Yellow Ribbon" plays and the women watch the column march away to confront Cochise, Emma Collingwood says of her husband and the other soldiers, "I can't see them. All I can see is the flags." In THE HURRICANE, an anti-colonial fighter became the collective symbol of a people's identity; in THE GRAPES OF WRATH, a union organizer; in FORT APACHE the flags are metonymically bound to the men who carry them. Death will tie them together, Irish, Anglo, Latino, Union soldier, and Confederate, all difference melting away in a community of blood and sacrifice. And when Emma Collingwood allows her husband to ride to his death, even her love for her man surrenders to love for their flag, for their community.

What began as an argument for social justice ends as an ironic justification for American militarism. As in THE GRAPES OF WRATH, what matters is the preservation of community. But here the survival of the community brought together by the flag justifies colonialism and, ultimately, genocide.

Yet the key to solving FORT Apache's cryptogram comes in one final scene, a kind of coda, after York lies to the reporters. A central subplot in the film involves the racial separation between the Irish and native born whites. This racial obsession plays out in the love affair between Thursday's daughter, Philadelphia (Shirley Temple) and West Point graduate Lt. Michael O'Rourke (John Agar). The Lieutenant is the son of the Fort's Irish Master-Sergeant. Colonel Thursday steps in to stop this racial crossing, bothered both by O'Rourke's Irish blood, and, in Thursday's words, by his "class." When Thursday dies on the battlefield, however, he's standing beside Master Sergeant O'Rourke. And the film ends with the gathered reporters meeting Philadelphia's and Michael's child, "Michael Owen Thursday York O'Rourke." The marriage taboo broken, Irish and Anglo meet upon the ground of a new common whiteness born (as in THE GRAPES OF WRATH) from blood sacrifice. Thus, it is precisely through this blood sacrifice, as well as through their commitment to the genocidal American project, that the Irish O'Rourkes become full members of the (white) community. As Slotkin notes, the Irish in FORT APACHE stand in for various immigrant groups and "ethnics" (Slotkin 1998: 336). The larger argument FORT APACHE seems to make is that through their participation in American imperial conquest, ethnics achieve full membership in white society. The price of whiteness is uncritical identification with the flag.

Although set in the post-Civil War period, Ford's film was an obvious and overt allegory about the American nation on the cusp of the Cold War. Simultaneously a narrative about ethnic divisions and labor relations, the community imagined by the conclusion of FORT APACHE is what C. Wright Mills calls a "garrison state" (1948: 233) in which divisions of ethnicity, and even class, disappear under the banner of the imperial nation. Class compromise and ethnic integration go hand in hand and the garrison protecting this compromise secures white citizenship for working class ethnics and immigrants, together with native born (but not Native) Americans, by excluding those who don't fall under the company's banner. The Apache may have a just claim against the United States; but in order for the Union to stand, and the Irish to become white, they must be slaughtered.

When compared to THE HURRICANE, FORT APACHE's narrative sets in clear relief the transformations in Ford's work. The earlier film metonymically identifies the (French) flag with colonial oppression; Thursday is simulacrum of De Laage; and both films take a sympathetic perspective toward colonized

peoples. But FORT APACHE's melancholy end documents its director's transformation, as he internalizes, even ironically, and externalizes, cinematically,
his new white nationalism. Like THE HURRICANE, both THE GRAPES OF
WRATH and FORT APACHE end with allegories of American collective identity; but the space between those representations offers a perspective on the
transformations in the American community between 1940 and 1948.

We'll have no more *Grapes of Wrath*...

The social senses embodied in Ford's New Deal cinema may have been bound
by a certain moral traditionalism; but they also reached beyond that traditionalism and promised at least the possibility of a more expansive class politics.
Ford's films represented an expression of the cultures of solidarity built in and
around the labor movement during the late 1930s. And although those cultures
were constructed, in part, to defend traditional social prerogatives of working
class men, the solidarities engendered had their own symbolic effects. As Rick
Fantasia argues, "In the process of defending rights and ways of life, new associations, institutions, and valuations may be required, representing a significant social *creation*" (Fantasia 1988: 231). Though built upon a foundation of
tradition, those affiliations had the potential to open new social and political
possibilities. Like the CIO itself, in 1940 Ford's cinema was politically ambivalent; but the failures of its best hopes, like the failure of the expansive dreams
of the CIO, cannot be blamed exclusively on ideological limitations. Although
his cinema attempted to re-shape his audience's sensibility, its sense depended
upon his viewers' semiotic pre-dispositions. Those dispositions were formed in
the fire of social struggle. As the cultures of solidarity built around the age of
the CIO decayed, Ford's cinematic rhetoric refracted that change as well. The
direction taken by Ford's work, and the force of its possibility, were thus shaped
by circumstance well outside of the controlled crucible of cinematic
reproduction.

Two political events made THE GRAPES OF WRATH—or at least its immense
popularity—possible: the collective trauma of the Great Depression; and the
emergence of cultures of solidarity associated with the Popular Front, the CIO,
and the array of counter-hegemonic activities and institutions that shaped the
mid and late 1930s (Denning 1998). But between 1940 and 1948 conditions
changed dramatically. Already, with the CIO's "no strike" pledge, the character
of industrial unionism began to change. Unions became instruments of industrial discipline and aimed at securing peaceful and uninterrupted production.
As a contemporary observer of this phenomenon, C. Wright Mills recognized

the meaning of the union movement's new position within national political economy. "The union bureaucracy stands between the company bureaucracy and the rank and file of the workers, operating as a shock absorber for both.... Responsibility is held for the contract signed with the company; to uphold this contract the union must often exert pressure upon the workers. Discipline must be brought to bear..." (Mills 1948: 224). Unions became the "personnel agents" for monopolistic capitalist firms. This shift became more dramatic with the passage of Taft-Hartley in 1947. After the war, the 1946 wildcat strike wave—the most direct cause for the passage of Taft-Hartley—helped further this emerging labor-State-capital coalition, as these three institutions came together to discipline and subdue popular discontent. The anti-Communism that followed solidified this coalition, nearly ended radical participation in the union movement, and left working people with little hope that their grievances could be redressed through the kind of collective political action that gave birth to the CIO's sit-down victories of 1937 (Lipsitz 1994: 157–181; Cassano 2006).

If the age of the CIO was a moment of opportunity for a critical American cinema, the post war period produced important new constraints. The distance between Ford the Popular Front democrat and Ford the Cold Warrior might be measured by his increasing distance from Popular Front liberal, Dudley Nichols. Between 1930 and 1940, Ford and Nichols made 13 films together. But their collaboration ended before the war. They partnered for just one more film, THE FUGITIVE (1947), a critical and box office failure (McBride 2001:437–441). As the director made clear in his interview with Eisenberg, in the 1930s, Nichols represented Ford's progressive political conscience (Eisenberg 2001). And throughout the 1930s and 1940s, Dudley Nichols was an active member of the Hollywood left, on the liberal edge of the Popular Front (Ceplair and Englund 2003; Nichols 1947). By 1949, however, Ford saw Nichols as "a sort of white nigger" (McBride 2001: 489). As Ford became increasingly committed to a white garrison state, Nichols was an embarrassment, too political, *too black*.

But such an assessment doesn't fully capture the constraints that shaped Ford's transformation over time. First, as this chapter argues, Ford's most economically radical analyses of capitalism come in two films he made without Nichols as collaborator, THE GRAPES OF WRATH and HOW GREEN WAS MY VALLEY. Just as important, when Ford and Nichols did reunite, after a seven year hiatus, the resulting film says as much about Nichols own transformation into a Cold War liberal as it does Ford's changes over time. The story of a persecuted Catholic priest (Henry Fonda) in a nameless, totalitarian, Latin American country, THE FUGITIVE bears comparison to THE HURRICANE. Like THE HURRICANE, THE FUGITIVE concerns itself with "the world's afflicted races." In the earlier film, that affliction came from the sting of the (white) colonist's whip (see Chapter 4). But in THE FUGITIVE, the police lieutenant (Pedro Armendáriz) oppresses the people in the name of an anti-clerical revolution and, yet, self identifies as "an Indian, like you." A paternalistic orientalism replaces the ambivalent anti-colonialism of the earlier film (Said 1978; Shohat and Stam 1994). The Indians are deceived by foreign ideas, and their revolution produces an oppressive regime. Early in the film, Ford visually illustrates the division between the interests of the "people" and the actions of this totalitarian State. The shot begins with an idyllic scene of peasants walking together through the village streets; guitar music plays; a tenor sings a Spanish song. The priest, finding temporary sanctuary in the community, walks together with the singing peasants, their livestock, and their smiling children. The music changes to ominous orchestration. The police lieutenant and his men ride into the village, hollering, chasing down women with babies in their arms, tearing the marketplace to pieces, and attacking villagers. As in THE HURRICANE, but now with a different purpose, the forces of modernity and civilization (here represented by the revolutionary regime) threaten and destroy structures of tradition and community.

The hopes of the age of the CIO were replaced with a new fear shared by conservatives, liberals, and many on the left: totalitarianism. Indeed, whatever their other differences, the liberal Heideggerianism of Hannah Arendt (1968) and the conservative Marxism of Adorno and Horkheimer (1987) meet on common ground when they project Stalinism and Fascism as two faces of the same post-Enlightenment phenomenon. The forces that gave birth to the modern personality now threatened to destroy that same individualism. Adorno and Horkheimer (1987) in 1944, Mills in 1948, Arendt (1968) in 1950, all represent the authoritarian repression of the individual as the fundamental threat of the 20th century. Likewise, Nichols and Ford use THE FUGITIVE to evoke that threat. While THE HURRICANE resisted the urge to provide an existential allegory about the agony of the lone individual, THE FUGITIVE is precisely such a story, with nearly the entire narrative focused upon the priest's struggle as he is hunted by the regime. So, while Ford and Nichols' final collaboration helps document this new cultural emphasis upon the fear of totalitarianism, it leaves a question: what does this cultural shift mean?

In the case of Nichols and Ford, their shared fear was shaped in some part by the conflict with European Fascism and the Second World War. But the director and writer had a more direct experience of forces of domination beyond individual control: the domination of industrialized methods in factory filmmaking. The same month THE FUGITIVE was released in theatres (November), Nichols published a column in the *New York Times*, "Speaking From Personal

Experience" (1947), in which he draws connections between the 20th century threat to individualism, the requirements of the capitalist market, the standardization of mass culture, and the new Red Scare in Hollywood.

Nichols' essay is meant as a kind of anticipatory defense for his upcoming film, MOURNING BECOMES ELECTRA (1947).[2] He begins by defining art as style, and style as individual expression. From there, the author bemoans the lack of such individual expression in most Hollywood cinema. Then the critique of Hollywood becomes a critique of capitalist mass culture, with Nichols echoing lines from Adorno and Horkheimer.

For Adorno and Horkheimer, industrialized art is necessarily standardized art.

> Not only are the hit songs, stars, and soap operas cyclically recurrent and rigidly invariable types, but the specific content of the entertainment itself is derived from them and only appears to change. The details are interchangeable.
>
> ADORNO AND HORKHEIMER 987: 125

Nichols takes an identical stand toward the lack of style in Hollywood movies.

> The unthinking may believe that the assembly line films of Hollywood (which comprise inevitably most of the product) have a style, because they are so much alike in their photography and technical finish, apart from content. Yet it is precisely because of this neat and sumptuous similarity that we can assert definitely that they have no style. For style is an individual thing...
>
> NICHOLS 1947

Adorno and Horkheimer find in assembly line standardization a necessary "exclusion of the new" (1987: 134). Because commercial concerns govern the "art" of cinema, producers exclude "the untried as a risk. The movie-makers distrust any manuscript which is not reassuringly backed by a bestseller" (ibid.: 134).

As Nichols puts it, seeming to continue their argument,

> ...no producing company is going to lay out millions so that individual craftsmen [sic] may experiment and attempt something other than factory finished films...Give me a good commercial picture is the cry [in Hollywood]. And you sympathize with that anguished cry because the

---

2   Like THE FUGITIVE, MOURNING BECOMES ELECTRA was a box office failure (AFI Catalog).

> company heads have got to have them or there will be someone else
> behind their desks next week.
> NICHOLS 1947

Here Nichols deploys radical economic analysis. Agency, intention and individuality may be the key to "style." But Hollywood, as a factory system dependent upon commercial success, has little to do with individual intentions. The good hearted welfare capitalist paying her workers a wage higher than her competitors will go out of business. So, too, the artist who ignores mass tastes and insists upon the individuality of style will lose the audience, because "the masses...resist anything new" (Nichols 1947).

At this point Nichols' logic takes a significant turn. From an analysis based in political economy, the essay becomes an argument about the dangers of the American masses. Films that evince style, individuality, social significance, "all these tend to empty theatres."

> The unhappy truth is that the American people, aided and abetted by the
> bulk of film critics and reviewers, are given precisely the motion pictures
> they want and deserve.... So long as the people demand witless
> entertainment[s]...they will continue to get them.
> NICHOLS 1947

The notion of "the People," a powerful New Deal symbol that captured the aspirations of the age of the CIO, reveals its dark side, for Nichols, as the tyranny of the majority (Denning 1998). The hopes he shared with Ford in 1936, for a "new kind of public," dashed by the Red Scare, Nichols valorizes a melancholy individualism now threatened by the very People he once celebrated. "Don't blame Hollywood for all this: blame yourselves" (Nichols 1947).

As he closes, Nichols adds an odd (and important) coda:

> Let us not repine: this is a part of the proud civilization we have forged---
> and now in the minds of some of our Congressmen in Washington it is
> becoming a crime to criticize our society and perhaps will become man-
> datory to exalt it!.
> NICHOLS 1947

These unexpected closing lines mark their historical context. The HUAC hearings that produced the blacklists began in October of that same year (Ceplair and Englund 2003: 254–298). Apart from this historical particular, the relationship between Nichols' remark and the rest of the text at first appears unclear. In fact, this obscurity reveals a moment of significant anxiety. Note that Nichols conflates "our proud civilization" both with constraints of mass culture and with "our [witch hunting] Congressmen in Washington." In each case, civilization represents the elimination of the individual: the elimination of style through the dominance of mass culture; the elimination of freedom of thought through repression by the State.

In this context, the casual orientalism that characterizes THE FUGITIVE begins to make sense. Like THE HURRICANE, THE FUGITIVE depends upon a central character portrayed by an actor in "brownface": Jon Hall as Terangi; Fonda as the priest. Both actors are altered by dark body paint; both actors affect native/peasant styles of speech. Just as 19th century "blackface" minstrel theatre allowed performers, and through them, the audience, to "act black," lifting certain censorship restrictions and allowing messages otherwise taboo, so Ford and Nichols represent these darkened others as avatars, imagined repositories of very real social conflicts (Roediger 1999). THE FUGITIVE puts on display Ford's and Nichol's own anxieties and despair at the futility of individual struggle with industrial filmmaking, as well as their fears concerning the incipient Red Scare. Its orientalism fuels the critique of a "white" civilization that has become inescapably authoritarian. The film's anxieties are displaced projections of the struggle with a bureaucratic, capitalist system that allowed little space for style, personality, art, and freedom. As Nichols puts it, the same civilization that destroys personal expression makes it a "crime to criticize our society."

THE FUGITIVE was filmed from November of 1946 to January of 1947, ending production eight months before the HUAC hearings (October 1947) that brought about the imprisonment of the Hollywood Ten (McBride 2001: 439; Langdon 2008: 301–353). However, two years before those hearings, and more than a year before the film was made, Eric Johnson assumed leadership of the industry group, the Motion Picture Producers Association (MPPA). Johnson was particularly concerned with the portrayal of American life and values in the context of the ideological struggle with the Soviet Union.

> Thus, soon after taking charge of the MPPA in September 1945, Johnston announced to a meeting of the Screen Writers Guild, "We'll have no more *Grapes of Wrath*, we'll have no more *Tobacco Roads*, we'll have no more films that deal with the seamy side of American life. We'll have no more films that treat the banker as a villain".
>
> LANGDON 2008: 307

Johnson's remarks prefigure the wave of censorship and persecution about to overtake Hollywood and the United States. Moreover, in his demonization of New Deal cinema and its critiques of American inequality, he directs particular disapprobation toward *two John Ford films*, TOBACCO ROAD (1941) and THE GRAPES OF WRATH. The fears Ford and Nichols projected into their orientalist representations thus probably had as much to do with the very real threat of a new American authoritarianism and Red Scare, as they did with some imagined totalitarianism abroad.

John Ford's disillusioned corporatism of the 1930s gave way to a radical traditionalism in the early 1940s and this radical traditionalism itself might have opened the way to another form of political narrative, no longer bound by the limitations of patriarchy and racial exclusion. After the War, however, the end of militant union activity and a renewed anti-Communism foreclosed the social channels of representation. At this new historical juncture, Ford shed his radicalism, but not his traditionalism. A racialized nationalism provided the imaginary community that he had once envisioned as a workers' republic. In FORT APACHE's melancholy narrative, John Ford surrendered the critique of class and capitalism in favor of an anti-Communism that preserved tradition at the cost of social justice. The two voices that inhabited HOW GREEN WAS MY VALLEY, continued to animate FORT APACHE, one arguing for tradition and honor (Thursday), the other for justice (York). At the end of the film, honor and tradition repress justice.

But such a conclusion still does not explain the discontinuous and ironic repression that ends FORT APACHE. True, the film takes the side of Cold War nationalism, and endorses an unjust genocidal policy against Native Americans, but this endorsement acknowledges and even emphasizes the critique that came before. After all, the audience knows that York has falsified history. With that contradictory representation, Ford recalls his Popular Front past even as buries it. When the director returns to York's story in RIO GRANDE (1950),[3] all the complexity of the previous Native American representations disappear, and the narrative has the monovocal quality of much Cold War propaganda. A paternalistic traditionalism replaces Ford's anticolonial critique, with the Indians standing in for any colonized peoples "duped" by Communism into resisting American military aggression. "Democracy and nation are now entirely identified with the military" (Slotkin 1998: 359). Thus, rather than the first of his Cold War westerns, FORT APACHE represents the last monument to Ford's Popular Front radicalism, and its irony serves as an anxious farewell to the "new kind of public" he discovered in the late 1930s. But perhaps most important for his imagined audience, the transition from FORT APACHE to RIO GRANDE marks the price of immigrant whiteness. The Irish turn white when the Indians become "Reds."

---

3   In RIO GRANDE, John Wayne's character is "Colonel Kirby Yorke," while in FORT APACHE, his last name is spelled "York." Whatever significance Ford had in mind with this change, if any, must surely had been lost on the audience, who only heard the name (AFI Film Catalog).

Epilogue
Psycho (1960) and the New Domestic Gaze

By the time FORT APACHE appeared in theatres, the Hollywood studios were in deep crisis. As Schatz puts it, "business was declining rapidly. In fact, the falling gross revenues and profits for all the studios would not only continue but accelerate over the coming years" (1999: 331). When the studios did begin to recover, Hollywood had lost its monopoly on the moving sound image. Television began to penetrate everyday life. So, in the late 20th century, cinema was no longer as central to the habits and practices of Americans as it had been during the period in which it alone had the power to move pictures, and thus people. In response, cinema began to dramatize this very transformation through its interrogation of the cinematic gaze.

The Gaze

Rather than defining the "cinematic gaze" in conceptual terms, let me describe the picture that most famously theorizes this gaze. I'm thinking of course of that seminal moment from Alfred Hitchcock's film PSYCHO (1960) that takes place about 45 minutes into the picture. Marion Crane (Janet Leigh) has arrived at the Bates Motel with a bag full of money stolen from her employer. After having dinner with Norman, she decides to shower, presumably to wash away her guilt. Norman Bates (Anthony Perkins), in an adjoining room, takes a painting from the wall. Behind the frame, a hole in the plaster through which Norman watches Marion undress. Here I offer the context, but the scene is important not only for its function in this specific narrative, but because of its formal structure; what that structure says about cinema itself, and about the viewer's symbolic participation in cinematic violence.

Norman looks at the hole in the wall. Then the camera angle changes, so that Norman is seen in profile. He slowly moves his face toward the peepshow. Around him, all is darkness. But his eye is illuminated from the light coming through the break in the plaster. Cut to Marion undressing to her undergarments, the picture oval framed by the black plaster so that it looks like some effect from a D.W. Griffith film. Then back to Norman's eye, now in extreme close-up and fully illuminated by Marion's room.

This shot only lasts a few seconds. But it's no accident that Norman's eye looks much like a film projector, projecting images into the darkness. Here Hitchcock offers, in allegorical form, a theory of cinema spectatorship.

Norman Bates is simultaneously the projector and the receiver of the image. Hitchcock argues the spectator is intimately implicated in the spectacle, in the construction of cinematic "reality." While it's true that the spectator, the audience member, does not create the image, the viewer nonetheless participates in that image. In the particular case of PSYCHO, Hitchcock seems to be asking a question: Why do spectators enjoy the spectacle of violence? And he answers that question: It satisfies something in their psyche, some dark and unacknowledged self that is every bit as bloodthirsty as Norman Bates. In the play of shadow and light, every audience member becomes a murderous psycho.

But there's something more to say about this theory of the cinematic gaze. From Hitchcock's VERTIGO (1958) and PSYCHO, as well as Michael Powell's masterwork, PEEPING TOM (1960), to contemporary horror filmmakers, this gaze has been directed toward women. In fact, PSYCHO's reflexive gaze implicates the viewer in the torture and murder of women. While there are certainly exceptions to this genre rule, often (especially in the "slasher" genre Hitchcock and Powell pioneered) the cinematic gaze is an unguarded expression of masculine domination that both reinforces domination and is reciprocally fueled by the energies of patriarchy circulating within the cinematic audiences (Bourdieu 2001).

Thus we arrive at the *sociological* significance of PSYCHO's cinematic gaze. This gaze signifies the spectator's participation in cinematic violence (directed, here, against women), while, at the same time, suggesting that the spectator is, in turn shaped (interpellated) by the cinematic object itself. In other words, the film looks back at the spectator. In doing so, the film calls the spectator into a certain system of domination. Thus, cinema creates the audience, even as the audience, reciprocally, creates the cinematic object by participating in its violent spectacle.

Interpellating Community

Writing on popular song as folklore, Gramsci argues that "what distinguishes a popular song...[is] the way it conceives the world and life, in contrast to official society" (Gramsci 1985: 195). True, cinema is not "popular song." But consider Gramsci's definition of the latter: "those [songs] written neither by the people nor for the people, but which the people adopt because they conform to their way of thinking and feeling" (ibid.). Now it becomes much easier to think about cinema through this Gramscian lens. Film is mediated by political and economic constraints, but within those constraints, certain films become popular, while others hardly seem to exist. This suggests that viewers, to some greater or lesser degree, claim some cinematic objects, recognize their significance; but when the audience lays claim to the object, the object lays claim to them.

Gramsci follows the above remark with a word about audience, which is also a word about class theory. He writes:

> ...the people themselves are not a homogenous cultural collectivity but present numerous and variously combined cultural stratifications which, in their pure form, cannot always be identified within specific historical collectivities. Of course, when one historically 'isolates' these collectivities to a greater or lesser degree, such an identification is at least partially possible.
>
> GRAMSCI 1985: 195

Gramsci is thinking about what constitutes an audience, because, in an audience is a kind of community. Nation-states that found themselves upon some concept of the "people's sovereignty" found themselves upon a kind of fiction. "The people" does not "exist." It must be imagined. In a sense, a cultural artifact, whether a popular song or, in this case, a film, imagines its audience, and in that imagining, helps construct the audience as a community. It isolates segments of a stratified cultural formation and, through mutual identification, creates something new.

From here, in order to reach the significance of the gaze, we need to think more generally about the social function of cinema, at least in the early 20th century. Every society has collective rituals that create and sustain social solidarity. During the early 20th century, cinema attendance was one such ritual. Within the cinema, the spectators were potentially bound together by the spectacle. The cinematic experience forged a new group, an "audience." With spectators and participants drawn from different strata, classes, occupations, ethnicities, and races, through cinema a kind of "Americanization" could take place, as it did in union halls, saloons and churches. (Barrett 1992) This Americanization process taught both official norms, as when Henry Ford Americanized his employees, and counter-hegemonic norms that sometimes resisted capitalist domination, and sometimes undermined traditional forms of masculine and racial domination. In short, through various cultural processes, including popular cultural processes, a new, national working class community emerged in the early twentieth century that re-socialized both new immigrants and native born workers. While not the only factor in this new cultural synthesis, cinema participated in crafting a new American working class sensibility.

In this study, I have documented the manner in which some Hollywood productions attempted to intervene in shaping that American working class sensibility. Those interventions presented a variety of political possibilities for envisioning solidarity, community, and the economy. When Hollywood did offer solutions to the problems of the Great Depression, those solutions were often of the corporatist variety, combining a demand for a moral capitalism with an argument for class compromise and cooperation. Films like BLACK FURY, RIFFRAFF, and MY MAN GODFREY put precisely such a corporatist politics to work, criticizing the excesses of capitalism, but not the system itself. On the other hand, Hollywood also produced the occasional radical analysis of irreconcilable contradictions between capitalism and community. Admittedly, such radical representations were always in the minority. For instance, in 1936 Hollywood produced more than 500 feature length films (AFI Catalog). Only a handful of those films offered critiques of American inequality; and of that handful, only a very few, statistically insignificant number provided something like a radical critique. Nonetheless, MODERN TIMES and SWING TIME, with their radical representations, were two of the most popular films of the year. That popularity suggests a new openness both on the part of the audience and the Hollywood cultural apparatus. And, as I show in the first chapters of this study, even films that explicitly reject radical analysis, like MY MAN GODFREY and RIFFRAFF, contain a demand for a moral capitalism that implies something inherently immoral about the capitalism that structures their world. They may be attempts at imaginary evasions, but even the evasion reveals something real about the traumas that mark the films' imagined audiences (On the popularity of the cinematic demand for a moral capitalism, see May 1998).

The contours of this imagined audience emerge from the persona projected by Ginger Rogers between 1939 and 1941. In a bid to establish her solo career once she separated from Fred Astaire, Rogers took on a number of roles written by members of the Hollywood left, most notably Dalton Trumbo, Allan Scott, and Paul Jarrico. And even in her less overtly political roles, like BACHELOR MOTHER, Rogers' films have important critical subtexts. By 1941, Rogers had created a somewhat consistent character, portraying her parts as an independent, class conscious supporter of the New Deal, with occasional left sympathies. But for all the projected independence of this character, each film ends in precisely the same manner, with Rogers' independence repressed and normalized by marriage and submission to masculine authority. In other words, like much Hollywood cinema, and even the left itself, Rogers' films were torn by ambivalence and contradiction. When her films attempted to mobilize the sentiments of the audience for class critique, the energies for that critique emerged from a radical paternalism that fretted over the immoral influences plaguing working women.

Thus, I have resisted the urge to label any particular film "radical," "conservative," "liberal," etc. Rather, films contain radical scenes or moments (analyses of irreconcilable contradictions), together with sometimes conservative cultural politics, or vice versa. The "radical" economic arguments I have found in New Deal Cinema usually have "conservative" foundations in racial privilege and masculine domination. Likewise, the "radical" critiques of gender inequality I have studied often depend upon a corporatist vision that rejects radical economic solutions. During the 1930s and 1940s, Hollywood cinema was not simply a mechanism for enforcing the dominant ideology and norms of the time. While cinema attempted to interpellate an audience, that interpellative call was full of lacunae, uncertainties, and contradictions. Thus, a film like RIFFRAFF (1936) offered a conventional attack upon Marxism, while both endorsing craft unionism and providing a radical critique of masculine domination. Four years later, THE GRAPES OF WRATH (1940) began with a radical critique of capitalist expropriation and exploitation, and, like KITTY FOYLE, based that class critique upon a normative system of patriarchal privilege and the trauma resulting from loss of that privilege.

But whatever the contradictions its messages contained, cinema was taking up the concerns, ideas, and sensibilities of the working class, even as it was attempting, in contradictory ways, to shape those sensibilities. Between 1934 and 1941, a moment of political possibility emerged in the United States; and while resurgent nationalism eclipsed working class politics during the war, the massive strike wave of 1946 provides some evidence that the cultures of solidarity forged during the New Deal continued to thrive. With the onset of the post-war Red Scare, the passage of Taft-Hartley, and the beginning of the Cold War, those working class cultures of solidarity were actively repressed (Lipsitz 1994; Schrecker 1998; Storrs 2013).

John Ford's films document this transformation and provide an explanation of the process itself. His paradoxical representations are a refraction of the contradictions and anxieties that shaped historical experience. In the 1930s, Ford created one of the most powerful indictments of colonialism and the construction of whiteness ever produced by Hollywood, THE HURRICANE. Yet the anti-colonialism Ford evinced in that film had its double in the stereotypical and racist representations of American blacks he produced throughout his career. This contradiction between progressive politics and an endorsement of traditional forms of domination shaped much of Ford's work during the New Deal. Like THE HURRICANE, FORT APACHE takes a critical attitude toward the social construction of whiteness, even as the latter film ironically displays the transformation of the Irish racial identity through military solidarity, spilt blood, and an uncritical commitment to the flag. In deconstructing the meaning of racialized solidarity, however, Ford ultimately asserts ethnic (Irish) whiteness, embracing the very category he challenges.

Thus while FORT APACHE represents the injustice of the genocidal attitude of the U.S. government toward the Apache, it ambivalently endorses that genocide in the name of a new garrison state that includes ethnics under a broadly conceived whiteness. As Ford put it in 1970:

> My sympathy was always with the Indians. Do you consider the invasion of the Black and Tan into Ireland a blot on English history? It's the same thing, all countries do the same thing. There's British doing it, Hitler doing it, there's Stalin. Genocide seems to be common place in our lives.
>
> Quoted in GALLAGHER 1988: 254

Genocide had become commonplace and injustice was justified by (genocidal) threats to the community. While THE GRAPES OF WRATH attacks capitalism because it corrupts community and buries tradition, by the time he made THE FUGITIVE and FORT APACHE, Ford turned his fear and anxieties primarily toward the threat of totalitarianism to a reified image of community founded upon reconstructed white privilege. Indeed, the later Ford openly rejected what he called "anti-racism," presumably because, under his anxious gaze, it was a cover for Communism.

> I'm worried about these riots. I'm worried about this anti-racism. It doesn't mean the Negroes are doing it. They're being influenced by outside. Some other country. They are agents, the people who are doing things...and the poor Negroes are getting the blame.
>
> PEARY 2001: 140

In these lines, Ford's attitude toward colonial subjects and his attitude toward black Americans intersect. Just as in THE FUGITIVE, paternalistic white nationalism turns critics of U.S. foreign and domestic policy into dupes of "agents" from "some other country." But by uncritically celebrating the garrison state as the only alternative to totalitarianism, he necessarily represses the claims of the world's afflicted races. Peter Bogdanovich asked the director if he agreed with the line from THE MAN WHO SHOT LIBERTY VALENCE, "When the legend becomes a fact, print the legend." Ford responded: "Yes—because it's good for the country" (quoted in Gallagher 1988: 253). And so through that familiar device, metonymy, John Ford solders the very fissures he once revealed. Repress the past, reinvent tradition, live for—and thus in—the flag.

The Loss of the Collective Spectacle

Yet even during the Red Scare, tears in the social fabric weren't so easily repressed. While Hitchcock began his film career in the 1920s, by the early 1950s, he was, like Ford, an archetypal Cold War filmmaker. Yet what's so perplexing about Hitchcock's pictures is neither their unthinking nationalism nor their casual misogyny, but the way the filmmaker sometimes undermines and contradicts the very normative and ideological notions the films seem to be endorsing.

Much of Hitchcock's American work seems to assert masculine authority and to privilege the male gaze, as many commentators have noted (see Modleski 1989: 1–15). And, yet, some of his work from the 1950s offers fragmentary critiques of masculine domination. Two films in particular come to mind: the second version of THE MAN WHO KNEW TOO MUCH (1956) and VERTIGO (1958). Both narratives are consumed by a central social and cultural crisis of the 1950s, the changing role of women in work and domestic life. And both films simultaneously support the domestic ideology of the time and deconstruct that ideology, offering subversive critiques of the masculine gaze and male power. In THE MAN WHO KNEW TOO MUCH, the central trauma clearly involves the relationship between women and work. Jo Conway McKenna (Doris Day) is a successful singer, forced by her doctor-husband, Ben McKenna (Jimmy Stewart), to retire. On a vacation trip in North Africa, their son is kidnapped by a spy ring. Throughout the film, Ben drugs Jo to keep her passive and under control. Meanwhile, each decision he makes proves to be wrong; each (ignored) suggestion she makes proves to be correct. Finally, despite the title of the film, Jo is the central protagonist: she both stops an assassination and recovers her lost child. And, more significant still, she finds her child by *singing*, doing the very work that her dominating husband had forbidden. In short, the film portrays men as incompetent, domineering, even hypocritical. And it is Jo, *the professional singer,* who preserves the family and rescues Ben's failing manhood.

VERTIGO also concerns itself with the relationship between women and work. But VERTIGO goes further, interrogating and critiquing the dominating and violent masculine gaze (Modleski 1989; Wood 2002). Kim Novak plays Judy Barton, a working class woman who impersonates a fantastic masculine idealization of a woman. She does so in order to involve Scottie Ferguson (Jimmy Stewart) in a criminal conspiracy and another woman's murder. Afterward, no longer impersonating this ideal, Judy meets Ferguson again. This time, he slowly transforms her into the part she had previously played. And, despite the danger to herself (she conspired in a murder), she allows this transformation out of love and desire.

These scenes deconstruct the masculine gaze, showing "femininity" as the conceptual product of masculine domination. Like BACHELOR MOTHER (1939), VERTIGO examines the manner in which masculine fantasy constrains and constructs women's identity. Near the end of the film, as Scottie becomes increasingly obsessed with transforming Judy's appearance into his lost fiction of love, she says in desperation:

> "Well I'll wear the darn clothes if you want me to, if you'll just...just like me.... If I let you change me, will that do it? If I do what you tell me, will you...love me?"

Both THE MAN WHO KNEW TOO MUCH and VERTIGO are about men's control over women. And rather than uncritically endorsing that control, both films deconstruct masculinity and masculine fantasy.

PSYCHO continues the examination of the gaze initiated by VERTIGO and, as in THE MAN WHO KNEW TOO MUCH, is centrally concerned with the relationship of working women to the dominant ideology of domestic life. At the same time, PSYCHO appears to end the critique of masculine domination so central in Hitchcock's previous films. Marion Crane is a working woman. But she has little of the complexity shown by Novak's tortured character, nor the strength of Doris Day's Jo McKenna. Instead, Marion is an unremarkable stereotype, the traditional and sexualized "working girl" whose life in the formal economy has led to a loose moral sensibility. She has premarital sex with men and steals money from her employer. Thus, despite regret over her crime, when Norman Bates murders her there's a certain cinematic justice at work. Through her murder Norman restores the normative order. The threat of the working woman is subdued. With this context, it becomes clear that Norman's gaze is not simply misogynistic. His misogyny and his violence are part of a reaction to the proletarianization of women. Unlike THE MAN WHO KNEW TOO MUCH, PSYCHO resolves the conflict between domestic norms and the new realities of women in the workplace with violence. The projected gaze restores domesticity by literally confining women to the domestic sphere (after all, the corpse of "Mother" never leaves the house) and murdering women who violate this ideology of domesticity. During the 1950s, Hitchcock's films were at war with themselves, both endorsing and critiquing masculine domination. By 1960, however, the war seemed to be over.

But let me return to the cinematic gaze. PSYCHO appeared in the wake of Hitchcock's tremendous success as a television writer, producer and director, and clearly shows its televised roots (Raubicheck and Srebnick 2011). While PSYCHO theorizes the cinematic gaze (as masculine domination), it transforms that collective experience into an individuated event. In other words, PSYCHO both analyzes film, and points toward television. Like Norman's sadistic gaze, television literally confines the viewer to the domestic sphere. By the time the film appeared, "television" and "living room" had become practical synonyms. And here recall one of the final shots of Marion Crane, a close-up of her dead eye, watching nothing. Hers are the lifeless eyes of the T.V. spectator.

New Deal Cinema contributed to, and was at times shaped by, a working class political culture. With the onset of the Cold War, that political culture was repressed. Despite their repression, political themes from New Deal cinema returned in new forms. Thus, the concern with women and work found in a film like RIFFRAFF (1936) reappears in Cold War filmmakers like Hitchcock. His films from the 1950s deconstruct and critique masculine domination. And yet that critique seems to end with PSYCHO. But to the extent that the film turns its gaze upon the gaze itself, it continues the critical work of Hitchcock's previous efforts. In fact, PSYCHO posits (and analyzes) the interpellating call for a social subject turned inward, whose gaze is entirely individualized, like the shot of Norman looking through the hole. Consider the theory of the cinematic gaze as articulated by 5th AVENUE GIRL (1939). When Borden stares at the tree branch in the park, a kind of community emerges, with multiple participants in this mini-spectacle. The gaze is a collective event, cinema as a shared, social and ritual practice. But PSYCHO points toward the advent of *television*. Norman watches alone. The cinema of the 1930s as the site of collective spectacle has been replaced by t.v.'s individuating experience. And, like film, television looks back at its spectators, remaking them. The televised spectacle represents a new moment of domesticity and confinement. Just as cinema helped create and anchor working class cultures of solidarity during the 1930s and 1940s, in PSYCHO the solitary gaze becomes the aesthetic and ritual anchor for a new domesticity that subjugates and isolates social agents through its sadistic look back.

References

Abel, Elizabeth. 2003. Shadows. *Representations*, November 84(1): 166–199.

Adorno, Theodor and Horkheimer Max. 1987. *Dialectic of Enlightenment*. New York: Continuum.

Althusser, Louis. 1971. Ideology and the Ideological State Apparatus. In *Lenin and Philosophy and Other Essays*. New York: Monthly Review Press.

Arendt, Hannah. 1968. *The Origins of Totalitarianism. New Edition*. San Diego, New York, and London: Harcourt.

Balio, Tino (ed.). 1995. *Grand Design: Hollywood as a Modern Business Enterprise, 1930–1939*. Berkeley: University of California Press.

Barrett, James R. 1992. Americanization from the Bottom Up: Immigration and the Remaking of the Working Class in the United States, 1880–1930. *The Journal of American History*, 79(3): 996-1020.

Beauchamp, Cari. 1997. *Without Lying Down: Frances Marion and the Powerful Women of Early Hollywood*. Berkeley: University of California Press.

Benjamin, Walter. 2003. On the Concept of History, pp. 389–400 in *Walter Benjamin: Selected Writings, Vol. 4: 1938–1940*. Cambridge, MA: The Belknap Press.

——, 1999. *The Arcades Project*. Cambridge, Mass: Belknap Press.

Bernstein, Irving. 1969. *Turbulent Years: A History of the American Worker, 1933–1941*. Boston: Houghton Mifflin Company.

Black, Gregory. 1994. *Hollywood Censored: Morality Codes, Catholics and the Movies*. Cambridge, U.K.: Cambridge University Press.

Blumer, Herbert. 1933. *Movies and Conduct*. New York: The Macmillan Company.

Bodnar, John. 2003. *Blue-Collar Hollywood: Liberalism, Democracy, and Working People in American Film*. Baltimore: Johns Hopkins University Press.

Bourdieu, Pierre. 1992. *Outline of a Theory of Practice*. Cambridge, UK: Cambridge University Press.

——, 2001. *Masculine Domination*. Stanford: Stanford University Press.

Brodkin, Karen. 1998. *How Jews Became White Folks & What That Says About Race in America*. New Brunswick: Rutgers University Press.

Buhle, Paul and Wagner, Dave. 2002. *Radical Hollywood: The Untold Story Behind America's Favorite Movies*. New York: The New Press.

Burke, Kenneth. 1935. *Permanence and Change*. Berkeley: University of California Press.

——, 1945. Four Master Tropes, pp. 503–517 in Burke, Kenneth, *A Grammar of Motives*. Berkeley: University of California Press.

Calhoun, Craig Jackson. 1983. The Radicalism of Tradition: Community Strength or Venerable Disguise and Borrowed Language? *American Journal of Sociology*. March. (88) 5: 886–914.

Cassano, Graham 2005a. Reification, Resistance, and Ironic Empiricism in Simmel's *Philosophy of Money*, *Rethinking Marxism*. October 17(4): 571–590.

——, 2005b. Stylistic Sabotage and Thorstein Veblen's Scientific Irony, *Journal of Economic Issues*. September 39(3): 741–764.

——, 2006. Labor, Desire, and the Wages of War, *Rethinking Marxism*. July 18(3): 453–462.

——, 2008. The Acquisitive Machine: Max Weber, Thorstein Veblen, and the Culture of Consumptive Individualism, pp. 177–189 in Chalcraft, David, Howell, Fanon Howell, Menendez, Marisol Lopez and Vera, Hector, eds., *Max Weber Matters: Interweaving Past and Present*. Burlington: Ashgate Publishers.

——, 2009a. Choosing Our Ancestors: Thorstein Veblen, Radical Institutionalism and Sociology, *Critical Sociology*. 35:3:367–377

——, 2009b. Symbolic Exploitation and the Social Dialectic of Desire, *Critical Sociology*. 35:3:379–393

——, 2009c. Introduction: Returning to the Popular Front, *Rethinking Marxism*. October (21)4: 476–479

Cassano, Graham (ed.). 2010. *Class Struggle on the Homefront: Work, Conflict and Exploitation in the Household,* New York, NY: Palgrave Macmillan.

Cassano, Graham and Rondinone, Troy. 2010. The Persistence of Republicanism: Class War Talk, American Style, *Labor Studies Journal*. September 35(3): 417–430

Ceplair, Larry. 2007. *The Marxist and the Movies: A Biography of Paul Jarrico*. Lexington: University of Kentucky Press.

Ceplair, Larry and Englund, Steve. 2003. *The Inquisition in Hollywood: Politics in the Film Community, 1930–1960*. Urbana and Chicago: University of Illinois Press.

Cohen, John, Seeger, Mike, and Wood, Hally. 1976. *Old-Time String Band Songbook*. New York and London: Oak Publications.

Cohen, Lizabeth. 1990. *Making a New Deal: Industrial Workers in Chicago, 1919–1939*. Cambridge, UK: Cambridge University Press.

Collins, Patricia Hill. 2005. *Black Sexual Politics: African Americans, Gender, and the New Racism*. New York: Routledge.

Connell, R.W. 1987. *Gender and Power: Society, the Person, and Sexual Politics*. Stanford: Stanford University Press.

Cooley, Charles Horton. 1922. *Human Nature and the Social Order. Rev. Edition*. New York: Charles Scribner & Sons.

Denning, Michael. 1998. *The Cultural Front: The Laboring of American Culture in the Twentieth Century*. London and New York: Verso.

Diggins, J.P. 1999. *Thorstein Veblen: Theorist of the Leisure Class*. Princeton: Princeton University Press.

Doane, Mary Ann. 1987. *The Desire to Desire: Woman's Film of the 1940s*. Bloomington and Indianapolis: Indiana University Press.

Ducrot, Oswald and Todorov, Tzvetan. 1979. *Encyclopedic Dictionary of the Science of Language*. Baltimore: Johns Hopkins University Press.

Durkheim, Emile. 1984. *The Division of Labor in Society*. New York: Free Press.

——, 1992. *Professional Ethics and Civic Morals*. New York: Routledge.

Eisenberg, Emanuel 2001. John Ford: Fighting Irish, pp. 255–260 in Studlar, Galyn and Bernstein, Matthew (eds), *John Ford Made Westerns: Filming the Legend in the Sound Era*. Bloomington: Indiana University Press.

Eyman, Scott. 1999. *Print the Legend: The Life and Times of John Ford*. Baltimore: Johns Hopkins University Press.

Fantasia, Rick. 1988. *Cultures of Solidarity: Consciousness, Action, and Contemporary American Workers*. Berkeley: University of California Press.

Fanon, Frantz. 1967. *Black Skin, White Masks*. New York: Grove Press.

Faue, Elizabeth. 1991. *Community of Suffering and Struggle: Women, Men, and the Labor Movement in Minneapolis, 1915–1945*. Chapel Hill: The University of North Carolina Press.

Fine, Sidney. 1969. *Sit-Down: The General Motors Strike of 1936–1936*. Ann Arbor: University of Michigan Press.

Fraad, Harriet, Resnick, Stephen, and Wolff, Richard. 1994. *Bringing it All Back Home: Class, Gender, & Power in the Modern Household*. London: Pluto Press.

Fraser, Steve. 1989. The 'Labor Question', pp. 55–84 in Fraser, Steve and Gerstle, Gary, *The Rise and Fall of the New Deal Order: 1930–1980*. Princeton: Princeton University Press.

Freud, Sigmund. 1989a. *Beyond the Pleasure Principle*. New York: Norton.

——, 1989b. *Group Psychology and the Analysis of the Ego*. New York: Norton.

Gallagher, Tag. 1988. *John Ford: The Man and His Films*. Berkeley: University of California Press.

Geertz, Clifford. 1983. *Local Knowledge: Further Essays in Interpretive Anthropology*. New York: Basic Books.

Gerstle, Gary. 2002. *Working-Class Americanism: The Politics of Labor in a Textile City, 1914–1960*. Princeton: Princeton University Press.

Glenn, Evelyn Nakano. 2002. *Unequal Freedoms: How Race and Gender Shaped American Citizenship and Labor*. Cambridge: Harvard University Press.

Gramsci, Antonio. 1985. *Selections from Cultural Writings*. Cambridge, MA: Harvard University Press.

Gutman, Herbert and Berlin, Irving. 1987. Class Composition and the Development of the American Working Class, 1840–1890, pp. 380–394 in Gutman, Herbert, *Power & Culture: Essays on the American Working Class*. New York: The New Press.

Hobsbawm, Eric. 1998. *Uncommon People: Resistance, Rebellion, and Jazz*. New York: The New Press.

Hochschild, Arlie. 2003. *The Second Shift*. New York: Penguin Books.

Hollier, Dennis. 1988. *The College of Sociology, 1937–39.* Minneapolis: University of Minnesota Press.

Horne, Gerald. 2001. *Class Struggle in Hollywood, 1930–1950: Moguls, Mobsters, Stars, Reds, and Trade Unionists.* Austin: University of Texas Press.

Huber, Patrick. 2008. *Lint Head Stomp: The Creation of Country Music in the Piedmont South.* Chapel Hill: University of North Carolina Press.

Jacobs, Lea. 1997. *The Wages of Sin: Censorship and the Fallen Woman Film, 1928–1942.* Berkeley: University of California Press.

——, 1999. Industry Self-Regulation and the Problem of Textual Determination, pp. 87–101 in Bernstein, Matthew (ed.), *Controlling Hollywood: Censorship and Regulation in the Studio Era.* New Brunswick: Rutgers University Press.

Jakobson, Roman. 1956. Two Aspects of Language and Two Types of Aphasic Disturbances, in Jakobson, Roman and Halle, Morris, *Fundamentals of Language.* The Hague: Mouton Publishers.

Jewell, Richard B. 1994. RKO film grosses, 1929–1951: The C.J. Tevlin ledger. *Historical Journal of Film, Radio & Television,* March 14(1)

Klein, Jennifer. 2003. *For All These Rights: Business, Labor, and the Shaping of America's Public-Private Welfare State.* Princeton: Princeton University Press.

Kojeve, Alexandre. 1969. *Introduction to the Reading of Hegel: Lectures on the Phenomenology of the Spirit.* Ithaca: Cornell University Press.

Koritz, Amy. 1994. Dancing the Orient for England: Maud Allan's 'The Vision of Salome'. *Theatre Journal.* March 46(1):63–78

Lacan, Jacques. 1977. The Mirror Stage as Formative of the Function of the I, in *Ecrits: Selected Writings.* New York: Norton.

——, 1985. *Feminine Sexuality.* Trans. Jacqueline Rose. New York: Norton.

Langdon, Jennifer E. 2008. *Caught in the Crossfire: Adrian Scott and the Politics of Americanism in 1940s Hollywood.* New York: Columbia University Press.

Leff, Leonard J. 1991. The Breening of America. *PMLA.* May 106(3):432–445.

Leff, Leonard J. and Simmons, Jerold L. 2001. *The Dame in the Kimono: Hollywood, Censorship, and the Production Code.* Second Edition. Lexington: The University Press of Kentucky.

Levine, Rhoda F. 1988. *Class Struggle and the New Deal: Industrial Labor, Industrial Capital, and the State.* Lawrence: University of Kansas Press.

Lichtenstein, Nelson. 1989. From Corporatism to Collective Bargaining: Organized Labor and the Eclipse of Social Democracy in the Postwar Era, pp. 122–152 in Fraser, Steve and Gerstle, Gary, *The Rise and Fall of the New Deal Order.* Princeton: Princeton University Press.

——, 1995. *Walter Reuther: The Most Dangerous Man in Detroit.* Urbana: University of Illinois Press.

——, 2002. *State of the Union: A Century of American Labor.* Princeton: Princeton University Press.

Lipsitz, George. 1994. *Rainbow at Midnight: Labor and Culture in the 1940s*. Chicago: University of Illinois Press.

Locke, Ralph P. 1998. Cutthroats and Casbah Dancers, Muezzins and Timeless Sands: Musical Images of the Middle East. *19th-Century Music*, Summer 22(1):20–53.

Lomax, Alan, Guthrie Woody, and Seeger, Pete. 1999. *Hard Hitting Songs for Hard-Hit People*. Lincoln: University of Nebraska Press.

Loos, Anita. 1966. *A Girl Like I*. New York: Viking Press.

Luhmann Niklas. 2000. *The Reality of the Mass Media*. Stanford: Stanford University Press.

Lynd, Robert S. and Lynd, Helen Merrell. 1937. *Middletown in Transition: A Study in Cultural Conflicts*. New York: Harcourt Brace Jovanovich.

Maland, Charles J. 2003. 'Powered by a Ford'?: Dudley Nichols, Authorship, and Cultural Ethos in *Stagecoach*, pp. 48–81 in Grant, Barry Keith (ed.), *John Ford's Stagecoach*. Cambridge, UK: Cambridge University Press.

Maltby, Richard. 1995. The Production Code and the Hays Office, pp. 37–72 in Balio, Tino (ed.), *Grand Design: Hollywood as a Modern Business Enterprise, 1930–1939*. Berkeley: University of California Press.

Maltz, Albert. 1935. What is Propaganda? *New York Times*. April 28.

Marchetti, Gina. 1994. *Romance and the Yellow Peril: Race, Sex and Discursive Strategies in Hollywood Fiction*. Berkeley: University of California Press.

Markels, Julian. 2003. *The Marxian Imagination: Representing Class in Literature*. New York: Monthly Review Press.

Martin, Christopher R. 2004. *Framed: Labor and the Corporate Media*. Ithaca and London: ILR/Cornell University Press.

Marx, Karl. 1902. *Wage-Labor and Capital*. New York: New York Labor News Company.

——, 1967. *Capital, Volume One*. New York: International Publishers.

Marx, Karl and Engels, Friedrich. 1988. *The German Ideology: Part One*. New York: International Publishers.

Mauss, Marcel. 1979. Body Techniques, in Mauss, Marcel, *Sociology and Psychology: Essays*. London: Routledge.

——, 1990. *The Gift: The form and reason for exchange in archaic societies*. London: Routledge.

May, Lary. 1998. *The Big Tomorrow: Hollywood and the Politics of the American Way*. Chicago: University of Chicago Press.

McBride, Joseph. 2001. *Searching for John Ford: A Life*. New York: St. Martin's Griffin Press.

McGilligan, Patrick and Buhle, Paul. 1997. *Tender Comrades: A Backstory of the Hollywood Blacklist*. Minneapolis: University of Minnesota Press.

Mead, George Herbert. 1967. *Mind, Self and Society: From the Standpoint of a Social Behaviorist*. Chicago: University of Chicago Press.

Melosh, Barbara. 1991. *Engendering Culture: Manhood and Womanhood in New Deal Public Art and Theater*. Washington: Smithsonian Institution Press.

Meyerowitz, Joanne. 1994. Beyond the Feminine Mystique: A Reassessment of Postwar Mass Culture, 1946–1958, pp. 229–262 in Meyerowitz, Joanne (ed.), *Not June Cleaver: Women and Gender in Postwar America, 1945–1960*. Philadelphia: Temple University Press.

Mills, C. Wright. 1948 [2001]. *The New Men of Power*. Urbana: University of Illinois Press.

——, 1959 [1967]. The Cultural Apparatus, pp. 405–422 in Mills, C. Wright, *Power, Politics & People: The Collected Essays of C. Wright Mills*. London: Oxford University Press.

Mink, Gwendolyn. 1996. *The Wages of Motherhood: Inequality in the Welfare State, 1917–1942*. Ithaca: Cornell University Press.

Modleski, Tania. 1989. *The Women Who Knew Too Much: Hitchcock and Feminist Theory*. New York and London: Routledge.

Moran, Kathleen and Rogin, Michael. 2000. "What's the matter with Capra?": Sullivan's Travels and the Popular Front. *Representations*. Summer. Number 71: 106–134.

Nichols, Dudley 1947. Speaking from Personal Experience. *New York Times*. November 4.

Nielsen, Mike and Mailes, Gene. 1995. *Hollywood's Other Blacklist: Union Struggles in the Studio System*. London: British Film Institute Publishing.

Peary, Gerald (ed.). 2001. *John Ford Interviews*. Jackson: University of Mississippi Press.

Porter Benson, Susan. 2007. *Household Accounts: Working Class Family Economies in the Interwar Years*. Ithaca, NY: Cornell University Press.

Puette, William J. 1992. *Through Jaundiced Eyes: How the Media View Organized Labor*. Ithaca and London: ILR/Cornell University Press.

Rabinowitz, Paula. 1991. *Labor & Desire: Women's Revolutionary Fiction in Depression America*. Chapel Hill: University of North Carolina Press.

Raubicheck, Walter and Srebnick, Walter. 2011. *Scripting Hitchcock: Psycho, The Birds, and Marnie*. Urbana, Chicago, and Springfield: University of Chicago Press.

Reuther, Walter P. 1940. 500 Planes A Day—A Program for the Utilization of the Automobile Industry for Mass Production of Defense Planes, pp. 1–12 in Reuther, Walter. *Walter P. Reuther: Selected Papers*. 1961. New York: MacMillan Company.

Resnick, Stephen and Wolff, Richard. 1987. *Knowledge and Class: A Marxian Critique of Political Economy*. Chicago: University of Chicago Press.

Roediger, David. 1999. *The Wages of Whiteness: Race and the Making of the American Working Class*. Revised Edition. London and New York: Verso.

——, 2005. *Working Toward Whiteness: How America's Immigrants Became White*. New York: Basic Books.

Roediger, David and Barrett, James R. 2002. In between Peoples: Race, Nationality and the 'New-Immigrant' Working Class, pp.138–168 in Roediger, David, *Colored White: Transcending the Racial Past*. Berkeley: University of California Press.

Rogers, Ginger. 1991. *Ginger: My Story*. New York: Harper Collins.

Rogin, Michael. 1992. Making America Home: Racial Masquerade and Ethnic Assimilation in the Transition to Talking Pictures. *The Journal of American History*. December 7(3): 1050–1077.

——, 1998. *Blackface, White Noise: Jewish Immigrants in the Hollywood Melting Pot.* Berkeley: University of California Press.

——, 2002. How the Working Class Saved Capitalism: The New Labor History and the Devil and Miss Jones. *The Journal of American History.* June. 89(1): 87–114.

Rondinone, Troy. 2010. *The Great Industrial War: Framing Class Conflict, 1865–1950.* New Brunswick, NJ: Rutgers University Press.

Roscigno, Vincent J. and Danaher, William. 2004. *The Voice of Southern Labor: Radio, Music, and the Textile Strikes, 1929–1934.* Minneapolis: University of Minnesota Press.

Ross, Murray (1941) *Stars and Strikes: Unionization of Hollywood.* New York: Columbia University Press.

Ross, Steven Jay. 1999. *Working Class Hollywood: Silent Film and the Shaping of Class in America.* Princeton, NJ: Princeton University Press.

Ryskind, Morrie. 1994. *I Shot an Elephant in My Pajamas: The Morrie Ryskind Story.* Lafayette: Huntington House Publishers.

Said, Edward. 1978. *Orientalism.* New York: Pantheon Books.

Schatz, Thomas. (ed.) 1999. *Boom and Bust: American Cinema in the 1940s.* Berkeley: University of California Press.

Schrecker, Ellen. 1998. *Many are the Crimes: McCarthyism in America.* Princeton: Princeton University Press.

Sedgwick, John. 1994. Richard B. Jewell's RKO film grosses, 1929–51: The C.J. Trevlin Ledger: A Comment. *Historical Journal of Film, Radio & Television*, March 14(1).

Shohat, Ella and Stam, Robert. 1994. *Unthinking Eurocentrism: Multiculturalism and the Media.* New York: Routledge.

Slotkin, Richard. 1998. *Gunfighter Nation: They Myth of the Frontier in Twentieth Century America.* Norman: University of Oklahoma Press.

Stansell, Christine. 1987. *City of Women: Sex and Class in New York, 1789–1860.* Chicago: University of Illinois Press.

Storrs, Landon. 2013. *The Second Red Scare and the Unmaking of the New Deal Left.* Princeton: Princeton University Press.

Stricker, Frank. 1990. Repressing the Working Class: Individualism and the Masses in Frank Capra's Films. *Labor History.* Fall 31(4): 454–467

Thompson, E.P. 1993. *Customs in Common: Studies in Traditional Popular Culture.* New York: The New Press.

Veblen, Thorstein. 1994. The Theory of the Leisure Class. New York: Dover Publications.

——, 1998. The Economic Theory of Woman's Dress, pp. 65–77 in Veblen, Thorstein, *Essays in our Changing Order.* New Brunswick: Transaction Publishing.

——, 1964. *The Vested Interests and the Common Man.* New York: Augustus M. Kelley.

——, 1990. *The Engineers and the Price System.* New Brunswick: Transaction Publishing.

Volosinov, V.N. 1973. *Marxism and the Philosophy of Language.* Cambridge, MA: MIT Press.

Walsh, Francis R. 1986. The Films We Never Saw: American Movies View Organized Labor, 1934–1954. *Labor History*. Fall 27(4): 564–580.

Weber, Max. 1946. *From Max Weber: Essays in Sociology*. New York: Oxford University Press.

Williams, Raymond. 1977. *Marxism and Literature*. Oxford: Oxford University Press.

Winnicott, D.W. 1971. *Playing and Reality*. London and New York: Tavistock Publishing.

Wolff, Rick. 2005. Ideological Apparatuses, Consumerism, and U.S. Capitalism: Lessons for the Left. *Rethinking Marxism*. April 17(2).

Wood, Ellen Meiksins and Wood, Neal. 1997. *A Trumpet of Sedition: Political Theory and the Rise of Capitalism*. New York: New York University Press.

Wood, Robin. 2001. Shall We Gather at the River? The Late Films of John Ford, pp. 23–41 in Studlar, Gayln and Bernstein, Matthew (eds), *John Ford Made Westerns: Filming the Legend in the Sound Era*. Bloomington: Indiana University Press.

——, 2002. *Hitchcock's Films Revisited. Revised Edition*. New York: Columbia University Press.

Worrell, Mark P. 2006. The Other Frankfurt School. *Fast Capitalism* 2(1).

——, 2009 *Dialectic of Solidarity: Labor, Antisemitism and the Frankfurt School*. New York: Haymarket Press.

Zieger, Robert H. 1997. *The CIO, 1935–1955*. Chapel Hill: University of North Carolina Press.

Zizek, Slavoj. 1989. *The Sublime Object of Ideology*. London and New York: Verso.

Zurier, Rebecca. 1988. *Art for the Masses: A Radical Magazine and its Graphics, 1911–1917*. Philadelphia: Temple University Press.

Films Cited

Source: The American Film Institute Catalog
http://www.afi.com/members/catalog/

5TH AVENUE GIRL, dir. Gregory La Cava, RKO, 1939.

BACHELOR MOTHER, dir. Garson Kanin, RKO, 1939.

THE BARKLEYS OF BROADWAY, dir. Charles Walters, MGM, 1949.

THE BATTLE OF MIDWAY, dir. John Ford, 1942.

BIG CITY, dir. Frank Borzage, MGM, 1937.

BIRD OF PARADISE, dir. King Vidor, RKO, 1932.

THE BIRTH OF A NATION, dir. D.W. Griffith, Epoch Producing Corp., 1915.

BLACK FURY, dir. Michael Curtiz, First National Pictures, 1935.

CASABLANCA, dir. Michael Curtiz, Warner Brothers, 1943.

CHEYENNE AUTUMN, dir. John Ford, Warner Brothers, 1964.

CROSSFIRE, dir. Edward Dmytryk, RKO, 1947.

DEAD END, dir. William Wyler, United Artists, 1937.

THE FUGITIVE, dir. John Ford, RKO, 1947.

FORT APACHE, dir. John Ford, RKO, 1948.

GOLD DIGGERS OF 1933, dir. Mervyn LeRoy, Warner Brothers, 1933.

THE GRAPES OF WRATH, dir. John Ford, Twentieth Century Fox, 1940.

HIS GIRL FRIDAY, dir. Howard Hawks, Columbia Pictures, 1940.

HOW GREEN WAS MY VALLEY, dir. John Ford, Twentieth Century Fox, 1941.

THE HURRICANE, dir. John Ford, United Artists, 1937.

KITTY FOYLE, dir. Sam Wood, RKO, 1940.

I AM A FUGITIVE FROM A CHAIN GANG, dir. Mervyn LeRoy, Warner Brothers, 1932.

THE JAZZ SINGER, dir. Alan Crosland, Warner Brothers, 1927.

JUDGE PRIEST, dir. John Ford, Twentieth Century Fox, 1934.

THE MAN WHO KNEW TOO MUCH, dir. Alfred Hitchcock, Paramount, 1956.

THE MAN WHO SHOT LIBERTY VALENCE, dir. John Ford, Paramount, 1962.

MANNEQUIN, dir. Frank Borzage, MGM, 1938.

MEET JOHN DOE, dir. Frank Capra, Warner Brothers, 1941.

METROPOLIS, dir. Fritz Lang, 1927.

MODERN TIMES, dir. Charlie Chaplin, United Artists, 1936.

MY MAN GODFREY, dir. Gregory La Cava, Universal, 1936.

NINOTCHKA, dir. Ernst Lubitsch, MGM, 1939.

PEEPING TOM, dir. Michael Powell, Astor Pictures, 1960.

PINKY, dir. Elia Kazan, Twentieth Century Fox, 1949.

PSYCHO, dir. Alfred Hitchcock, Paramount, 1960.

THE PUBLIC ENEMY, dir. William A. Wellman, Warner Brothers, 1931.

ROMANCE IN MANHATTAN, dir. Stephen Roberts, RKO, 1935.

RIFFRAFF, dir. J. Walter Ruben, Twentieth Century Fox, 1936.

SALT OF THE EARTH, dir. Herbert J. Biberman, Independent Production Corp., 1954.

SCARFACE, dir. Howard Hawks, United Artists, 1932.

THE SEARCHERS, dir. John Ford, Warner Brothers, 1956.

STAGECOACH, dir. John Ford, United Artists, 1939.

THE STORY OF VERNON AND IRENE CASTLE, dir. H.C. Potter, RKO, 1939.

SULLIVAN'S TRAVELS, dir. Preston Sturges, Paramount, 1942.

THE SUN SHINES BRIGHT, dir. John Ford, Republic Pictures, 1953.

SWING TIME, dir. George Stevens, RKO, 1936.

TENDER COMRADE, dir. Edward Dmytryk, RKO, 1944.

THEY WERE EXPENDABLE, dir. John Ford, MGM, 1945.

TOM, Dick and Harry, dir. Garson Kanin, RKO, 1941.

TOP HAT, dir. Mark Sandrich, RKO, 1935.

VERTIGO, dir. Alfred Hitchcock, Paramount, 1958.

THE WEDDING NIGHT, dir. King Vidor, United Artists, 1935.

THE WIZARD OF OZ, dir. Victor Fleming, MGM, 1939.

YOUNG MR LINCOLN, dir. John Ford, Twentieth Century Fox, 1939.

YO YO, dir. Pierre Étaix, Magna Pictures, 1967.

Index